"In a troubling debate, resolution of which is currently out of sight, this extended monograph is a must-read for all who care about biblical authority, Christian relationships, and well-ordered church life. Laboriously and exhaustively, with clarity, charity, and a scholar's objectivity, Wayne Grudem sifts through many current challenges to the Bible's apparent teaching on men and women. This is the fullest and most informative analysis available, and no one will be able to deny the cumulative strength of the case this author makes, as he vindicates the older paths."

—J. I. Packer
Professor of Theology, Regent College

"Wayne Grudem provides evangelical churches with a reverent, kind, thoughtful, and ultimately decisive answer to the shaky logic and questionable exegesis often advocated by feminists, who wish to overturn twenty centuries of Christian history and the clear witness of Holy Scripture."

—Paige Patterson
President, Southwestern Baptist Theological Seminary

"After the Bible, I cannot imagine a more useful book for finding reliable help in understanding God's will for manhood and womanhood in the church and the home. The practical design of this book will help laypeople find answers without having to read eight hundred pages. But the rigor of scholarship, the amazing thoroughness, and the unparalleled clarity (which Wayne Grudem is justly famous for!) will make this book the standard complementarian manifesto for many years to come. I thank God and stand in respectful awe of Grudem's achievement."

—John Piper
Pastor for Preaching and Vision, Bethlehem Baptist Church
Minneapolis, Minnesota

"With diplomacy and world-class scholarship, Wayne Grudem has taken on not just some of the thorny questions, but the entire briar patch! This book will be used and referenced by scholars, church leaders, and laymen and laywomen for decades."

—Dennis Rainey
President, FamilyLife

"The evangelical world has waited a long time for such a comprehensive work on what has become, sadly, a controversial topic. This is the most thorough, balanced, and biblically accurate treatment of feminism and the Bible I have seen. It also exudes kindness and grace, qualities sorely needed for meaningful dialogue on this foundational issue."

—Stu Weber
Author of *Tender Warrior*

COUNTERING
THE CLAIMS OF
EVANGELICAL
FEMINISM

WAYNE
GRUDEM

Multnomah® Publishers, *Colorado Springs, Colorado*

COUNTERING THE CLAIMS OF EVANGELICAL FEMINISM
published by Multnomah Publishers, *A division of Random House Inc.*
© 2006 by Wayne Grudem
International Standard Book Number: 1-59052-518-3
ISBN-13: 978-1-590-52518-0
Interior design and typeset by Katherine Lloyd, The DESK, Sisters, OR

Unless otherwise indicated, Scripture quotations are from:
The Holy Bible, English Standard Version
© 2001 by Crossway Bibles, a division of Good News Publishers.
Used by permission. All rights reserved.
New American Standard Bible (NASB) © 1960, 1977, 1995
by the Lockman Foundation. Used by permission.
The Holy Bible, King James Version (KJV)
The Holy Bible, New International Version (NIV)
© 1973, 1984 by International Bible Society,
Used by permission of Zondervan Publishing House
Revised Standard Version Bible (RSV)
© 1946, 1952 by the Division of Christian Education of the
National Council of the Churches of Christ in the United States of America
Italics in Scripture quotations are the author's emphasis.

Multnomah is a trademark of Multnomah Publishers,
and is registered in the U.S. Patent and Trademark Office.
The colophon is a trademark of Multnomah Publishers.
Printed in the United States of America

For information:
MULTNOMAH PUBLISHERS
12265 Oracle Boulevard, Suite 200
Colorado Springs, CO 80921

¹505686²7

To John Piper:

faithful pastor,
godly example,
lifelong friend

TABLE OF CONTENTS

PREFACE

This is a book for anyone who wants a quick overview of the main issues in the controversy over the Bible's teachings about men's and women's roles in the home and the church. It is a condensation of my 856-page comprehensive study, *Evangelical Feminism and Biblical Truth: An Analysis of More Than 100 Disputed Questions* (Sisters, OR: Multnomah, 2004). Its intended audience is evangelical Christians who do not want to wade through that larger book but want an accurate, Bible-based analysis of the major biblical teachings about manhood and womanhood, together with answers to the major evangelical feminist claims from a "complementarian" position.

But I have also added to this book some material that is not in the 2004 book, particularly some specific interaction with the recent egalitarian book *Discovering Biblical Equality: Complementarity without Hierarchy*, edited by Ronald W. Pierce and Rebecca Groothuis (Downers Grove, IL: InterVarsity, 2004).[1]

In the first two chapters of this book I attempt to cast a clear, biblical vision of manhood and womanhood, first with respect to creation and marriage and then with respect to the church. In the remainder of the book I interact with challenges and objections that egalitarians have brought against the vision expressed in these first two chapters.

I think it would be helpful if I could explain how this present book differs from the five other books I have written or edited on this topic:

(1) *Recovering Biblical Manhood and Womanhood* (Wheaton: Crossway, 1991; 566 pages), which John Piper and I edited, contains 26 essays by 22 different authors who were experts in various fields such as Old Testament, New Testament, theology, history, sociology, psychology, biology, law, and pastoral ministry. It remains the classic statement of the complementarian position and was named

---

1. A chapter-by-chapter response to *Discovering Biblical Equality* can also be found in the entire issue of *Journal for Biblical Manhood and Womanhood* (JBMW) 10:1 (Spring, 2005).

"Book of the Year" in 1992 by *Christianity Today* (based on a poll of readers). It continues to be widely read and has just been reprinted in an updated edition with a new preface (2006).

(2) *Biblical Foundations for Manhood and Womanhood* (Wheaton: Crossway, 2002), which I edited, contains ten chapters by various scholarly specialists on biblical, theological, and ethical topics related to this topic. Several of these essays are found nowhere else.

(3) *Pastoral Leadership for Manhood and Womanhood* (Wheaton: Crossway, 2002), which Dennis Rainey and I edited, contains fifteen chapters by fourteen authors, all of them veteran pastors or ministry leaders, on practical issues involved with teaching and practicing biblical manhood and womanhood in the ministry of a local church. Many church leaders have found this the most practical of all of these books.

(4) *Evangelical Feminism and Biblical Truth: An Analysis of More Than 100 Disputed Questions* (Sisters, OR: Multnomah, 2004; 856 pages), is a comprehensive reference work covering every aspect of the controversy in significant detail. It contains the results of everything I have learned in over twenty years of writing, research, and speaking on this topic, and interacts with 118 egalitarian claims.

(5) *Evangelical Feminism: A New Path to Liberalism?* (Wheaton: Crossway, 2006), documents 25 different arguments used by evangelical feminists that undermine the effective authority of Scripture in our lives. It shows how the same arguments used by more liberal denominations to approve the ordination of women in the 1970s are now being used by evangelical feminists, and traces the historical pattern that has led several groups from the ordination of women to the approval of homosexuality and the ordination of homosexual clergy.

I intend a book like this to be useful for all Christians who are wondering what to believe about biblical manhood and womanhood. It should especially be useful for college and seminary students, church study committees, and pastors and Bible study leaders who are looking for a shorter summary of arguments on both sides of this issue. It will also provide a useful handbook for Christians to consult when they are seeking answers to arguments proposed by their egalitarian friends.

I think the book will also be useful for those who are not engaged in any controversy but who simply want to understand more deeply what the Bible teaches about men and women and about our similarities and differences as created by God in His infinite wisdom.

Controversy is never easy, but God in His grace often allows controversies to bring us to deeper understanding of His Word and deeper love and trust for Him. This has been true throughout history as Christians have grown in their understanding of the Bible when they had to ponder and seek to answer controversial viewpoints on topics such as the Trinity, the person of Christ, justification by faith, the inerrancy of the Bible, and so forth. And so it has been in this controversy as well. As I have taught and written and debated about this topic for the past twenty-seven years, I know that God has given me a deeper love and appreciation for my wife Margaret, a deeper respect for the wisdom that God gives to both women and men, a deeper desire to see women as well as men using all the gifts God has given them for the good of the church, and a deeper appreciation for the amazing wisdom of God in creating men and women so wonderfully equal in many ways, yet so delightfully different in many other ways.

One danger of controversy is that it can overwhelm us to the point that we lose our joy. With regard to this issue, there is a risk of being so entangled in controversy that we lose the joy of being men and women. I hope this book will enable women to rejoice once again that God has made them women, and men to rejoice once again that God has made them men. I hope that we will be able to look at each other once again as brothers and sisters in God's family and feel something of the joy that God felt just after he first created us male and female:

> And God saw everything that he had made, and behold, *it was very good.* (Genesis 1:31)

Another danger of controversy is that we can lose our tempers or lash out in anger at those with whom we disagree. When we do this we forget what the New Testament teaches us about how we are to disagree with others:

> And the Lord's servant must not be quarrelsome but kind to everyone, able to teach, patiently enduring evil, correcting his opponents with gentleness. God may perhaps grant them repentance leading to a knowledge of the truth. (2 Timothy 2:24–25)

Who is wise and understanding among you? By his good conduct let him show his works in the meekness of wisdom.... But the wisdom from above is first pure, then peaceable, gentle, open to reason, full of mercy and good fruits, impartial and sincere. And a harvest of righteousness is sown in peace by those who make peace. (James 3:13, 17–18)

I have tried to follow these principles even when I disagree very directly with my egalitarian brothers and sisters in this book. I hope others who read this book will seek to obey these verses as well, and I hope readers will call it to my attention if I have been unfaithful to these verses in anything I wrote in this book.

Another danger of controversy is the temptation to passivity and to avoidance of an important issue that the Lord is asking us to deal with in our generation. I have been saddened to hear of churches and institutions that decide not to take any position regarding roles of men and women in marriage and the church. "It's too controversial," people have told me.

But this was not the practice of the apostle Paul. He was the greatest evangelist in the history of the world, but his concern to reach the lost did not lead him to shrink back from declaring unpopular doctrines if they were part of the Word of God. He told the elders of the church at Ephesus:

I testify to you this day that I am innocent of the blood of all of you, for I did not shrink from declaring to you the whole counsel of God. (Acts 20:26–27)

The implication is that if he had avoided some unpopular teachings in the Word of God, he would have to answer to the Lord for his negligence on the Last Day (see 2 Corinthians 5:10).

There is a parallel today. If a pastor or other ministry leader decides not to teach about male headship in the home, and if marriages in his church begin to experience the conflict and disintegration that results from the dominant feminist mindset of our secular culture, then he cannot say like Paul, "I am innocent of the blood of all of you." He cannot say at the end of his life that he has been a faithful steward of the responsibility entrusted to him (1 Corinthians 4:1–5). Those who avoid teaching on unpopular topics that are taught in God's Word have forgotten their accountability before God for their congregations: "They are keeping watch over your souls, as those who will have to give account" (Hebrews 13:17).

Churches and institutions that decide not to take any position on this issue are in fact taking a position anyway. They are setting themselves up for continual leftward movement and continual erosion of their level of obedience to Scripture (see chapter 44 for some examples). A church or organization that decides to have no policy on this issue will keep ratcheting left one cog at a time, in the direction of the main pressures of the culture. I hope this book will keep that process from happening in many churches and parachurch organizations.

THE NAME "COMPLEMENTARIAN"

I need to say something at the outset about the term "complementarian." I have used this term to refer to my position throughout this book, as I have for the last eighteen years. But one curious feature of *Discovering Biblical Equality*, the 2004 compendium of egalitarian essays,[2] is its attempt to apply the word "complementarian" to the book's egalitarian position (note the subtitle, *Complementarity without Hierarchy*). This can only result in confusing the debate. Since the first public announcement of the Council on Biblical Manhood and Womanhood (CBMW) at the Evangelical Theological Society meeting at Wheaton College in Wheaton, Illinois, on November 17, 1988, CBMW has used the word "complementarian" to refer to its position.[3] In fact, I was present when the CBMW executive committee coined that word (as far as we knew it had not previously been used in this controversy, or perhaps not at all) at a breakfast meeting at the Lisle Hilton in Lisle, Illinois, prior to our press conference announcing the formation of CBMW. We wanted one term that would summarize our position that men and women are equal in value and personhood before God, but different in roles. We coined the word "complementarian" to reflect the fact that men and women "complement" each other in our equality and differences.

Then in 1991 John Piper and I wrote in the "Preface" to *Recovering Biblical Manhood and Womanhood,*

2. Pierce and Groothuis, *Discovering Biblical Equality: Complementarity without Hierarchy.*

3. The CBMW web site, www.cbmw.org, now has hundreds of resources supporting and defending a complementarian position.

A brief note about terms: If one word must be used to describe our position, we prefer the term *complementarian,* since it suggests both equality and beneficial differences between men and women. We are uncomfortable with the term "traditionalist" because it implies an unwillingness to let Scripture challenge traditional patterns of behavior, and we certainly reject the term "hierarchicalist" because it overemphasizes structured authority while giving no suggestion of equality or the beauty of mutual interdependence.[4]

The editors of *Discovering Biblical Equality,* however, do not want us to use the word "complementarian" to identify our position. They say,

"This term must be challenged because egalitarians also believe in gender complementarity—yet *complementarity without hierarchy.*"[5]

My response is that the terms "complementarian" (on the one side) and "egalitarian" or "evangelical feminist" (on the other side) can now be found literally thousands of times in the literature on this topic over the last eighteen years. It will only bring confusion to try to apply "complementarian" to the egalitarian position at this point. A Google search for "complementarian" turned up 55,800 hits! The Wikipedia entry for "complementarianism" (accessed July 28, 2006) was accurate:

Complementarianism is a view of the relationship between the genders that differs from gender equalism, in that it believes that both men and women are equal in status, but can have different and complementary roles.

In Christian Theology, this view is promoted by the Council on Biblical Manhood and Womanhood. Groups of churches that broadly support this

---

4. John Piper and Wayne Grudem, eds., *Recovering Biblical Manhood and Womanhood: A Response to Evangelical Feminism* (Wheaton, IL: Crossway Books, 1991), p. xiv.
5. Rebecca Groothuis and Ronald Pierce, "Introduction," in *Discovering Biblical Equality,* 15. They also note that the most common terms used to describe their position have been "evangelical feminism," "egalitarianism," and "biblical equality" (pp. 15–16), and I think it significant that they had to use the word "egalitarians" in this very sentence to make clear to readers what group they were talking about!

positon include Newfrontiers, Sovereign Grace Ministries, the Southern Baptist Convention, the Presbyterian Church of America and the Anglican Diocese of Sydney, amongst many others.

Noted theologians and Christian thinkers who support this position include Wayne Grudem, Albert Mohler, Mark Dever, C.J. Mahaney, Joshua Harris, Ligon Duncan, Terry Virgo, and John Piper.

The complementarian position has clear implications for the Christian view of marriage as well as the Ordination of women. Complementarians tend to view women's roles in ministry, particularly in church settings, as limited to one extent or another. For example, few complementarians would support placing women in roles of leadership, such as that of pastor or priest, though specifically what ministry roles are open to women varies widely among complementarians.[6]

The objection of Groothuis and Pierce to the effect that "egalitarians also believe in gender complementarity" does not decide the question. It would be as if Presbyterians suddenly started calling themselves "Baptists," saying, "We also believe in baptism." Or if Baptists started calling themselves "Lutherans," saying, "We also trace our heritage to the Reformation started by Martin Luther." This turns ordinary conversation into nonsense.

Therefore in this book, and in all my other writing, I will continue to use the term "complementarian" for my own position and that of CBMW, and to use the terms "egalitarian" or "evangelical feminist" to refer to the position of *Discovering Biblical Equality* and that of Christians for Biblical Equality (CBE) and dozens of other egalitarian writers (see the Bibliography, pp. 308–13, for a list of many egalitarian books).

Those who helped in various ways with my earlier book *Evangelical Feminism and Biblical Truth* also deserve thanks for this condensation of that book (see EFBT, 20–21, for a list of many names). For this book in particular I wish especially to thank my son Elliot Grudem, pastor of Christ Our Comfort Presbyterian Church (PCA) in Raleigh, NC, for his initial work in shortening the first section of this book. Then, in addition to my own editing work, a huge amount of work in short-

---

6. http://en.wikipedia.org/wiki/Complementarian, accessed July 28, 2006.

ening the longer book was done very skillfully by Brian Thomasson at Multnomah Publishers. In addition, Chris Davis, Ben Burdick, and Travis Buchanan helped me with the editing process at various stages, and Ron Dickison again took time from his busy schedule to solve my computer problems from time to time. I am also grateful to Multnomah Publishers for their encouragement in pursuing this project of a condensed, more popular version of *Evangelical Feminism and Biblical Truth*.

My wife Margaret, my best advisor and best friend, has once again been a great encouragement to me in this writing process. I am thankful for the thirty-seven wonderful years of marriage that the Lord has given us and glad that we can look forward to many more years together, until the Lord himself calls us home.

Wayne Grudem
Scottsdale, AZ
July 28, 2006

ABBREVIATIONS

ANF: *Ante-Nicene Fathers*, 5th ed., ed. Alexander Roberts, James Donaldson, et al., 10 vols. (Grand Rapids: Wm. B. Eerdmans, 1969; first published 1885).

BDAG: *A Greek-English Lexicon of the New Testament and Other Early ChristianLiterature*, 3rd ed., rev. and ed. Frederick William Danker (Chicago and London: University of Chicago Press, 2000).

BDB: Francis Brown, S. R. Driver, and Charles A. Briggs, *A Hebrew and English Lexicon of the Old Testament* (Oxford: Clarendon Press, 1968).

DBE: *Discovering Biblical Equality: Complementarity without Hierarchy*, ed. Ronald W. Pierce and Rebecca Merrill Groothuis (Downers Grove: InterVarsity, 2004).

DNTB: *Dictionary of New Testament Background*, ed. Craig A. Evans and Stanley E. Porter (Downers Grove, IL: InterVarsity Press, 2000).

DPL: *Dictionary of Paul and His Letters*, ed. Gerald F. Hawthorne, Ralph P. Martin, and Daniel G. Reid (Downers Grove, IL: InterVarsity Press, 1993).

EDT: *Evangelical Dictionary of Theology*, ed. Walter Elwell (Grand Rapids: Baker Book House, 1984).

EFBT: Wayne Grudem, *Evangelical Feminism and Biblical Truth: An Analysis of More Than 100 Disputed Questions* (Sisters, OR: Multnomah, 2004).

ICC: *The International Critical Commentary*, ed. J. A. Emerton, C. E. B. Cranfield, and G. N. Stanton (Edinburgh: T & T Clark).

JBMW: Journal for Biblical Manhood and Womanhood.

JETS: Journal of the Evangelical Theological Society.

LS: *Greek-English Lexicon with a Revised Supplement*, ed. H. G. Liddell and R. Scott (Oxford: Clarendon Press, 1996).

NIDOTTE: *The New International Dictionary of Old Testament Theology and Exegesis*, ed. Willem A. VanGemeren, 10 vols. (Grand Rapids: Zondervan, 1997).

NPNF: *The Nicene and Post-Nicene Fathers,* Series 1 and 2, ed. Philip Schaff, et al., 26 vols. (Grand Rapids: Wm. B. Eerdmans, 1974).

TDNT: *Theological Dictionary of the New Testament,* ed. Gerhard Kittel and Gerhard Freidrich, trans. and ed. Geoffrey W. Bromiley, 9 vols. (Grand Rapids: Wm. B. Eerdmans Publishing Co., 1964–1974).

TrinJ: Trinity Journal.

PART ONE

A BIBLICAL VISION OF MANHOOD AND WOMANHOOD

In this first section of the book I give an overview of manhood and womanhood in marriage as it was first created by God (chapter 1), and then summarize the Bible's teaching on the roles that God has given for both men and women in the church (chapter 2).

I make reference from time to time to the Council on Biblical Manhood and Womanhood (CBMW). I was a cofounder of that organization in 1987 and have remained on its board ever since. CBMW continues to publish and distribute material representing essentially the same "complementarian" position that I advocate in this book. It is the primary organization defining and defending a complementarian position on men and women in the evangelical world today. Its website (www.cbmw.org) is an exceptionally valuable source of information.

The official statement of principles adopted by CBMW in December, 1987, is the Danvers Statement, which can be found on pp. 304–07.

A BIBLICAL VISION
OF MANHOOD AND
WOMANHOOD
AS CREATED BY GOD

MAN AND WOMAN:
EQUALLY VALUED, EQUALLY DIGNIFIED

The first thing the Bible tells us about human beings is that they were created "male and female" and that both men and women were created "in the image of God": "So God created man in his own image, in the image of God he created him; male and female he created them" (Genesis 1:27). This is a tremendous privilege and honor—to bear God's image—and it is something that the Bible clearly teaches is shared by both men and women: Both men and women are more like God than anything else in the universe.

Therefore, from the very beginning, the Bible clearly states that men are not superior to women and women are not inferior to men. They both have equal importance and value to God. Whenever men and women do not listen respectfully and thoughtfully to the other's viewpoints, do not value the wisdom of the other, or do not value the other's gifts and preferences as much as their own, they are neglecting the teaching found in Genesis 1:27.

DIFFERENT ROLES IN MARRIAGE

But while the Bible does teach that men and women were created with equal value and dignity before God, it also teaches that they were created to fill different roles in marriage; specifically, the husband "has the God-given responsibility to provide for, to protect, and to lead his family."[1]

Even before the Fall, we see that God has established this distinct leadership role—male headship—for the husband in marriage. Following are ten clear, biblical evidences of this headship:

1. The order: This idea of male headship in marriage is seen first in the order that men and women were created. Man (Adam) was created first, and woman (Eve) was created second (see Genesis 2:7, 18–23). The order of creation is no minor detail, but instead sets an important biblical precedent. This is evident when Paul uses the fact that "Adam was formed first, then Eve" (1 Timothy 2:13) as a reason for men and women having different roles in the life of the New Testament church.[2]

2. The representation: It was Adam, not Eve, who had a special role in representing the human race. Though Eve sinned before Adam (Genesis 3:6), the Bible tells us: "For as in Adam all die, so also in Christ shall all be made alive" (1 Corinthians 15:22; see also 1 Corinthians 15:45–49 and Romans 5:12–21). Adam and Eve did not represent the human race together. Adam alone represented the human race because of a particular leadership role God gave him, a role that Eve did not share.

3. The naming of woman: Not only was Adam created before his wife; he was also given the responsibility of naming her: "She shall be called Woman, because she was taken out of Man" (Genesis 2:23). Given the larger context of the naming activities in Genesis 1–2, the original readers would have recognized that the person given the responsibility to name created things is always the person who has authority over those things. This is seen in God's naming different parts of His creation in Genesis 1–2 and parents naming their children (see, for example, Genesis 4:25, 26; 5:3, 28–29; 16:15; 19:37, 38; 21:3).[3]

---

1. This wording is taken from *The Baptist Faith and Message* as adopted by the Southern Baptist Convention June 14, 2000, and taken from www.sbc.net/bfm/bfm2000.asp (accessed May 9, 2006). See a longer quotation in Grudem, EFBT, 716.
2. See below, pp. 77–78, for an answer to the egalitarian claim that if being created first gave Adam authority, then animals would have authority over us.
3. For an answer to the egalitarian objections that Adam did not really name Eve in Genesis 2, and that naming does not imply authority, see Grudem, EFBT, 31–34.

4. The naming of the human race: Genesis 5:1–2 records God's naming the human race: "When God created man, he made him in the likeness of God. Male and female he created them, and he blessed them and named them Man when they were created." As we have seen, both men and women were created in the image of God, so both have equal value and importance. But when God chose to name the human race, He chose a distinctively male term (in the context of Genesis 1–5)[4] to indicate male leadership. "God's naming of the race 'man' whispers male headship."[5]

5. The primary accountability: And it was Adam who God first called to account after he and Eve sinned. "The LORD God called to the man and said to him, 'Where are you?'" (Genesis 3:9). In doing so, God demonstrated that Adam, as the leader, had the primary accountability for his family, even though the serpent spoke first to Eve and though Eve sinned first (Genesis 3:1, 6).

6. The purpose: When God created Eve, He created her as a helper for Adam. "Then the LORD God said, 'It is not good that the man should be alone; I will make him a helper fit for him'" (Genesis 2:18). Though a "helper" can take differing roles in terms of leadership (more, equal, or lesser authority),[6] the broader context indicates a helper who by virtue of creation serves in a role of lesser authority in the relationship. Yet "helper" does not mean someone who is inferior, for God Himself is often called our "helper" in the Bible (see Psalm 33:20; 70:5; 115:9; yet with regard to tasks for which we are still primarily responsible). In addition, the word translated "fit for him" means "a help corresponding to him" that is "equal and adequate to himself."[7]

7. The conflict: Sin brought conflict into Adam and Eve's relationship by creating a distortion of the roles God set out for them. It did not create new roles; it just made the current ones more difficult to fulfill. When God spoke to Eve in judgment after the Fall, He said: "Your *desire* shall be for your husband, and he shall

---

4. For more specific information about the Hebrew word translated "man" (Hebrew *'ādām*), see Grudem, EFBT, 34–36.
5. Raymond C. Ortlund Jr., "Male-Female Equality and Male Headship," in Piper and Grudem, *Recovering Biblical Manhood and Womanhood*, 98.
6. See Grudem, EFBT, 36–37 and 117–19 for more information on the word translated "helper" (Hebrew *'ēzer*); see also pp. 74–76, below.
7. BDB, 617.

rule over you" (Genesis 3:16). A similar phrase using the same unusual Hebrew word translated "desire" is found in Genesis 4:7, when God says to Cain: "Sin is crouching at the door. Its *desire* is for you, but you must rule over it." In both cases, the word "desire" (Hebrew *teshûqāh*) probably implies a "desire to conquer or rule over" (not sexual desire, as some believe). And the word translated "rule over" in Genesis 3:16 refers to Adam's later harsh leadership over Eve—not one of equals, but one who rules by virtue of power and strength (even sometimes harshly and with force).[8]

So it is clear from Genesis 3:16 that part of the curse of sin was pain and conflict in the relationship between husband and wife. The wife would have an impulse or desire to rule against her husband and his leadership, and the husband would have a tendency to rule his wife out of his strength, in a way that was forceful and at times harsh. Because Genesis 3:16 is one of the results of the curse, this is not something we should try to promote. Just as we weed our gardens and take steps to prevent pain in childbirth (thus seeking to overcome two other results of the curse), so we should do everything we can to overcome this conflict and distortion in the relationship between men and women.

8. The restoration: The good news is that when Jesus came, He came to bring restoration—in the words of the Christmas hymn *Joy to the World,* He came "to make his blessings flow, far as the curse is found." And in Colossians 3:18–19 we find Paul explaining an unraveling of Genesis 3:16: "Wives, *submit to your husbands,* as is fitting in the Lord. Husbands, *love your wives, and do not be harsh with them.*" While we see a foreshadowing of this in the Old Testament (the relationship of Ruth and Boaz, for example), we see clearly in this and other passages in both the Old and New Testament that God's design for marriage was for the wife to be subject to her husband and for the husband to love his wife and lead her in a way that was not harsh—the way Adam and Eve related before the Fall.

---

8. See Grudem, EFBT, 37–40, for more information on the words translated "desire" and "rule." Interestingly, the chapter on Genesis 1–3 in the recent egalitarian book *Discovering Biblical Equality* agrees with this understanding of Genesis 3:16. Richard Hess writes, "Susan Foh suggests that a woman's desire here is not a sexual desire but a desire to dominate, just as sin has a 'desire' to 'rule over' Cain (Gen. 4:7).... On this point Foh appears to have gotten it right and to have made an important contribution" (Richard Hess, "Equality with and without Innocence: Genesis 1–3," in DBE, 92).

9. The mystery: Though Adam and Eve did not know it, their relationship prior to the Fall represented the relationship between Christ and His church. That is why Paul, writing of the marriage relationship, quotes the command given by God in Genesis 2:

> "Therefore a man shall leave his father and mother and hold fast to his wife, and the two shall become one flesh." This mystery is profound, and I am saying that it refers to Christ and the church. (Ephesians 5:31–32)

The profound "mystery" Paul refers to is that the marriage relationship was only faintly, if at all, understood in the Old Testament to be a reference to the relationship between Christ and the church. But in the New Testament, Paul says that *from the beginning,* God designed marriage to show us how Jesus relates to the church, His bride. That is why Paul writes, "For the husband is the head of the wife even as Christ is the head of the church" (Ephesians 5:23).

Now the relationship between Christ and the church is not culturally variable. It is the same for all generations. And it is not reversible. There is a leadership or headship role that belongs to Christ that the church does not have. This is the same with marriage. God created within marriage a leadership or headship role that belongs to the husband that the wife does not have. The relationship was there from the beginning of creation, in the beautiful marriage between Adam and Eve in the Garden.

10. The parallel with the Trinity: Just as in the Trinity there are equality, differences, and unity among Father, Son, and Holy Spirit, so in marriage there are equality, differences, and unity that reflect the relationships within the Trinity. Adam and Eve's differences before the Fall reflect the eternal differences between the Father and Son in the Trinity, as Paul specifies in 1 Corinthians 11:3: "But I want you to understand that the head of every man is Christ, the head of a wife is her husband, and the head of Christ is God."

So there are at least ten reasons showing that Adam and Eve had distinct roles before the Fall. This was God's purpose in creating them.[9]

---

9. Richard Hess's essay, "Equality with and without Innocence," in DBE, 79–95, argues that Genesis 1–2 affirms equality, but then claims, with respect to several specific details of the narrative in Genesis 2, that male headship is nowhere explicitly affirmed. For example, "Genesis 2 nowhere suggests a hierarchical relationship between the man and the woman, and certainly not because of the 'order of creation'" (85), or "The text nowhere states that the man exercised authority over the animals by naming them" (87). (*Note 9 continued at right.*)

WHEN ROLES GO WRONG

When the roles designed by God for the marriage relationship are distorted, danger can arise in the relationship. Distortion can come either in the form of aggressiveness or passivity; such distortions can come from either the husband or the wife.

Errors of aggression are those that have their beginnings in Genesis 3:16: The husband can be selfish, harsh, domineering, or tyrannical. This is not biblical headship. On the other hand, if the wife resists the husband's leadership by trying to usurp it, then she is not following God's pattern for marriage.

Opposite the errors of aggression are errors of passivity. They are equally as wrong. When a husband abdicates his leadership responsibilities by not disciplining his children, not caring for the family's physical or spiritual needs, or not defending his wife and children when verbally attacked by a friend or relative (these are just a few of many examples), then his acting as a wimp does not fit the role God designed for him in marriage. Or when a wife chooses not to participate in family decisions, does not express her preferences or opinions, does not speak up when her children or husband are doing wrong, or does not object to her husband's physical or verbal abuse, then she is not being submissive, but instead is acting as a doormat, and out of line with the role God designed for her in the marriage relationship.

Here is a chart showing the dangers of both active and passive distortion of biblical responsibilities:

	Errors of passivity	Biblical ideal	Errors of aggressiveness
Husband	Wimp	Loving, humble headship	Tyrant
Wife	Doormat	Joyful, intelligent submission	Usurper

But Hess fails to take adequate account of the fact that it is the nature of narrative to *report* events, even though the immediate context does not always provide specific *interpretation* of those events. The way certain actions and events are treated in the rest of the Bible gives us the larger context in which these events would have been understood by Old Testament readers, events such as (1) Adam naming the animals and then naming Eve, or (2) Adam being created before Eve, or (3) God speaking to Adam first before creating Eve, or (4) God speaking to Adam first after the Fall, or (5) God naming the human race "Man." As I have argued above, and more extensively in EFBT, 29–42, there is significant evidence that these things all indicate a leadership role for Adam before the Fall.

The biblical ideal is that the husband is to be both loving and humble in his leadership. The wife is to be both joyful and intelligent in her submission. Practically, this means that they will frequently talk about many decisions, both large and small. This also means that both the husband and wife will listen to the other's unique wisdom and insight related to the decision. Often, one will defer to the other in the decision; rarely will they differ greatly on the decision (for the Lord has made them "one flesh").

But in every decision that involves both the husband and wife, whether large or small, and whether they agree or not, the responsibility to make the decision rests with the husband. Therefore, male headship makes a difference every day in the marriage relationship. This is not because the husband is wiser or a better leader or a better decision maker, but because that headship is part of the God-given role for the husband. It is part of God's good design for the marriage relationship.

DIFFERENT ROLES, DIFFERENT RESPONSIBILITIES

As has been hinted at up to this point, it seems God designed both the husband and wife to bear primary responsibility for different roles within the marriage. First, Adam had a responsibility to lead in a way that was pleasing to God, and Eve had a responsibility to be submissive to and supportive of Adam in his leadership role. In addition, Adam is assumed to have the primary responsibility for *providing for* his family, for it is Adam who is told that he will suffer pain as he tills the earth (Genesis 3:17–19). Eve is assumed to have the primary responsibility for *caring for the home and children*, for it is Eve who is told she will suffer pain in bearing children (Genesis 3:14–16). This is not to say that the husband should not assist in the child care (see Deuteronomy 6:7 and Ephesians 6:4, for example). It also does not mean that a wife cannot ever provide for her family or help to provide (see Proverbs 31:16–18 and Acts 16:14, for example). It does, however, mean that the husband has the *primary* responsibility to provide for his wife and family, and the wife has the *primary* responsibility to care for the home and children.

This is seen not only in Genesis 3, but also throughout the Scriptures.[10] For

---

10. For additional biblical evidence, see Grudem, EFBT, 44–45.

example, the church is commanded to care for widows, not widowers, in 1 Timothy 5:3–16. In addition, older women are encouraged to teach younger women to work at home (Titus 2:5).

In addition, it is men who bear the primary responsibility of *protecting* their families. The laws concerning warfare in Deuteronomy 20:7–8 and elsewhere are addressed to men and it is thought shameful for a nation to send women to combat (see also Num. 1:2–3; Deut. 3:18–19; 24:5; Judg. 4:8–10; Josh. 1:14; 23:10; Judg. 9:54; 1 Sam. 4:9; Neh. 4:13–14; Jer. 50:37; Nah. 3:13). A man's responsibility to protect even involves a willingness to lay down his life for his wife (Ephesians 5:25).

EQUALITY AND DIFFERENCES IN GOD HIMSELF

There is more at stake in this argument, though, than how a husband and wife relate in their marriage or the meaning of one or two words in the Bible. For at the heart of this issue is a question about the very nature of God Himself.

For example, as I mentioned before, in 1 Corinthians 11:3, Paul writes, "But I want you to understand that the *head* of every man is Christ, the *head* of a wife is her husband, and the *head* of Christ is God." The Greek word translated "head" (the word *kephalē*) refers to one in a position of authority, as is the case here when Paul writes of both the relationship between a husband and wife and the relationship between God the Father and God the Son.

Just as God the Father and God the Son are equal in deity, equal in attributes, but *different in role*, so a husband and wife are equal in personhood, equal in value, but *different in the roles* God gave them. Just as God the Son is eternally subject to the authority of God the Father, so wives are to be subject to the authority of their husbands. This is God's design.

Some have challenged the idea that the Son is eternally subject to the authority of the Father within the Trinity, but there is abundant evidence for it. Scripture tells us that the Father "gave" His only Son (John 3:16) and "sent" the Son into the world (John 3:17, 34; 4:34; 8:42; Galatians 4:4). In addition, John 12:49 tells us that the Son is obedient to the Father's commands.

In Ephesians 1:4, Paul writes that the Father "chose us" in the Son "before the foundation of the world." In order for this to be true, the Father must eternally be the Father, and the Son must eternally be the Son. First Corinthians 15:28 confirms this: "When all things are subjected to him, then the Son himself will also be subjected to him who put all things in subjection under him, that God may be all in all." Relationally, the Son has and always will be subject to the authority of the Father. Never in Scripture do we find the opposite stated.[11]

It is clear that the idea of headship and submission within a personal relationship was not simply a cultural ideal whose time has passed, a power grab by patriarchal men, or something that came to be after Adam and Eve's fall into sin in Genesis 3. The idea of headship and submission existed before the creation of the world.

In fact, the idea of headship and submission has always existed, for it is part of the eternal nature of God Himself. The Father has always had a leadership role as He relates to the Son. In addition, the Father and Son have eternally had a leadership role or an authority with respect to the Holy Spirit. Since all members of the Trinity have equal attributes and perfections, such leadership and submission is not based on gifts or abilities; it is just there. It is a fundamental difference between the Father, Son, and Spirit.

Submission to a rightful authority is a noble virtue. It is a privilege. It is a virtue that the Son of God has demonstrated forever. It does not lessen the value of the Son. Nor is it something He regretted (John 4:34); nor did it make Him inferior (Colossians 1:18).

Therefore, when Paul writes, "The head of every man is Christ, the head of a wife is her husband, and the head of Christ is God" (1 Corinthians 11:3), he demonstrates how important these roles are in marriage. For to change or modify these roles would likely lead to changing or modifying the scriptural role of the Father and the Son.

IT WAS VERY GOOD

After God made man and woman, He commented on all of His creation. His statement is found in Genesis 1:31: "And God saw everything that he had made,

---

11. For more discussion of this idea see below, 230–56, and also Grudem, EFBT, 45–48, 405–43.

and behold, it was *very good*." The way God created men and women—each one made in His image, each one equal in status, and each one differing in roles—God said was "very good." Though it may seem that both the popular and academic cultures are hostile to the idea of equality and difference when it comes to the relational roles of men and women, God thought the way He created things was "very good."

Therefore, such order is fair. Though some may say it is not fair for men to have a leadership role in marriage, God designed this role from the beginning of human existence. God the Father thought it was "very good." God the Son also thought such a relationship was good, as He fulfilled the Psalm that said, "I desire to do your will, O my God" (Psalm 4:8; compare Hebrews 10:7). In addition, Jesus said of His relationship with God the Father, "I always do the things that are pleasing to him" (John 8:29). Just as the relationships between the Father, Son, and Spirit are good and fair, so is the relationship between a man and woman that God established in marriage.

Such a relationship is also best for us because it comes from the all-wise Creator. This is the pattern God established to honor both men and women, to guard against abuse (each has equal value before God), and to encourage each to exercise their gifts and wisdom as they were created to use them. A marriage exercising this God-designed relationship is the marriage relationship that God called "very good."

And this created order is beautiful. God's created order for marriage is beautiful because it is God's way to bring amazing unity to people who are as different as men and women. This unity and diversity finds its beautiful expression in sexuality within the marriage relationship. When a man leaves his father and mother to "hold fast to his wife," and they "become one flesh" (Genesis 2:24), such unity and diversity is expressed in a truly beautiful way. As husband and wife, we are most attracted to the parts of each other that are the most different. Our greatest unity comes at the places of greatest difference. Such unity expresses not only a physical union, but also an emotional and spiritual union as well. God delights in such unity within diversity. And He considers it "very good."

Marriage is a wonderful expression of love. It is not only an expression of love between a man and woman, but also between God and His creation. It is also a wonderful God-designed expression to reflect the equality, difference, and unity He planned for such a relationship. Equal in value and different in roles: God's excellent design both for marriage and for our good.

2

A BIBLICAL VISION OF MANHOOD AND WOMANHOOD IN THE CHURCH

I n the previous chapter, I discussed a biblical vision of manhood and womanhood as they were created by God—sharing equally in status, value, and dignity as bearers of His image—from the beginning and as they should function in marriage, in obedience to God's Word today. But how will this picture of manhood and womanhood work itself out in the life of the church? What does the Bible teach about the roles of men and women in the church, and how should this teaching be applied in the practical details of church life?

WHAT THE BIBLE SAYS ABOUT ROLES IN THE CHURCH

In the New Testament, the Holy Spirit is poured out in a new kind of fullness on both men and women. On the Day of Pentecost, Peter says that the prophecy of Joel is fulfilled:

"And in the last days it shall be, God declares,
that I will pour out my Spirit on all flesh,
and *your sons and your daughters* shall prophesy,
and your young men shall see visions,

31

and your old men shall dream dreams;
even on my *male servants and female servants*
in those days I will pour out my Spirit, and they shall prophesy."
(Acts 2:17–18)

From Pentecost onward, this New Covenant work of the Holy Spirit would involve giving spiritual gifts to both men *and women*, and to sons *and daughters*. All will have spiritual gifts for various kinds of ministries. (See also 1 Corinthians 12:7, 11; 1 Peter 4:10; Acts 8:12.) The practical implication of this is that Paul expects that *every believer* will have at least one spiritual gift to be used for the benefit of others in the church. Therefore women as well as men will have such gifts.

Another reminder of our equal value before God is Paul's affirmation of our unity in the body of Christ, rather than being divided into groups who are "more important" and "less important," or who have higher or lower status. Paul says, "There is neither Jew nor Greek, there is neither slave nor free, *there is neither male nor female, for you are all one* in Christ Jesus" (Galatians 3:28).

These passages should cause us to ask whether our churches have rightly and fully utilized the gifts and ministries of women in the past. I hope that many church leaders reading this chapter will decide that they have not done enough to encourage various kinds of ministries by women. Although I argue below that God restricts the office of elder or pastor to men, there are many other activities in the church in which women should be actively involved.

For example, nothing in Scripture prohibits women from chairing various committees within the church, as long as that does not involve functioning as an elder with authority over the whole church. Similarly, I see no persuasive reason why only church officers should serve Communion, though the pastor or some other elder should officiate. There is also nothing in Scripture that prohibits a woman from being a paid full-time staff member in a church, such as a director of educational ministries, or a women's ministry director, or in a youth ministry position, or in a role as a part-time or full-time counselor.

I discuss a number of these activities under the heading "But What *Should* Women Do in the Church?" in the last part of this chapter. But at this point, it suffices to say that *we should not make rules that the Bible does not support*, and *we should not add restrictions to ministry positions when the Bible does not justify these restrictions.*

Where the Bible allows freedom, we should encourage ministries by women as well as by men. In the current controversy, God has provided us with an excellent opportunity to reexamine the Scriptures to see if they really do support all the restrictions we have inherited from tradition.[1]

TEACHING AND SPEAKING BY WOMEN THAT THE BIBLE RESTRICTS

As in every area of life and practice, we must measure all ministry in the church by the Bible. And there are several passages that clearly restrict some governing and teaching roles in the church to men. We begin with 1 Timothy 2:11–15:

> Let a woman learn quietly with all submissiveness. I do not permit a woman to teach or to exercise authority over a man; rather, she is to remain quiet. For Adam was formed first, then Eve; and Adam was not deceived, but the woman was deceived and became a transgressor. Yet she will be saved through childbearing—if they continue in faith and love and holiness, with self-control.

The setting for this passage is *the assembled church*. Just a few verses earlier, Paul says:

> I desire then that in every place the men should pray, lifting holy hands without anger or quarreling; likewise also that women should adorn themselves in respectable apparel, with modesty and self-control, not with braided hair and gold or pearls or costly attire, but with what is proper for women who profess godliness—with good works. (1 Timothy 2:8–10)

---

1. Egalitarian literature contains many real-life stories of wrongful repression of women's gifts and viewpoints, such as Ruth Tucker's carefully stated but evidently painful memory of trying to serve as a pastor's wife when her husband would repeatedly put her down by quoting "Women should be silent in the churches" whenever she said something in a Bible study or church business meeting (Ruth Tucker, *Women in the Maze*, 121–22). Though I differ with Dr. Tucker and with other egalitarians at several places throughout this book, I hope that I and my fellow complementarians will resolve also to oppose such a harsh, repressive view whenever we encounter it and thus fully honor the wisdom and gifting that God has given to women in His church.

This is a setting in which men lift "holy hands" to pray, and they do so "without anger or quarreling," which implies that Paul is thinking of them in a group, when they get together as an assembled church. Similarly, the demand that women dress "with modesty" implies that Paul is thinking about a time when other people are present, as when the church gathers together.

The phrase "in every place" in verse 8 indicates that it applies wherever groups of Christians might meet for prayer, worship, and instruction.

In fact, Paul's instructions in this section generally have to do with the church, because in 1 Timothy 3:1–7, he talks about the requirements for elders, and then in verses 8–13, he talks about the requirements for deacons, and both of these offices pertain to the entire church. Then immediately after that, Paul says he is writing these things to Timothy "so that, if I delay, you may know how one ought to behave in the household of God, which is the church of the living God, a pillar and buttress of truth" (v. 15).

Therefore, according to the context of this passage, the setting in which Paul does not allow a woman to teach and have authority over a man is the assembled church, where Bible teaching would be done.

What kind of "teaching" does Paul have in mind? Certainly this passage does not exclude women from teaching men mathematics or geography or a foreign language or any of hundreds of other subjects. That is not what the verb "teach" (*didaskō*) would have meant in this context to the Christians who read Paul's letter. Paul was talking about what should happen when the whole church came together, and in such a setting, *the kind of "teaching" that would be done was Bible teaching*. For example, when Paul and Barnabas were at Antioch, we read that they were "teaching and preaching *the word of the Lord*" (Acts 15:35). Or when Paul was at Corinth, "He stayed a year and six months, *teaching the word of God* among them" (Acts 18:11). In other cases, Paul commands Timothy to "teach" what Paul himself has written or taught, since such apostolic teachings had the same status as Scripture, and in fact Paul's written words had the authority of Scripture (see 1 Corinthians 14:37; 1 Timothy 4:11; 6:2; 2 Timothy 2:2). Using the related noun *didaskalia*, "teaching, instruction," Paul says that "all Scripture is breathed out by God and profitable for *teaching*" (2 Timothy 3:16).

The conclusion is that Paul did not allow women to teach *the Bible* or have governing authority over the assembled church. But this text would not prevent women from teaching *skills* (such as Greek or Hebrew or counseling) or teaching *information* (such as reporting on missionary activity or giving a personal testimony) to the church. The passage talks about Bible teaching, and therefore it is appropriate to distinguish between teaching *the Bible* and teaching *skills* or *information.*

But does Paul's command regarding women not teaching the Bible to or having authority over a man apply to Christians today as it did in the first century? Or was this just a temporary command given for a specific local situation?

In chapters 25–28 and 31–34 of this book, I examine different arguments that this is just a temporary command, given to a specific situation at Ephesus.[2] But at this point we should realize that Paul's words do not at all give the appearance of a temporary command for a specific situation, for he grounds his instructions in the situation of Adam and Eve before the Fall:

> Let a woman learn quietly with all submissiveness. I do not permit a woman to teach or to exercise authority over a man; rather, she is to remain quiet. For Adam was formed first, then Eve; and Adam was not deceived, but the woman was deceived and became a transgressor. Yet she will be saved through childbearing—if they continue in faith and love and holiness, with self-control. (1 Timothy 2:11–15)

Paul's first reason is the order of creation: "For Adam was formed first, then Eve." Paul does not use some local situation in Ephesus for a reason, such as saying, "For women aren't as well educated there in Ephesus," or "For you have some disruptive women teaching false doctrine there in Ephesus." No, he points back to the original time of creation, before there was any sin in the world, and sees that there was a purpose of God indicated in the order of creation: "For Adam was formed first, then Eve." Paul simply assumes that his readers will understand that when God created Adam first, and then gave commands to him alone (Genesis 2:7, 15–17), and then later created Eve (v. 22), God was giving a leadership role to Adam.

People in the ancient world, where the firstborn son had a leadership role in

---

2. See below, pp. 161–82 and 199–220, and also Grudem, EFBT, 280–302 and 329–61.

the family, would have understood this. But we do not need to assume that Paul was endorsing the entire system of "primogeniture," at least not in all its details. It is enough simply to say that people who were familiar with that system would have had no trouble understanding Paul's reasoning: The firstborn male in any family is assumed to be the leader in that family in his generation, and Adam was the firstborn in his generation, so he was the leader.

It does not really matter whether we think such a system is right today, or whether we practice some elements of such a system in families today, in order for this text of Scripture to be true. What matters is that Paul the apostle, writing under the guidance of the Holy Spirit, sees a leadership function that God indicated by creating Adam first, and then Eve. This leadership function had implications even for Christian churches in the first century, because Paul gives it as a reason why a woman should not teach or have authority over a man in the assembled congregation.

Sometimes egalitarians object, "If being created first means that one is a leader, then the animals should have authority over human beings!" But that objection fails to understand that authority relationships among human beings apply only to human beings. It would be foolishness to think otherwise, because God gave to human beings the responsibility to rule over the creation and to subdue the earth for His glory (see Genesis 1:28).

When Paul bases his argument on the order of creation of Adam and Eve, it indicates that his command about women not teaching or having authority in the assembled congregation transcends cultures and societies. It applies to men and women as they were created by God at the beginning, and it is not due to any distortion brought on by sin or the Fall. It applies, then, to all churches for all time, and it is a means by which the beauty of manhood and womanhood as God created them can be manifested in the life of the church.

Paul gives a second reason in verse 1 Timothy 2:14: "And Adam was not deceived, but the woman was deceived and became a transgressor."

Paul must have in mind something about the way the first sins of Adam and Eve came about, and he must be trying to avoid having a similar kind of disobedience in the New Testament church. Therefore, Paul must be pointing to something in the nature of Adam and Eve, or something in the roles in which God created them, that was violated when "Adam was not deceived, but the woman was deceived and became a transgressor." What was that?

There are two main interpretations of 1 Timothy 2:14.[3] The first interpretation says that verse 14 refers to a *role reversal* in the Fall. The idea is that Eve took the initiative and made the decision to eat the forbidden fruit on her own, but in doing this she took a leadership role that belonged to Adam. In this way, Paul is pointing out what happens when women take the leadership role that God has reserved for men.

We could paraphrase this "role reversal" interpretation as follows: "Women should not teach or have authority over men because Adam was not the first one deceived, but Eve was first deceived by the serpent when she took leadership instead of deferring to the leadership of her husband." Paul is not saying anything about the natural abilities of men and women or about their natural tendencies or preferences, but is simply saying that tragic results follow when people abandon God's plan for male leadership, and Eve is an example of that.

While this interpretation has some able defenders,[4] Paul does not specify that he is talking about who was deceived first and who was deceived second. He does not say, "And Adam was not deceived first, but the woman was deceived first." He says that Adam was not deceived *at all*: "And Adam *was not deceived.*" If Paul simply meant that Eve was deceived first and then Adam was deceived second, it seems unlikely that he would have started this clause by emphasizing that "Adam was not deceived." Rather, Paul is saying that Eve was convinced to believe something false, and she sinned as a result, but that Adam knew it was wrong and went ahead and sinned intentionally. Paul is not excusing either Adam or Eve, for both sinned, but he identifies a difference in the way their sins came about.

The second major interpretation of verse 14 is that Paul is saying something about the nature of men and women as God created them. This is by far the most common viewpoint in the history of interpretation of this passage.[5] While some

---

3. For further discussion, see especially the detailed studies by William Mounce, *Pastoral Epistles*, 135–43, and Thomas R. Schreiner, "An Interpretation of 1 Timothy 2:9–15: A Dialogue with Scholarship," in Köstenberger, *Women in the Church*, 140–46, and for a history of interpretation of the passage, see Doriani, "A History of the Interpretation of 1 Timothy 2," in Köstenberger, *Women in the Church*, 213–67, and especially his summary on pp. 262–67.
4. See, for example, Douglas Moo, "What Does It Mean Not to Teach or Have Authority over Men?" in Piper and Grudem, *Recovering Biblical Manhood and Womanhood*, 190.
5. See Doriani, "A History of the Interpretation of 1 Timothy 2," 213–68.

authors have wrongly understood this text to be teaching the intellectual inferiority of women, that misunderstanding is certainly not necessary to the passage, nor am I aware of any modern author who holds that view today. Rather, this interpretation says that while God made men and women (in general) with equal intellectual abilities, there are still differences in preferences and inclinations, and those differences are consistent or "congruent" with God's purposes in entrusting leadership in the church to men.

Thomas Schreiner adopts this second view of 1 Timothy 2:14:

> God's order of creation is mirrored in the nature of men and women. Satan approached the woman first not only because of the order of creation but also because of the different inclinations present in Adam and Eve. Generally speaking, women are more relational and nurturing and men are more given to rational analysis and objectivity.... Appointing women to the teaching office is prohibited because they are less likely to draw a line on doctrinal non-negotiables, and thus deception and false teaching will more easily enter the church. This is not to say women are intellectually deficient or inferior to men.... Their kinder and gentler nature inhibits them from excluding people for doctrinal error. There is the danger of stereotyping here, for obviously some women are more inclined to objectivity and are "tougher" and less nurturing than other women. But as a general rule women are more relational and caring than men. This explains why most women have many more close friends than men. The different inclinations of women (and men!) do not imply that they are inferior or superior to men. It simply demonstrates that men and women are profoundly different. Women have some strengths that men do not have, and men have some strengths that are generally lacking in women.[6]

This explanation seems to me to best suit the wording in 1 Timothy 2:14. Paul is saying that women should not teach or have authority over men in the congregation of God's people for two reasons: (1) Because God gave Adam a leadership role when He created him first and Eve second (v. 13), and (2) God gave men, in

---

6. Schreiner, "Interpretation of 1 Timothy 2:9–15," 145–46. A recent scientific analysis of the neurological basis for different inclinations of men and women is a book by neuropsychiatrist Louann Brizendine, *The Female Brain* (New York: Morgan Road, 2006).

general, a disposition that is better suited to teaching and governing in the church, a disposition that inclines more to rational, logical analysis of doctrine and a desire to protect the doctrinal purity of the church, and God gave women, in general, a disposition that inclines more toward a relational, nurturing emphasis that places a higher value on unity and community in the church (v. 14). Both emphases are needed, of course, and both men and women have some measure of both tendencies. But Paul understands the kinder, gentler, more relational nature of women as something that made Eve less inclined to oppose the deceptive serpent and more inclined to accept his words as something helpful and true.

To say this is not at all to say that men are better than women or that women are inferior to men. That would be contrary to the entire biblical testimony. But if in fact God has created us to be different, then it is inevitable that women will be better at some things (in general) and men will be better at other things (in general).

In the same way, it seems that 1 Timothy 2:14 is saying that men are better suited for the task of governing and of safeguarding the doctrine of the church. This does not mean that women *could not* do this task and do it well, at least in certain cases. But it does mean that God has both established men in that responsibility and has given inclinations and abilities that are well suited to that responsibility.

Yet we must be cautious at this point. We should not say, "Since Paul's reasoning is based on different general tendencies in men and women, there will be some unusual women who can be elders because they don't fit the generalizations but reason and relate more like men." We should not say that because Paul does not say that; he prohibits *all women* from teaching and governing the assembled congregation, not just those with certain abilities and tendencies.[7]

And he does so first because of the order in which God created Adam and Eve (v. 13) and second because he sees something in Eve that is representative of womanhood generally (v. 14) and therefore applies broadly and in principle to all women, as they are representatives of womanhood as well.

What then is the meaning of verse 15: "Yet she will be saved through childbearing—if they continue in faith and love and holiness, with self-control"?

The general force of the sentence is clear, although people differ about the

---

7. In the same way, all men have a responsibility for leadership in their marriages, even though some men are not as naturally inclined or gifted for leadership.

details. Paul has just finished saying that "the woman was deceived and became a transgressor." In this final comment his purpose is to assure readers that Eve's sin was not the final word regarding women! Though Eve sinned, salvation is now possible through Christ.

The phrase "through childbearing" is probably best understood as an *example* of being obedient to God's calling on one's life. Women are not to teach or govern the church, but God has given them a special responsibility, the awesome responsibility of bearing and raising children. Paul understands that not all women will be able to have children (for the Old Testament and life experience both testify to that fact), and he also gives a long section on widows in 1 Timothy 5:3–16, so he knows there are many women in the church at Ephesus who do not have husbands.

But Paul is speaking of "childbearing" as a *representative example* of how a woman should be obedient to God's calling on her life and fulfill the role or roles God has called her to, whether that includes bearing and raising children, or showing "hospitality" (1 Timothy 5:10), or caring for the afflicted (v. 10), or managing their households (v. 14), or ministering through "supplications and prayers" (v. 5), or training younger women (Titus 2:4–5), or any mixture of these or other callings. Paul takes "childbearing" as one obvious and representative example of a woman's distinctive role and calling from God.

What does it mean then to say that "she will be saved through childbearing"? It surely does not mean that a woman is justified or forgiven of her sins because of childbearing or fulfilling other tasks to which God calls her, for Paul clearly teaches that salvation in this sense is a "gift of God, not a result of works, so that no one may boast" (Ephesians 2:8–9) and it comes "through faith" (v. 8). "Salvation" in that sense is what Paul refers to when he says, "The free gift of God is eternal life in Christ Jesus our Lord" (Romans 6:23), and when he says that we "are justified by his grace as a gift, through the redemption that is in Christ Jesus" (3:24).

But Paul can use "salvation" and related terms in another sense, to refer to the Christian life from initial conversion until our death, a life in which we live in increasing obedience to God and see more and more good works as a consequence and as evidence of the change God has brought about in our lives. It is this sense of "salvation" that Paul uses when he tells believers to "work out your own *salvation* with fear and trembling, for it is God who works in you, both to will and to work for his good pleasure" (Philippians 2:12–13). In theological terms, this aspect of salvation is often called "perseverance." After our initial conversion, we continue or "persevere" in the Christian faith until the day of our death.[8]

So Paul means that a woman will be "saved"—she will continue to work out the results of her salvation—"through childbearing," that is, through being obedient to God in the various tasks and roles that He calls her to, rather than attempting to teach or govern the church, a role God has not called women to.

In the last part of the verse, Paul switches from a singular example of a woman who will be saved ("yet she will be saved") to a plural statement about all women who are Christians. Though the sentence forms a rather irregular construction in Greek, and is therefore a bit difficult to translate due to the shift from singular to plural, Paul is making a general statement that persevering in the Christian life and working out the results and implications of one's "salvation" (in the sense of perseverance) depends on continuing in faith and obedience. He says, "*if they* continue in faith and love and holiness, with self-control" (1 Timothy 2:15). This is consistent with Paul's teaching elsewhere that Christians, if they are genuine Christians, must continue trusting in Christ and being obedient to Him throughout their lives. For example, he says that Christ's purpose is to "present you holy and blameless and above reproach before him," but he adds that Christians must continue believing, for he says, "*if indeed you continue in the faith*, stable and steadfast, not shifting from the hope of the gospel that you heard" (Colossians 1:22–23).

So the point of 1 Timothy 2:15 is that women are not eternally lost because of Eve's sin, but they will be saved and will experience the outworking of their salvation throughout their Christian lives if they follow the roles God has given to them and continue in faith and obedience.[9]

Another important text with regard to the restrictions placed on women in the church context is 1 Corinthians 14:33–35:

---

8. Another possible explanation of "saved" here is "kept safe from Satan's deception." See Andreas Köstenberger, "Saved Through Childbearing: A Fresh Look at 1 Timothy 2:15 Points to Protection from Satan's Deception," *CBMW News* 2:4 (September 1997): 1–5.

9. Some other interpretations of 1 Timothy 2:15 have been proposed, and it is beyond the purpose of this book to analyze every one of them. For an explanation of many of these other, see Mounce, *Pastoral Epistles*, 143–47; also, on the whole of 1 Timothy 2:8–15, see the detailed exegesis of George Knight, *The Pastoral Epistles*, 130–49. However, on any of these interpretations, the main point of verse 15 is still clear: Though Eve sinned, salvation for women is still possible, and thus Paul ends the chapter on a positive and reassuring note.

As in all the churches of the saints, the women should keep silent in the churches. For they are not permitted to speak, but should be in submission, as the Law also says. If there is anything they desire to learn, let them ask their husbands at home. For it is shameful for a woman to speak in church.

Paul cannot mean that women are to be completely silent at all times in church, for he had just finished saying in 1 Corinthians 11:5 that they should not pray or prophesy unless they had a head covering. And surely women along with men should join in congregational singing (see Colossians 3:16), which is not exactly being silent! So then what kind of silence does Paul mean? The best explanation is that Paul means "women should keep silent in the churches" *with respect to the topic under discussion in this context.* This section begins at verse 29, where Paul says, "Let two or three prophets speak, and let the others weigh what is said." In verses 30–33a, Paul gives an explanation for the first half of verse 29 ("Let two or three prophets speak"). But now in verses 33b[10]–36 Paul goes on to explain the judging of prophecies, something he had mentioned in the second half of verse 29: "And let the others weigh what is said."

Paul says that when people are weighing and evaluating a prophetic message, the women should be silent and not speak up to judge the prophecies. This understanding fits the context well because it relates to the topic that is already under discussion, namely, prophesying and judging prophecies.

This understanding of 1 Corinthians 14:33b–36 is consistent with the teachings of the rest of the New Testament on appropriate roles for women in the church. Speaking out and judging prophecies before the assembled congregation is a governing role over the assembled church, and Paul reserves that role for men.

What then shall we say about verse 35, "If there is anything they desire to learn, let them ask their husbands at home. For it is shameful for a woman to speak in church"? If we have understood verse 34 correctly, then verse 35 is understandable. Suppose that some women in Corinth had wanted to evade the force of Paul's direc-

---

10. Verse numbers were not in what Paul wrote, but were added for the first time in 1551 in the fourth edition of the Greek text that was published by Stephanus (also referred to as Robert Estienne, 1503–1559). He inserted the verse divisions while on a journey from Paris to Lyons. For discussion, see Bruce Metzger, *Text of the New Testament*, 104–270.

tive. The easy way to do this would be to say, "We'll do just as Paul says. We won't speak up and criticize prophecies. But surely no one would mind if we asked a few questions! We just want to learn more about what these prophets are saying." Then such questioning could be used as a platform for expressing in none-too-veiled form the very criticisms Paul forbids. If a "prophet" proclaimed that "Jesus is coming back ten days from now," rather than saying, "That is contrary to what Jesus taught," a woman could ask a question: "You said that Jesus is coming back in ten days, but didn't Jesus say that no one can know the day or the hour of His return?"[11]

Paul anticipates this possible evasion and writes, "If there is anything they desire to learn, let them ask their husbands at home." Of course, some women were unmarried and would not have had a husband to ask. But there would have been other men within their family circles, or within the fellowship of the church, with whom they could discuss the content of the prophecies. Paul's general guideline is clear, even though he did not make pedantic qualifications to deal with each specific case.

To apply this to a hypothetical modern situation, if Fred stands up in a church service and says, "I believe the Lord has said to me that He is coming back next Thursday," then it would not be right for a woman to stand up and say, "Fred's prophecy is wrong, because Jesus says in Matthew 25:13 that we can know neither the day nor the hour of His return." Rather, it would be the role of some man in the congregation to do this. In this way, Paul reserves for men the function of governing and protecting doctrine in the church, and this is similar to what he says in 1 Timothy 2:12. (See further discussion of 1 Corinthians 14:34–35 on pp. 142–45.)

Men are to govern the church not only when it comes to dealing with prophecy, but in all other matters as well in their capacity as elders. In two different places, 1 Timothy 3:2 and Titus 1:6, Paul affirms that the office of elder (which he also calls the office of "overseer" or "bishop") should be filled by someone who is the "*husband of one wife*."[12]

Therefore an overseer must be above reproach, *the husband of one wife.* (1 Timothy 3:2)

---

11. See Matthew 25:13.

12. For further discussion of the phrase "husband of one wife," see Grudem, *Systematic Theology*, 916–17.

This is why I left you in Crete, so that you might put what remained into order, and appoint elders in every town as I directed you—if anyone is above reproach, *the husband of one wife.* (Titus 1:5–6)

It is evident that only a man can be a "husband." In fact, the Greek term here, *anēr,* can mean either "man" or "husband," but with either meaning it is the Greek term that specifically designates a male human being. This means elders had to be men.

This is important because Paul is not restricting the office of elder to men in the city of Ephesus alone (assuming some kind of unique situation there), but elders were required to be men also in Crete, and not just at one or two locations in Crete but "in every town."

The phrase "husband of one wife" is best understood to mean that a polygamist could not be an elder in a church. Therefore this expression is not intended to rule out a single man (such as Jesus or Paul) from being an elder or to rule out someone who had been divorced and then remarried. Though polygamy was not common in the first century, it was practiced, especially among the Jews. The Jewish historian Josephus says, "For it is an ancestral custom of ours to have several wives at the same time," and several sections in rabbinic legislation regulated the inheritance customs and other aspects that would apply in cases of polygamy.[13]

TEACHING AND SPEAKING BY WOMEN THAT THE BIBLE ENCOURAGES

It is important to understand 1 Timothy 2:12, 1 Corinthians 14:33–35, 1 Timothy 3:2, and Titus 1:6 in the light of other passages that view some kinds of teaching by women in a positive way. For example, we read in Acts 18:26 concerning Apollos, a man competent in the Scriptures but who did not understand fully the good news of salvation in Christ (Acts 18:24–25), that both Aquila and Priscilla explained the way of God more accurately to him:

---

13. See Josephus, *Antiquities* 17.14; also see *Mishnah,* Yebamoth 4:11; Ketuboth 10:1, 4–5; Sanhedrin 2:4; Kerithoth 3:7; Kiddushin 2:7; Bechoroth 8:4. [Passages in the *Mishnah* can be found in Herbert Danby, *The Mishnah* (Oxford: Oxford University Press, 1933).]

He began to speak boldly in the synagogue, but when Priscilla and Aquila heard him, *they* took him and *explained to him* the way of God more accurately. (Acts 18:26)

The word translated "explained" (Greek *ektithēmi*) is plural and it indicates that *both* Aquila and Priscilla were involved in explaining the way of God more fully to Apollos. This incident is viewed with approval in the book of Acts, for there is no indication that anything was wrong with this conduct as it fits the ongoing narrative of the spread of the gospel to many Gentile cities. Therefore *this passage gives warrant for women and men to talk together about the meaning of biblical passages and to "teach" one another privately, outside the context of the assembled congregation.*

A parallel example in modern church life would be a home Bible study where both men and women contribute to the discussion of the meaning and application of Scripture. In such discussions, everyone is able to "teach" everyone else in some sense, for such discussions of the meaning of the Word of God are not the authoritative teaching that would be done by a pastor or elder to an assembled congregation, as in 1 Timothy 2.

Another modern parallel to the private conversation between Priscilla and Aquila and Apollos would be *the writing of books on the Bible and theology by women.* When I read a Bible commentary written by a woman, it is as if the author were talking privately to me, explaining her interpretation of the Bible, much as Priscilla talked to Apollos in Acts 18:26. Reading a book by a woman author is much like having a private conversation with a woman author. The woman author does not have teaching authority over an assembled congregation or a group of men.[14]

Another example of an activity in the church that Scripture approves is *praying and prophesying aloud before the assembled congregation,* because Paul says:

---

14. There is another point of difference: Preaching to a church is generally endorsed by the church, while publishing a book is not. We can see this in the fact that churches carefully guard the responsibility of preaching to the congregation, so that, in general, the congregation knows that those who preach from the pulpit have the endorsement and approval of the church leadership. But we all read many things we disagree with, and churches do not usually try to keep their members from reading a variety of viewpoints. Bible teaching to the assembled congregation has the general endorsement of that church (and thus carries authority over that church) in a way that publishing a book does not.

Every man who prays or prophesies with his head covered dishonors his head, but every wife who prays or prophesies with her head uncovered dishonors her head—it is the same as if her head were shaven. (1 Corinthians 11:4–5)

Paul implies that it would be normal and natural in the church at Corinth for women to pray and to prophesy aloud. If it were wrong for women to pray or prophesy in the church service, Paul would not have said they should have their heads covered when they do so!

This passage also implies that giving prophecies aloud in the assembled congregation is appropriate for women (in churches that allow this gift today). As I explain more fully later in this book, giving prophecy is simply reporting something that God has spontaneously brought to mind.[15] Prophecy is always listed as a separate gift from teaching in the New Testament, and prophecy is always to be subject to the governing authority of the elders and is to be tested for its conformity to Scripture (see 1 Corinthians 14:29; 1 Thessalonians 5:20–21).

Paul encourages another kind of teaching activity by women when he says:

Older women…are to teach what is good, and so *train the young women* to love their husbands and children, to be self-controlled, pure, working at home, kind, and submissive to their own husbands, that the word of God may not be reviled. (Titus 2:3–5)

All kinds of Bible teaching ministries from women to other women are encouraged by this passage. Organizations such as Bible Study Fellowship have outstanding ministries in training women in the knowledge of the Word of God, and in the United States at least, some excellent women Bible teachers will speak to conferences of several thousand women at one time. These are valuable ministries that should be encouraged. They are not the kind of teaching or having authority over men that Paul prohibits in 1 Timothy 2.

Furthermore, evangelism of all kinds is another activity not restricted to men

---

15. See below, pp. 136–41, and EFBT, 78–80 and 227–32, on the reasons why women can prophesy but not teach. See also Wayne Grudem, *The Gift of Prophecy in the New Testament and Today.*

alone but open to men and women alike. For example, the woman at the well in Samaria went and told her village about Jesus:

> So the woman left her water jar and went away into town and said to the people, "Come, see a man who told me all that I ever did. Can this be the Christ?" They went out of the town and were coming to him. (John 4:28–30)

The women at the tomb became the first eyewitnesses of the Resurrection, and Jesus sent them to tell His disciples about the Resurrection. This was an affirmation of the principle of women as evangelists in the New Covenant age:

> But the angel said to the women, "Do not be afraid, for I know that you seek Jesus who was crucified. He is not here, for he has risen, as he said. Come, see the place where he lay. Then go quickly and tell his disciples that he has risen from the dead, and behold, he is going before you to Galilee; there you will see him. See, I have told you." So they departed quickly from the tomb with fear and great joy, and ran to tell his disciples. And behold, Jesus met them and said, "Greetings!" And they came up and took hold of his feet and worshiped him. Then Jesus said to them, "Do not be afraid; go and tell my brothers to go to Galilee, and there they will see me." (Matthew 28:5–10)

These passages seem to indicate that it would be appropriate for women to do evangelism in any setting, whether privately or in large groups. In speaking to non-Christians,[16] they are not having the kind of teaching or governing authority over the church that Paul prohibits in 1 Timothy 2, because the unbelievers who hear the gospel message are not a congregation of assembled believers.

---

16. One qualification is necessary here: In some evangelical churches, an "evangelistic service" may have one percent or fewer non-Christians and 99 percent Christians. Preaching to such an assembled group in the church is exactly what Paul said not to do in 1 Timothy 2:12. What I have in mind in this section is an audience that is primarily non-Christians (though some Christians may be in attendance), and the message is addressed to non-Christians. There will no doubt be borderline cases where people in the situation will need wisdom to decide what is right, but the distinction between evangelism and Bible teaching to the church is still a valid one and is not disproved by the existence of mixed situations.

The history of missions has many stories of courageous women who went by themselves to proclaim the gospel to unreached people. For example, Wycliffe Bible translator Joanne Shetler tells a beautiful story of her work with the Balangao people in the Philippines, and her interaction with a man in the village (her "daddy") who had adopted her into his family and who was reading pages of the New Testament for her as she produced it:

> I continued translating in Timothy with my daddy. And we came to a verse where Paul says to Timothy, "I don't allow women to teach men." My daddy didn't bat an eyelash. But that afternoon, after we'd finished work, he said to me, "Now what is that we're going to study on Sunday?" I thought he was just curious. I didn't know what was on his mind since fathers don't report to their children. So I told him. Sunday morning came, and before I could stand up to start, he stood up and said, "My daughter here knows more about this than I do, but we found in the Bible that women aren't supposed to teach men. So I guess I have to be the one!" And that was the end of my career, and the beginning of their teaching.[17]

It was a beautiful picture of a key turning point in the transition from an informal group of new Christians to an established congregation with indigenous male leadership naturally taking charge. Situations similar to this have probably occurred hundreds of times throughout the history of the church, and no doubt God gives much grace as new Christians seek to be faithful to His Word, even when it might be difficult to say exactly what point a transition should occur without being present in the actual situation. The important point is that the transition does occur, and male leadership is established in the church.

Other kinds of speech activities by women are also appropriate in the assembled church. Examples include giving a personal testimony of God's work in a woman's own life or in the lives of others (such as in youth work or in a mission activity), reading Scripture, singing a solo or singing in a group, acting as part of a dramatic presentation—whatever goes on in the assembled church other than

---

17. Joanne Shetler, "Faithful in Obedience," can be found at www.urbana.org/_today.cfm (accessed January 28, 2004).

what is explicitly prohibited by Scripture (Bible teaching and governing over the congregation of God's people).

SUMMARY

What then does the Bible forbid for women to do? People have suggested all sorts of complicated answers, but my answer is really quite simple: *when there is an assembled group of Christians, women should not teach the Bible to men or exercise governing authority over men.* That is what Paul said in 1 Timothy 2, with respect to an assembled group of Christians: "I do not permit a woman to teach or to exercise authority over a man" (1 Timothy 2:12). My position is that this verse is not hard to understand, and that God simply wants us to obey it. Apart from these two activities (and the office of elder or its equivalent, which involves these activities), all other ministries and activities in churches and parachurch organizations are open to women and men alike.

THE RELATIONSHIP BETWEEN
THE FAMILY AND THE CHURCH

In analyzing what the Bible teaches about the distinct roles of men and women in church, it is important to see that *the New Testament sees a close relationship between male leadership in the home and male leadership in the church.* This is in part because the church is viewed as a "family," and patterns of church life are imitated in the family, while patterns of family life are to be imitated in the church. Therefore Paul can say that a candidate for the office of elder (or overseer) "must manage his own household well, with all dignity keeping his children submissive, for if someone does not know how to manage his own household, how will he care for God's church?" (1 Timothy 3:4–5).

A little later Paul tells Timothy to relate to people in the church as he would relate to people in his own family:

> Do not rebuke an older man but encourage him *as you would a father.* Treat younger men *like brothers,* older women *like mothers,* younger women *like sisters,* in all purity. (1 Timothy 5:1–2)

This indicates that male leadership in the home and in the church are closely tied together, and that in today's controversy, male leadership in the home and in the church will likely stand or fall together. If we begin to abandon the requirement for men to be pastors and elders in our churches, and if we begin establishing women in positions of teaching and governing authority over our churches, then we will likely see an erosion of male leadership in the home as well. For how can a man come to church and sit under the teaching and authority of his wife—teaching and authority that applies to all areas of life—and yet the minute he walks out the church door expect that he will be the head of his household and she will be subject to his authority? And such erosion of male leadership would affect not only the family of the woman doing the Bible teaching, but also (by implication and example) all the other families in the church.

The close connection in the New Testament between church and family is, therefore, another argument in favor of restricting to men some governing and teaching roles in the church.[18]

THE SELECTION OF THE APOSTLES

When it comes to the most prominent positions of governing over the church, Jesus selected only men for the task. If Jesus had wanted to establish a truly egalitarian church, He could easily have chosen six men and six women to be apostles, and there would be no room for argument. While some people object that it would have been culturally offensive for Him to do this, if it had been Christ's intention for His church, then He would have done it, for He never hesitated to do culturally unpopular things when they were morally right.

But Jesus did not choose six men and six women as apostles. He chose twelve men (Matthew 10:2–4; see also Acts 1:24–26, where Matthias was chosen to replace Judas). These twelve apostles, under Jesus Christ as the head of the church, have the positions of highest authority in the church throughout its history. And they are all men. In fact, their authority will continue into the age to come, because Jesus tells these twelve, "Truly I say to you, in the new world, when the Son of Man

---

18. See also Vern Poythress, "The Church as Family," in Piper and Grudem, *Recovering Biblical Manhood and Womanhood*, 233–47.

will sit on his glorious throne, you who have followed me will also sit on twelve thrones, judging the twelve tribes of Israel" (Matthew 19:28).[19]

The highest positions of human authority in the age to come are not given to six men and six women equally but to twelve men, the twelve apostles.

When we see the heavenly city, the book of Revelation tells us that we will see twelve men's names on the foundation of this city: "And the wall of the city had twelve foundations, and on them were the twelve names of the twelve apostles of the Lamb" (21:14).

Therefore, for all eternity, we will see that Jesus has called to Himself a great family of God's people in which the highest leadership positions are not distributed equally to men and to women, but are all held by men.

MALE TEACHING AND LEADERSHIP THROUGHOUT THE BIBLE

From beginning to end, the Bible is simply not an egalitarian book. Think of the Bible as a whole, from Genesis to Revelation. Where is there one example *in the entire Bible* of a woman publicly teaching an assembled group of God's people? There is none. Sometimes people mention Deborah in Judges 4, but she did not teach the people publicly, for people came to her privately to hear her wise decisions in disputed cases: "She used to sit under the palm of Deborah between Ramah and Bethel in the hill country of Ephraim, and the people of Israel came up to her for judgment" (v. 5). (See chapter 7, pp. 80-4 on Deborah.) In the Old Testament the priests were responsible to teach the people, and the priests were all men.[20]

Therefore, there is a consistent pattern in Scripture: Men teach and lead God's people. On rare occasions where women gained power as queens in Israel or Judah (such as Jezebel in 1 Kings 16–21 or Athaliah in 2 Kings 11), they led the people into evil, so they can hardly be used as positive examples of women having governing authority over the people of God.[21] In its consistent patterns of male governing

---

19. For further response to the objection that they were all men because that was necessary in the first century culture, see below, chapter 12, pp. 98–101.
20. See Leviticus 10:11; Malachi 2:6–7. Women prophets did not teach God's people: See the discussion in chapter 8, pp. 85–87.
21. See further discussion on women as queens in Grudem, EFBT, 138–40.

and teaching, therefore, the entire Bible supports the idea of restricting to men the role of teaching and governing the assembly of God's people.

ROLES THROUGHOUT
THE HISTORY OF THE CHURCH

While women's gifts and ministries have been valued and affirmed throughout the history of the church, the dominant view by far has been that only men should govern and teach God's people in the role of pastors or elders (or in the role of priests in the Roman Catholic and Episcopal and Eastern Orthodox traditions). While this is not an argument directly from the Bible, and thus does not carry the same authority, it is nevertheless useful.

William Weinrich says that up until the nineteenth century "the only significant group that denied the continuing applicability of Paul's prohibitions was the Society of Friends (Quakers).... George Fox (d. 1671), founder of the Quakers, and especially Margaret Fell (d. 1702) argued that the authority of the indwelling Spirit gave women equal right and obligation to speak, even in public assemblies."[22] He notes that John Wesley (d. 1791) expected that Methodists would follow the ordinary rule of discipline and women would be in subjection in the congregation, but he would allow from time to time for "an extraordinary impulse of the Spirit" that would allow a woman to speak in public on rare occasions. Otherwise, Weinrich says,

> The Anabaptists, the Anglicans, the Puritans, and the Separatists all prohibited women from the public ministry of preaching and teaching. While groups that emphasized religious experience and interior calling did allow women to assume (more or less restricted) public preaching, not until the nineteenth century did women begin to make significant strides toward a ready acceptance of any public ministry. It has been only *in the last half of the twentieth century* that the major Protestant church bodies have begun to accept women as regular preachers and pastors.[23]

---

22. William Weinrich, "Women in the History of the Church: Learned and Holy, but Not Pastors," in Piper and Grudem, *Recovering Biblical Manhood and Womanhood*, 278.

23. For further discussion see Weinrich, "Women in the History of the Church," 263–79. See also Ruth Tucker and Walter Liefeld, *Daughters of the Church*, and see also chapter 11 for further discussion of the roles of women in the history of the church. See also the extended comment from Richard John Neuhaus cited in chapter 41, pp. 269–71.

In many of those cases, the leadership of those denominations was already in the hands of liberals who did not accept the full authority of the Bible as the inerrant Word of God.[24]

This of course does not prove that the complementarian position is correct, but it does mean that anyone who accepts the egalitarian position must conclude that the overwhelming majority of interpreters throughout the history of the church have all been wrong on this matter.

BUT WHAT SHOULD WOMEN DO IN THE CHURCH?

Probably the most frequent question I hear when I speak to Christian groups about this topic is this: "Okay, I agree with you that only men should be pastors and elders. But what about *other* activities in the church? Can they teach adult Sunday school classes? What about serving communion? We want to follow Scripture, but we can't find any verses that talk about these specific things."

While I gave a very brief, simple answer above (see p. 49), in this section I will try to answer those questions in more detail and with respect to many specific activities, partly in the hope of encouraging churches to examine their traditions to see if there are more areas of ministry they could open to women as well as men. On the other hand, I also want to explain why I think certain kinds of activities are restricted to men.

Generally the restrictions on the roles women may fill in the church fall in three areas, and almost all the questions of application pertain to at least one of these areas:

1. governing authority
2. Bible teaching
3. public recognition or visibility

Note that I have included the third area, public recognition or visibility, because it is closely related to the other two. There are some highly visible activities in the church that do not include governing or teaching authority, and people

---

24. See the discussion of the relationship between liberalism and an egalitarian view of women in the church in chapter 44, below, and especially in Wayne Grudem, *Evangelical Feminism: A New Path to Liberalism?* (Wheaton: Crossway, 2006).

easily combine and maybe confuse these in their minds. If we keep this area distinct, it helps us think more clearly about specific applications.

What follows here are three lists of activities. In List 1, I proceed from areas of greater governing authority to areas of lesser authority. In List 2, I proceed from areas of greater teaching responsibility and influence on the beliefs of the church to areas of lesser teaching responsibility and lesser influence on the beliefs of the church. In List 3, I proceed from areas of greater public recognition and visibility to areas of lesser visibility.

Before I give these lists, one word of caution is appropriate: These lists are *not* rankings of value or importance to the church! Paul tells us that *all* the members of the body are needed and that "the parts of the body that seem to be weaker are indispensable, and on those parts of the body that we think less honorable we bestow the greater honor" (1 Corinthians 12:22–23).

And Jesus said, "Whoever would be great among you must be your servant" (Mark 10:43). These statements remind us that when we talk about levels of governing authority, or levels of Bible teaching responsibility, or levels of public recognition, we are not talking about greatness or importance.

Then why talk about such levels at all? We must do so because Scripture tells us that *some* kinds of governing and teaching are inappropriate for women. In order to think clearly about what those roles are, we first must list the activities we are talking about. Then we can ask, in each case, if this was the kind of governing or teaching that Scripture intended us to understand in these passages. In short, we need to make such lists for purposes of clearer thinking on this issue.

• List 1: Areas of Governing Authority:

WHICH OFFICES OR ACTIVITIES SHOULD BE RESTRICTED TO MEN?

(listed in order of greatest to least amount of authority over men)

GOVERNING ACTIVITIES THAT SHOULD BE RESTRICTED TO MEN:

1. President of a denomination
2. Member of the governing board of a denomination
3. Regional governing authority (such as district superintendent, bishop, or similar office)
4. Member of regional governing board

5. Senior pastor in local church (or associate pastor with many similar responsibilities to the senior pastor)
6. Member of governing board with authority over whole church (this would be the office of elder in many churches, while it would be the office of deacon or board member or church council member in others)
7. Presiding over a baptism or communion service (but see List 3 for serving communion or performing a baptism)
8. Giving spoken judgment on a prophecy given to the congregation (1 Corinthians 14:33–36)
9. Permanent leader of a fellowship group meeting in a home (both men and women members)

GOVERNING ACTIVITIES THAT SHOULD BE OPEN TO BOTH MEN AND WOMEN:

10. Committee chairman (or chairperson)[25]
11. Director of Christian education[26]
12. Sunday school superintendent[27]
13. Missionary responsibilities (many administrative responsibilities in missionary work in other countries)
14. Moderating a Bible discussion in a home Bible study group
15. Choir director
16. Leading singing on Sunday morning[28]
17. Deacon (in churches where this does not involve governing authority over the entire congregation)[29]

---

25. I have put this item here because this activity and the following two have *some* kind of authority in the church, but it is less than the authority over the whole congregation that Paul has in mind in 1 Corinthians 14:33–36; 1 Timothy 2:12; 3; and Titus 1.
26. See footnote to item 10.
27. See footnote to item 10.
28. I understand that others may differ with me and may decide to list leading singing between 8 and 9. Such a decision would depend on how a church and the worship leader understand the degree of authority over the assembled congregation that is involved in leading a singing or worship time.
29. But see item 6 when "deacons" are the primary governing board over the congregation. However, some people may wish to restrict deacons to men based on 1 Timothy 3:12; see discussion on pp. 156–57 and also Grudem, EFBT, 263–68.

18. Administrative assistant to senior pastor
19. Church treasurer
20. Church secretary
21. Member of advisory council to regional governing authority
22. Meeting periodically with church governing board to give counsel and advice
23. Regular conversations between elders and their wives over matters coming before the elder board (with understanding that confidentiality is preserved)
24. Formally counseling one man[30]
25. Formally counseling a couple together[31]
26. Formally counseling one woman[32]
27. Speaking in congregational business meetings
28. Voting in congregational business meetings[33]

Once we reach a conviction that Bible teaching and governing the assembled congregation are restricted to men, it seems clear that this principle would prohibit activities 1–8 for women, and probably also item 9: The office of senior pastor and

---

30. I put items 24, 25, and 26 in this "Governing Authority" column (List 1) and also in the "Bible Teaching" column (List 2) because there is some amount of authority and some amount of Bible teaching involved in these counseling activities. I am not here commenting on whether it is ordinarily wise or most effective for one woman to counsel one man; I am just listing these activities according to the degree of governing or teaching authority they exhibit over the congregation of a church. I also realize that others may decide to put these activities at different places on these lists, depending on the style of counseling and the degree of authority they think attaches to it. It seems to me that these three items are quite similar to the positive example of Priscilla and Aquila together explaining to Apollos the way of God more accurately in a private setting in Acts 18:26.

31. See footnote to item 24.

32. See footnote to item 24.

33. Some may argue that when a woman votes she "exercises authority" over the congregation. I disagree. I believe she exercises some influence on the congregation, but so does everyone else who votes, and surely not everyone who votes is able or even qualified to exercise governing authority over the congregation. There is a huge difference between *exercising influence* through voting and *exercising authority* through governing the congregation (as an elder or a senior pastor would do). To take an analogy, an eighteen-year-old American can vote for the president of the United States, but cannot be president of the United States, and the authority residing in the office of president far exceeds the authority of any individual voter.

the office of elder (or equivalent), together with activities specifically connected to those positions, are not open to women. But all the other activities on the list, from item 10 to the end, are open to women.

I put item 9 in the first section because I do not think it appropriate for a woman to be a permanent leader of a home fellowship group, especially if the group regularly carries out pastoral care of its members and functions as a mini-church within the church. It seems to me that the leader of such a group carries a governing authority that is very similar to the authority over the assembled congregation that Paul mentions in 1 Timothy 2. Given the small size of churches meeting in homes in the first century, and given the pastoral nature of leading a home fellowship group, I think Paul would have included this in 1 Timothy 2:12, "I do not permit a woman to teach or to exercise authority over a man."

But that is my personal judgment and others who hold a complementarian view may differ with me on this point. At one time I was a member of a church that had some women leading home fellowship groups. I disagreed with that decision, but I found that I could in good conscience continue as an active and supportive member of the church. However, I don't think that I could have participated in a fellowship group in which a woman functioned in that pastoral role with regard to my wife and me.

So I would draw a line between items 9 and 10. From item 10 onward, I think it is right to encourage women to be involved in all the rest of the types of governing authority on the list. For example, I would approve of a woman as director of Christian education (item 11) or superintendent of the Sunday school (item 12), or as a committee chair (item 13). These activities do not carry the sort of authority over the whole congregation that Paul has in view in 1 Timothy 2, or when he specifies that elders should be men (1 Timothy 3; Titus 1).

• List 2: Areas of Bible Teaching:

WHICH ACTIVITIES SHOULD BE RESTRICTED TO MEN?
(listed in order of greatest to least teaching influence over men in a group or congregation)

TEACHING ACTIVITIES THAT SHOULD BE RESTRICTED TO MEN:

1. Teaching Bible or theology in a theological seminary
2. Teaching Bible or theology in a Christian college

3. Preaching (teaching the Bible) at a nationwide denominational meeting or at a nationwide Christian conference

4. Preaching (teaching the Bible) at a regional meeting of churches or at a regional Christian conference

5. Preaching (teaching the Bible) regularly to the whole church on Sunday mornings

6. Occasional preaching (teaching the Bible) to the whole church on Sunday mornings

7. Occasional Bible teaching at less formal meetings of the whole church (such as Sunday evening or at a midweek service)

8. Bible teaching to an adult Sunday school class (both men and women members)

9. Bible teaching at a home Bible study (both men and women members)

10. Bible teaching to a college-age Sunday school class

TEACHING ACTIVITIES THAT SHOULD BE OPEN TO BOTH MEN AND WOMEN:

11. Bible teaching to a high school Sunday school class

12. Writing a book on Bible doctrines[34]

13. Writing or editing a study Bible

14. Writing a commentary on a book of the Bible

15. Writing notes in a study Bible

16. Writing or editing other kinds of Christian books

17. Bible teaching to a women's Sunday school class

18. Bible teaching to a women's Bible study group during the week

19. Bible teaching to a junior high Sunday school class

---

34. I have put four examples of writing activities here on the list because the author of a book is doing some kind of teaching, but it is different from the teaching of the assembled congregation that Paul prohibits in 1 Timothy 2. The teaching relationship of an author to a reader is much more like the one-to-one kind of teaching that Priscilla and Aquila did when they explained the way of God more accurately to Apollos in Acts 18:26. When I am reading a book, it is similar to having a private conversation with the author of the book. And there is another difference: Christians often read books they disagree with, but we do not expect the sermon on Sunday morning to be given by someone we fundamentally disagree with. One more difference is that authors of books do not think of themselves as having any governing authority over their readers.

20. Teaching as a Bible professor on a secular university campus[35]
21. Evangelistic speaking to large groups of non-Christians (for example, an evangelistic rally on a college campus)
22. Working as an evangelistic missionary in other cultures
23. Moderating a discussion in a small group Bible study (men and women members)
24. Reading Scripture aloud on Sunday morning
25. Reading Scripture to other, less formal meetings of the church
26. Giving a personal testimony before the congregation (a story of how God has worked in one's own or others' lives)
27. Participating in a discussion in a home Bible study (men and women members)
28. Formally counseling one man[36]
29. Formally counseling a married couple
30. Formally counseling a woman
31. Teaching children's Sunday school class
32. Teaching Vacation Bible School
33. Singing a solo on Sunday morning (this is a form of teaching, since the lyrics often have biblical content and exhortation)
34. Singing to the congregation as a member of the choir
35. Singing hymns with the congregation (in this activity, sometimes we teach and exhort one another in some sense, see Colossians 3:16)

When we turn to these various areas of Bible teaching here in List 2, my own personal judgment is that a line should be drawn between items 10 and 11.[37] There are several considerations that weighed in my decision of where to draw the

---

35. I have put this here on the list because I see this task as essentially a combination of evangelism and teaching about the Bible as literature, mainly to non-Christians. Even though there may be Christians in some classes, the professor has no church-authorized authority or doctrinal endorsement, as there would be with a Bible teacher in a church or a professor in a Christian college or seminary. I realize that others would disagree with me on this point and would think that this activity should be considered the same as item 2 on the list.

36. See footnote to item 24 in List 1 (p. 56 above) for an explanation of why I put this item and the next two at this point in the list, and why I included these three items on both lists.

37. The Danvers Statement takes a broader perspective on this issue, (see Affirmation 6, p. 304 below) stating simply that "*some* governing and teaching roles within the church are restricted to men." This

line. As I mentioned when discussing List 1, there is a strong similarity between a home Bible study taught by a woman (item 9) and a local church meeting in a home in the ancient world.

Therefore, I do not think it is appropriate for a woman to be the regular instructor in a home Bible study. On the other hand, I believe that moderating a discussion in a small group Bible study (item 23) is appropriate for women. The teaching and governing component is less than it would be if she were regularly teaching or had pastoral responsibility over the group, and does not resemble the teaching authority over the assembled congregation that Paul prohibits in 1 Timothy 2.

For similar reasons, I think it is inappropriate for a woman to be the Bible teacher in an adult Sunday school class (item 8). This looks so much like what Paul prohibited in 1 Timothy 2 that I cannot endorse it. (I have heard many stories of women doing such teaching effectively, but I don't want to base my decision on people's experiences. I am trying to decide how Scripture applies and then let Scripture govern our experiences, not our experiences govern Scripture. It seems to me that teaching an adult Bible class is doing just what Paul is saying not to do—though God may bless His Word with good fruit at times even if women are disobedient to Scripture in teaching it to men.[38] The final question still must be what Scripture tells us to do and not to do.)

When do children become adults, and when does teaching *boys* become teaching *men*?[39] This will vary from society to society and from culture to culture. It may even vary from subculture to subculture. In our own culture, if children graduate from high school, move away from home, and begin to support themselves, then surely they are functioning as adults. A new household has been formed. In that

---

[37. *continued*] statement still draws a definite line and differs decisively with all egalitarians, because they simply could not agree with it. They would insist that all should be open to women and men alike. For more discussion of this subject, see EFBT pp. 97–99.

38. See chapter 42, pp. 272–77, for a discussion of how God can bring some blessing to women when they do Bible teaching to groups of men and women, even though this is contrary to what Scripture directs.

39. A boy would not have been called an *anēr* ("man") in the ordinary use of Greek in Paul's time. A male child could be called a *brephos* ("infant"), a *nēpios* ("young child"), a *pais* ("child"), a *paidarion* ("youth"), a *teknon* ("child"), or a *huios* ("son"), but not an *anēr* ("man"). But in 1 Timothy 2:12, Paul speaks of not teaching or exercising authority over an *anēr*, a man.

case, the young men are adult men, and it would not be appropriate for a woman to teach a class with them as members.

Many college students also live away from home, support themselves at least in part, and function in our society in all other ways as independent adults. Most college students would be insulted if you called them children! For these reasons, I believe that a college-age Sunday school class (item 10) should have a male teacher.

The situation with a high school class is different because high school students are still at home and still under the instruction of their mothers. Sunday school class might be seen as an extension of this home instruction, and therefore I do not think it is wrong for a woman to be a Bible teacher in a high school Sunday school class. However, many churches may think it *preferable* for a man to teach a high school class because of the modeling of male leadership in the church that these young adults will grow to appreciate and imitate. But I do not think having a woman teacher would be disobeying 1 Timothy 2:12.

• List 3: Areas of Public Visibility or Recognition:

WHICH ACTIVITIES SHOULD BE RESTRICTED TO MEN?

(listed in order of greatest to least public visibility or recognition in a local congregation)

PUBLIC RECOGNITION THAT SHOULD BE RESTRICTED TO MEN:

1. Ordination as pastor (member of the clergy) in a denomination[40]

   PUBLIC RECOGNITION THAT SHOULD BE OPEN TO BOTH MEN AND WOMEN:

2. Being licensed to perform some ministerial functions within a denomination
3. Paid member of pastoral staff (such as youth worker, music director, counselor, Christian education director)
4. Paid member of administrative church staff (church secretary or treasurer, for example)

---

40. I think this also includes ordination as a military chaplain; see Grudem, EFBT, p. 389.

5. Performing a baptism (in churches where this is not exclusively the role of clergy or elders)
6. Helping to serve the Lord's Supper (in churches where this is not exclusively the role of clergy or elders)
7. Giving announcements at the Sunday morning service
8. Taking the offering
9. Public reading of Scripture
10. Public prayer
11. Prophesying in public (according to 1 Corinthians 11:5 and 14:29, where this is not understood as having authority equal to Scripture or Bible teaching)
12. Singing a solo on Sunday mornings
13. Giving a personal testimony in church
14. Giving a prayer request in church
15. Being a member of a prayer team that prays for people individually after the service
16. Welcoming people at the door (a greeter)
17. Editing the church newsletter
18. Singing in the choir
19. Singing of hymns with the congregation on Sunday morning
20. Participating in the responsive reading of Scripture on Sunday morning

As for List 3 (areas of public visibility or recognition), since Scripture indicates that the office of pastor/elder should be restricted to men, I draw a line after item 1, the ordination to the clergy, which in most or all denominations implies recognition of an ability to serve as senior pastor, as restricted to men. But all other items, from item 2 to the end, are open to women as well as men. So, for example, I think it is appropriate for women to hold other full-time positions on the "ministry staff" of the church (such as youth worker or music director or professional counselor).

Even such long lists are, of course, incomplete. For one thing, there are specialized ministries (parachurch organizations such as Campus Crusade for Christ,

InterVarsity Christian Fellowship, the Navigators, Focus on the Family, or Prison Fellowship) that would have similar lists of activities but often with different titles.

In addition, this *list of activities* cannot include the *variation in attitudes* that can make a big difference in the actual level of governing authority in a specific situation. (Does a particular woman who chairs a committee have a domineering attitude or a gracious servant heart?)

This list also cannot take into account any *variation in goals* that a person is trying to attain. (Is a woman seeking more and more authority over men, or is she genuinely seeking to use gifts for the benefit of the church?) Where churches see a borderline situation, it may be hard to decide the matter in advance, and the decision may well depend on variations in the attitudes and goals of the people involved.

Moreover, these lists cannot take into account the wide *variation in situations* that occur in different churches. One church may have a college-age class of three students, while another may have a college-age class of five hundred. Surely what it means to teach and have authority over men applies differently in the two situations. In such borderline situations, churches will need to use mature wisdom and sound judgment to make a correct evaluation of what is appropriate in light of biblical principles. But I think these lists, though not exhaustive, are still helpful.

CONCLUSION

I hope these guidelines will help many churches come to their own understanding of where to draw a line on what is appropriate for women and what is inappropriate. I realize that many churches will draw a more restrictive line than what I have proposed here, and others will be less restrictive. I simply encourage churches to be careful not to prohibit what the Bible doesn't prohibit, while they also attempt to preserve male leadership in the way Scripture directs.

I also recognize that some complementarians who agree with CBMW's Danvers Statement (see pp. 304–07) would allow more teaching activities by women than I would. Some would allow women to do occasional Bible teaching to men (items 6–10 on List 2, above). While I differ with their judgment (for reasons I have explained above), I would still consider them "complementarians," for they still agree that "some governing and teaching roles in the church are restricted to men" (Danvers Statement, affirmation 6), and that is something to which no egalitarian could agree.

What should be evident is that on all three lists, many activities are fully open to women. And these include a number of activities that have not traditionally been open to them. In addition, I have not even mentioned hundreds of *other* kinds of ministries in a local church that both women and men are already carrying out but that do not occur on any of these lists because they belong to other categories of activities.

I hope this controversy in the evangelical world will prompt churches to give earnest consideration to the possibilities of many more ministries for women than have been open to them in the past. It is the Council on Biblical Manhood and Womanhood's sincere desire to open the doors wide to all the areas of ministry that God intends for women to have. These areas of ministry may indeed be more numerous, more visible, and more prominent in the life of the church than we have previously thought. If that happens, this entire controversy will have served a wonderful purpose, and the church will be far stronger and far more pleasing to God as it carries out its ministry until Christ returns.

PART TWO

EVANGELICAL FEMINIST CLAIMS FROM GENESIS 1–3

In the first part of this book, we have seen a detailed portrait of the Bible's teaching regarding men and women. God created us equal in His sight, equal in value and dignity, and equal in that we are both in the image of God. But He also created us with differences in roles, differences that find expression in the way we relate to each other in marriage and in the church. Therefore we have in Scripture a beautiful picture of *both equality and differences between men and women*, reflecting the equality and differences among the members of the Trinity.

But this biblical teaching has been strongly challenged by evangelical feminists in the last thirty years. Can we continue to hold to the view presented in the Bible after considering the counterclaims of evangelical feminists? The remainder of this book is devoted to answering some of the key claims that evangelical feminists have made. Following a simple, "Claims and Answers" format, I will first state an evangelical feminist claim (carefully documenting it from the evangelical feminist writings) and then provide one or more responses to it.

I should also state here, for readers who are interested in more detailed analysis, that every one of the claims in the remainder of this present book is also answered in more detail, with more extensive scholarly documentation, in my longer book, *Evangelical Feminism and Biblical Truth: An Analysis of More Than 100 Disputed Questions* (Sisters, Ore.: Multnomah, 2004). I also treat more than fifty additional claims in that longer book. But this book still retains the most frequent and most important claims, and contains key points of response for every claim.

Now in this second part of the book, we consider evangelical feminist (or "egalitarian," an interchangeable term) claims regarding Genesis 1–3. If Adam and Eve were equal in God's sight, how could there be any difference in role or authority? And isn't male headship a result of sin and the Fall, and therefore something we should not perpetuate today? These and other egalitarian objections will be considered in this part.

3

CREATED EQUAL

↶ EGALITARIAN CLAIM: In Genesis 1, Adam and Eve Were Created Equal; Therefore, There Could Be No Difference in Role or Authority Between Them.

This is probably the most fundamental egalitarian argument, and it is the unspoken assumption behind a large number of specific egalitarian arguments. The assumption is that equality is incompatible with difference in roles and specifically with differences in authority. This argument was stated well by Linda Belleville in commenting on Genesis 1–2:

Does being male and female distinguish who we are and what we can do in ways that are non-interchangeable and divinely ordered—a biblical manhood and womanhood so to speak? Although some are quick to say *yes*, the creation accounts offer no support. Instead, the note that is clearly sounded throughout Genesis 1 and 2 is that of *equality*. For one, there is an *equality* of personhood. Both male and female are created in the image of God.... There is also *equality* in the social realm.... There is likewise *equality* in the family realm.... Finally, there is *equality* in the spiritual realm.[1]

---

1. Linda Belleville, *Women Leaders and the Church*, 99–101 (italics added). See also Rebecca Groothuis, *Good News for Women*, 122–23; Judy Brown, *Women Ministers*, 23; and several of the arguments of Gilbert Bilezikian, *Beyond Sex Roles*, 21–37.

Aida Spencer also states this clearly, regarding Adam and Eve in Genesis 1–2:

> Their similar tasks necessitate the work of *equals*. Adam and Eve are *equal* in rank, *equal* in image. Genesis 2, like Genesis 1, declares and explains male and female *equality*, joint rulership, and interrelationship.[2]

— Answer #1: We must distinguish different senses of "equal." It is true that Adam and Eve were created equal in several ways, but equal value does not imply sameness in authority or roles.

I agree that Adam and Eve were created equal in many ways. They were equal in that both were "in the image of God" (Genesis 1:27). To be in the image of God means that they were like God and they represented God on the earth. This implies that men and women have *equal value* to God, and men and women deserve *equal honor and respect*. They were also *equal in their personhood*, their possession of the qualities that make a truly human person (though they no doubt *differed* in many of their abilities and preferences, as all human beings do). And Adam and Eve were *equal in their importance* to the human race and importance to God. The human race, and God's plans for the human race, would not have gone very far if one of them had been missing!

But equal value and equal honor and equal personhood and equal importance do not require that people have the *same roles* or the *same authority*. A fundamental egalitarian error is constantly to blur the distinctions and to assume that being equal in the image of God means that people have to be equal (or the same) in authority. This assumption runs throughout Gilbert Bilezikian's treatment of Genesis 1–2,[3] for example, but it is merely an unproven assumption, and it simply is not true.

— Answer #2: Many relationships among people involve equal value but difference in roles and authority.

To take a modern example, think of the 2001 World Series, which was won by the Arizona Diamondbacks the year my wife and I moved to Arizona. Who was more

---

2. Aida Spencer, *Beyond the Curse*, 29 (italics added).

3. Bilezikian, *Beyond Sex Roles*, 21–37.

valuable to the Diamondbacks, the manager Bob Brenly or the winning pitchers Randy Johnson and Curt Schilling?

Of course, callers to a radio talk show could argue about that kind of question for hours. Some would say that Johnson and Schilling were most valuable since they shared the Most Valuable Player award. Others would say that Brenly was most valuable since he alone had the skill to coach a young team to the world championship. The argument is pointless since the Diamondbacks needed both the coach and the pitchers, as well as many other players, to win. The truth is that Brenly, Johnson, and Schilling were equally valuable and deserved equal honor.

But one thing is not in question: Bob Brenly had far greater *authority* than any player. He told Johnson and Schilling when they could play and when they had to come out of the game, and even if they didn't like it, they followed his instructions. Different roles, different authority, but equal value and importance.

In fact, greater authority did not result in greater honor in this case. Even though the manager had greater authority, the players got much more honor from fans. The players were the true heroes in Arizona in 2001, and they were the ones who received the loudest cheers from the crowds.

The same holds true in many other human activities. In a university, the president and the board have greater authority than the faculty, but students come because of what they will learn from the professors. Both the administration and the faculty are valuable, at least equal in value, but they are not equal in authority or the same in their roles.

In a church, the elders (or other leaders) have greater authority, but all Christians are equal in value before God. In a church committee, the head of the committee has greater authority but no greater value as a person. In a family, the parents have authority over their children, but the children are just as valuable to God. In a city, the mayor has greater authority but no greater value to the city than many of the citizens.

So the fundamental egalitarian claim, "If men and women have different God-given roles and authority, then we can't be equal," is an unproven assumption and just does not hold true in human experience.

Jesus taught the same thing:

"You know that the rulers of the Gentiles lord it over them, and their great ones exercise authority over them. It shall not be so among you. But whoever would be great among you must be your servant, and whoever would be first among you must be your slave, even as the Son of Man came not to be served but to serve, and to give his life as a ransom for many." (Matthew 20:25–28)

To have greater authority does not necessarily mean being great in God's sight. From the Bible's perspective, having authority over others and having value in God's kingdom are completely separate things.[4]

---

4. See chapter 39, 254–57, and Grudem, EFBT, 437–43, for a response to Rebecca Groothuis's claim that it is wrong to use analogies to other kinds of human subordination with equality because the subordination of women to men is different, since: It is not based on ability or choice, and it is based on a woman's very being.

4

MALE HEADSHIP
A RESULT OF THE FALL

⌐· EGALITARIAN CLAIM: In Genesis 1–3,
Male Headship Did Not Come About Until
After the Fall and Is Therefore a Product of Sin.

T his is a fundamental claim of every egalitarian writer I know. Gilbert Bilezikian writes of Adam and Eve:

Instead of meeting her desire and providing a mutually supportive and nurturing family environment, he will rule over her.… The clearest implication of this statement [Gen. 3:16], conferring rulership to Adam as a result of the fall, is that he was not Eve's ruler prior to the fall.[1]

And Rebecca Groothuis says:

In fact, there is no mention of either spouse ruling over the other—until after their fall into sin, when God declares to the woman that "he will rule over you" (3:16). This is stated by God not as a command, but as a consequence of their sin.[2]

---

1. Gilbert Bilezikian, *Beyond Sex Roles*, 55, and 264–12.
2. Rebecca Groothuis, *Good News for Women*, 123. Many other egalitarian writers make similar statements. For example, see Judy Brown, *Women Ministers*, 51, 55, and Richard Hess, "Equality with and without Innocence: Genesis 1–3," in *Discovering Biblical Equality*, ed. Ronald Pierce and Rebecca Groothuis, 79–95.

— Answer #1: There are at least ten arguments that prove there was male headship before the Fall.

I have explained these ten in Chapter 1. In summary form, they are:

1. *The order:* Adam was created first, then Eve (note the sequence in Genesis 2:7 and 2:18–23; 1 Timothy 2:13).
2. *The representation:* Adam, not Eve, had a special role in representing the human race (1 Corinthians 15:22, 45–49; Romans 5:12–21).
3. *The naming of woman:* Adam named Eve; Eve did not name Adam (Genesis 2:23).
4. *The naming of the human race:* God named the human race "Man," not "Woman" (Genesis 5:2).
5. *The primary accountability:* God called Adam to account first after the Fall (Genesis 3:9).
6. *The purpose:* Eve was created as a helper for Adam, not Adam as a helper for Eve (Genesis 2:18; 1 Corinthians 11:9).
7. *The conflict:* The curse brought a distortion of previous roles, not the introduction of new roles (Genesis 3:16).
8. *The restoration:* Salvation in Christ in the New Testament reaffirms the creation order (Colossians 3:18–19).
9. *The mystery:* Marriage from the beginning of creation was a picture of the relationship between Christ and the church (Ephesians 5:32–33).
10. *The parallel with the Trinity:* The equality, differences, and unity between men and women reflect the equality, differences, and unity in the Trinity (1 Corinthians 11:3).

—Answer #2: It is true that oppressive male rule did not come about until after the Fall, but male headship and unique male authority in marriage did exist before the Fall.

As explained in chapter 1, when God punished Adam and Eve after the Fall, His statement "he shall rule over you" (Genesis 3:16) indicated a rule by means of greater power, which among sinful human beings will often result in a harsh and oppressive rule. But this is part of God's curse following sin, and we should not support it or perpetuate it.

Instead of harsh, oppressive rule, the Bible restores the beauty of Adam and Eve's situation before the Fall when it says, "Wives, submit to your husbands, as is fitting in the Lord. Husbands, love your wives, and do not be harsh with them" (Colossians 3:18–19).

This is the beauty of the original relationship between Adam and Eve that the New Testament is restoring in our new creation in Christ.

5

HELPER IMPLIES EQUALITY

⌐· EGALITARIAN CLAIM: The Word Helper, Which Is Applied to Eve, Implies That Eve Is Equal in Status or Even Superior to Adam.

R ebecca Groothuis says:

If the term "helper" most frequently refers to God, whose status is clearly superior to ours…then there is no justification for inferring a subordinate status from the woman's designation as "helper."[1]

Stanley Grenz claims something similar:

The debate over Genesis 2 verses 18 and 20 hinges on the meaning of the phrase *'ēzer kenegdô* (helper fit). Egalitarians not only dispute the complementarian claim that *helper* means "subordinate," but they also claim that the Hebrew designation clearly indicates the equality of the sexes. Alvera Mickelsen, for example, notes that in the Bible the word *'ēzer* (translated "helper") is *never* used of a subordinate.[2]

---

1. Rebecca Groothuis, *Good News for Women*, 134.
2. Stanley Grenz, *Women in the Church*, 164. See also Judy Brown, *Women Ministers*, 27.

Helper *Implies Equality*

— Answer #1: The word helper (Hebrew *'ezer*) is used of God, so the role of helper is an honorable one.

I agree with egalitarians that this Hebrew word is used most often to refer to God in the Old Testament. For example, "Our soul waits for the LORD; he is our *help* and our shield" (Psalm 33:20), or "My *help* comes from the LORD, who made heaven and earth" (Psalm 121:2).

Though the word can also be used in other ways, the fact that God calls Himself our "helper" imparts dignity and honor to this role and this title.

— Answer #2: The word helper (Hebrew *'ezer*) cannot settle the question of superior or inferior authority or rank.

A person who helps can be superior to, equal to, or inferior to the person being helped.

Sometimes God is called our helper (see above), and He is superior to us. On the other hand, the "helper" can be one of lesser rank or authority, as when God says about the prince of Jerusalem, "I will scatter toward every wind all who are around him, his *helpers* and all his troops, and I will unsheathe the sword after them" (Ezekiel 12:14). (This means that egalitarians are incorrect when they claim that this word is never used of someone of inferior status or rank.)[3] And the closely related feminine form of this noun can be used of an equal, as when one army helps another. For example, God said to the king of Judah, "Behold, Pharaoh's army that came to *help* you [literally, that came to you as a helper] is about to return to Egypt, to its own land" (Jeremiah 37:7).[4] If we expand our consideration to the related verb "to help" (*'āzar*), there are many more examples of someone with lesser rank or authority or power giving help (see for example 2 Samuel 21:17; 1 Chronicles 12:1).[5] So *helper* (*'ezer*)

---

3. Aida Spencer is incorrect when she says, "At no time does *'ezer* indicate a subordinate helper unless the two references to 'helper' in Genesis 2:18, 20 are considered exceptions" (*Beyond the Curse*, 27). The statement by Grenz (quoting Alvera Mickelsen) cited above is also incorrect.

4. Jeremiah 37:7 has the feminine form *'ezrāh*, but the lexicons show no difference in meaning between *'ezer* and *'ezrāh* (see BDB, 740–41; NIDOTTE 3:378–79).

5. These verses were pointed out by William Webb, *Slaves, Women and Homosexuals*, 128. Webb's own count indicates that when both noun and verb forms are included, in 18 percent of the cases the "helper" is of equal status, and in 10 percent, of lower status than the one being helped.

75

itself cannot settle the issue for us; it has to be decided on other grounds.

Since the Old Testament deals almost entirely with various ways that God helps His people, it is not surprising that this word often refers to God as our helper. But that does not by itself imply that the helper is necessarily of greater authority or rank, any more than it implies that a helper is divine, or is godlike, or anything else. The word just means that the helper is a person who helps, in whatever way the context specifies.

— Answer #3: Eve's creation as a "helper...for him" indicates a created role as helper who would bring benefit to Adam.

It is important to read the whole sentence in Genesis 2:18. As already noted in chapter 1, God made Eve to provide Adam with a helper, one who by virtue of creation would function as Adam's helper.

> Then the LORD God said, "It is not good that the man should be alone;
> I will make him a helper fit for him." (Genesis 2:18)

The Hebrew text can be translated literally, "I will make *for him* [Hebrew *le-*] a helper fit for him." The apostle Paul understands this accurately, because in 1 Corinthians 11 he writes, "Neither was man created *for* woman, but woman *for* man" (v. 9). Eve's role, and the purpose that God had in mind when He created her, was that she would be "for him...a helper." Egalitarians regularly focus on the word *helper* by itself, which decides nothing, and fail to consider that the apostle Paul was emphasizing the relationship implied by the "for him" in the phrase "I will make for him a helper."

Yet in the same sentence God emphasizes that the woman is not to help the man as one who is inferior to him. Rather, she is to be a helper "fit for him" and here the Hebrew word *kenegdô* means a help *"corresponding to him,"* that is "equal and adequate to himself."[6] So Eve was created as a helper, but as a helper who was Adam's equal, and one who differed from him, but who differed from him in ways that would exactly complement who Adam was.

---

6. BDB, 617.

PRIOR CREATION AND ANIMAL RULE

∼· EGALITARIAN CLAIM: If Prior Creation Gave Authority to Adam, Then the Same Logic Would Require That the Animals Rule over Us Since They Were Created First.

This is a common egalitarian claim. Gilbert Bilezikian writes:

As soon as primal origination becomes a norm that confers dominance to the first in line, both Adam and Eve fall under the rulership of animals. According to Genesis 1, animals were created before humans. Therefore, they should rule over humans. The absurdity of such a theory is evident. Temporal primacy of itself does not confer superior rank.[1]

Similarly, Linda Belleville says:

The account in Genesis 2 certainly attaches no significance to the order of male then female. Indeed, the fact that the animals were created before the male should caution us against drawing a conclusion of this kind.[2]

---

1. Gilbert Bilezikian, *Beyond Sex Roles*, 30.
2. Linda Belleville, *Women Leaders and the Church*, 103. See also Judy Brown, *Women Ministers*, 24–25.

— Answer #1: Authority relationships among human beings apply only to human beings.

The Bible clearly gives human beings authority to rule over the animal kingdom: "fill the earth and subdue it and have dominion over the fish of the sea and over the birds of the heavens and over every living thing that moves on the earth" (Genesis 1:28). So we see from Genesis itself that authority belonging to things created first is not an *absolute* rule that applies to everything ever created. It is a *limited* principle that applied to the creation of Adam and Eve, and that is clear because the Bible views it that way.

In fact, when the idea of primogeniture (the idea that leadership in a family belongs to the firstborn son) is applied in later Old Testament narratives, it is not an absolute principle either. It applies only to the oldest son, not to the firstborn daughter. It applies only within each family, not to children born earlier in neighboring families. And it surely does not apply to animals born in the household before the children! The concept is a limited principle that applies within human families, and there is no inconsistency in limiting its application in that way in the story of Adam and Eve. (See also p. 21, above.)

— Answer #2: Paul views Adam's prior creation as important for the relationship between men and women.

Whether or not we think there is anything significant about the fact that Adam was created before Eve, the apostle Paul thought it significant enough to influence the way men and women should relate to each other in the New Testament church age: "I do not permit a woman to teach or to exercise authority over a man.... *For* Adam was formed first, then Eve" (1 Timothy 2:12–13). To object, "Well that can't be right because then animals would rule over us," is to object to the reasoning of the Word of God itself. If we are going to remain subject to the authority of Scripture, then we should accept Paul's reasoning as valid.

EVANGELICAL FEMINIST CLAIMS FROM THE REST OF THE OLD TESTAMENT

It is best to conclude from Genesis 1–3 that God created Adam and Eve equal in personhood, importance, and dignity, but also different in role. As part of that difference in role, God gave Adam a responsibility for leadership in the marriage before there was any sin in the world. Male leadership in marriage was not a result of the Fall, but was part of the original created order of which God said, "It was very good" (Genesis 1:31).

The egalitarian objections considered so far have not been able to undermine this teaching. Nor have they made a persuasive case for an egalitarian position in Genesis 1–3. But what about the rest of the Old Testament? Doesn't Deborah's example show that women can assume leadership over men? And what about other women who were prophets in the Old Testament? Aren't there examples of women exercising leadership roles and being blessed by God?

Part 3 considers these questions.

7

DEBORAH

⌁· EGALITARIAN CLAIM: Deborah's Leadership in Israel (Judges 4) Shows That God Can Call Women to Leadership Roles.

E galitarian writers regularly appeal to the example of Deborah. Linda Belleville says:

> Deborah is called "prophetess" (Judg. 4:4 NIV), "judge" (Judg. 4:5 NRSV), and "mother in Israel" (Judg. 5:7). She held court in the hill country of Ephraim and all of Israel (men and women alike) came to her to have their disputes settled (Judg. 4:5). So respected was Deborah that the commander of her troops refused to go into battle without her (Judg. 4:8).[1]

⌁ Answer #1: We should be thankful for Deborah.

In Judges 4–5, Deborah is a "prophetess" who faithfully delivered God's messages to Barak (4:6–7), courageously accompanied Barak to the place where he was assembling troops for battle (4:10), demonstrated strong faith by encouraging Barak that the Lord would be with him (4:14), and joined Barak in a lengthy song of praise and thanksgiving to God (5:1–31). She also must have spoken with much wisdom from God, because we read:

---

1. Linda Belleville, *Women Leaders and the Church*, 44. Others who see much significance in Deborah's leadership role include Gilbert Bilezikian, *Beyond Sex Roles*, 70–71; Cindy Jacobs, *Women of Destiny*, 179–80; Judy Brown, *Women Ministers*, 104; and J. Lee Grady, *Ten Lies the Church Tells Women*, 37. Jacobs says, "Deborah ruled the nation as the senior judge of all the judges" (179).

> Now Deborah, a prophetess, the wife of Lappidoth, was judging Israel
> at that time. She used to sit under the palm of Deborah between
> Ramah and Bethel in the hill country of Ephraim, and the people of
> Israel came up to her for judgment. (Judges 4:4–5)

For all these things, we should be thankful to God. For all generations, Deborah will serve as an example of faith, courage, worship, love for God, and godly wisdom. We must be careful not to let the disputes over Deborah cloud our appreciation for her or diminish the honor that Scripture accords to her.

— Answer #2: Deborah affirmed male leadership over God's people.

Deborah did not summon the people of Israel to battle, but encouraged Barak to do this (Judges 4:6–7, 14). Thus, rather than asserting leadership and authority for herself, she affirmed the rightness of male leadership. Then when Barak hesitated and insisted that Deborah accompany him to the battle (4:8), she announced a word of rebuke on Barak, and a loss of honor: "I will surely go with you. Nevertheless, the road on which you are going will not lead to your glory, for the LORD will sell Sisera into the hand of a woman" (4:9). This implies that Barak should not have insisted that Deborah come with him. He should have acted like a man and led on his own.

— Answer #3: The text does not say that Deborah ruled over God's people or taught them publicly or led them militarily.

It is important to examine the text of Judges 4 to see exactly what Deborah did and did not do:

1. She gave "judgment" (Hebrew *mishpāt*) to the people privately when
   they came to her. When the text says that "Deborah...was judging
   Israel at that time" (Judges 4:4), the Hebrew verb *shāphat,* "to judge,"
   in this context does not mean "to rule or govern," but rather has
   the sense "decide controversy, discriminate between persons in civil,
   political, domestic and religious questions."[2] That is evident because

---

2. BDB, 1047, 2.

the next verse tells how she was "judging": she "used to sit...under the palm of Deborah" and "the people of Israel came up to her for judgment." This is not a picture of public leadership like that of a king or queen, but of private settling of disputes through both arbitration and judicial decisions.[3] If we decide to take this as an example for today, we might see it as justification for women to serve as counselors and as civil judges. But the text of Scripture does not say that Deborah ruled over God's people.

2. Deborah is never said to have taught the people in any assembled group or congregation. While Deborah did give private judgments when people came to her, (Judges 4:5) she was never a priest, and in the Old Testament, it was the role of the priests to teach Scripture to the people. (See Leviticus 10:11.)

3. Deborah refused to lead the people in military battle, but insisted that a man do this (Judges 4:6–7, 14). In fact, Tom Schreiner points out that Deborah is the only judge in the book of Judges who has no military function.[4] When Linda Belleville claims that Deborah "united" the tribes of Israel and "led them on to victory,"[5] her assertions are contrary to the text of Judges 4, which says that Deborah prophesied that God was commanding *Barak* to "gather your men" (v. 6). The text says that *Barak*, not Deborah, "called out Zebulun and Naphtali," and that "10,000 men went up at *his* heels" (v. 10), not Deborah's. It says that "*Barak* went down from Mount Tabor with 10,000 men following *him*" (v. 14), not Deborah. It says that "the LORD routed Sisera and all his chariots and all his army *before Barak* by the edge of the sword" (v. 15). Belleville actually

---

3. The NIV is alone among standard translations in rendering Judges 4:4 as "Deborah...was *leading* Israel at that time." This is a rather loose paraphrase rather than lexically supported translation, since the meaning "lead" is not given for *shāphat* in BDB, 1047–48. Other standard translations all translate the verb *shāphat* in Judges 4:4 as "judging": ESV, NASB, KJV, NKJV, RSV, and NRSV. The Septuagint agrees, translating with *krinō*, "to judge."

4. Thomas Schreiner, "The Valuable Ministries of Women in the Context of Male Leadership," in Piper and Grudem, *Recovering Biblical Manhood and Womanhood*, 216.

5. Belleville, "Women in Ministry", 93.

speaks of the army of Israel as *Deborah's* troops ("her troops"),[6] but the Bible contains no such language. Belleville claims that Deborah "led them to victory," but the Bible says no such thing. Belleville is inserting into her reports of Scripture things that are not there and are not true. Deborah encouraged the male leadership of Barak, and the Bible says several times that he led Israel to victory.[7]

4. Deborah functioned as a "prophetess" (Judges 4:4). In this role, she delivered messages from God to the people, but this is a different role from the governing role of a king or the teaching role of a priest. (See chapter 8.)

— Answer #4: The Bible views Deborah's judgeship as a rebuke against the absence of male leadership.

Judges 4:4 suggests some amazement at the unusual nature of the situation in which a woman actually has to judge Israel, because it piles up a string of redundant words to emphasize that Deborah is a woman: translating the Hebrew text literally, the verse says, "And *Deborah*, a *woman*, a *prophetess*, the *wife* of Lappidoth, *she* was judging Israel at that time." Something is abnormal, something is wrong—there are no men to function as judge! This impression is confirmed when we read of Barak's timidity and the rebuke implied in his subsequent loss of glory: "The road on which you are going will not lead to your glory, for the LORD will sell Sisera into the hand of a woman" (4:9).

Does the story of Deborah then show that women can lead the people of God in churches where the men are passive and not leading? No, for Deborah did not do this. *The story of Deborah should motivate women in such situations to do what Deborah did: encourage and exhort a man to take the leadership role to which God has called him*, as Deborah encouraged and exhorted Barak (4:6–9, 14).

Barak finally did lead and defeated the Canaanites. Then in subsequent biblical passages that speak of this period of the judges, Barak's leadership alone is

---

6. Ibid.

7. Sarah Sumner similarly makes an inaccurate claim about what the Bible says when she writes, "Deborah is commended for leading ten thousand men into a battle against King Jabin and his army" (Sumner, *Men and Women in the Church*, 109). Contrary to Sumner's claim, the Bible says that Deborah spoke to Barak, and Barak led the ten thousand men.

mentioned: Samuel tells the people, "And the LORD sent Jerubbaal and *Barak* and Jephthah and Samuel and delivered you out of the hand of your enemies on every side" (1 Samuel 12:11). And the author of Hebrews says, "And what more shall I say? For time would fail me to tell of Gideon, *Barak*, Samson, Jephthah, of David and Samuel and the prophets" (Hebrews 11:32).

— Answer #5: We must use caution in drawing examples to imitate from the book of Judges.

The book of Judges has many examples of people doing things that we are not to imitate, such as Samson's marriage to a Philistine woman (14:1–4), or his visiting a prostitute (16:1), or Jephthah's foolish vow (11:30–31, 34–39), or the men of Benjamin lying in wait to snatch wives from the women dancing in the feast at Shiloh (21:19–23). The situation at the end of the book is summarized this way: "In those days there was no king in Israel. Everyone did what was right in his own eyes" (21:25). The unusual nature of Judges should also warn us that it is not a good source for examples of how the New Testament church should be governed.

8

WOMEN PROPHETS

～· EGALITARIAN CLAIM: Old Testament Examples of Women Prophets Like Miriam, Deborah, and Huldah Give Precedents for Women in Leadership Roles Today.

Once again, egalitarians commonly use this argument. Gilbert Bilezikian says:

> The prophetic ministry was the highest religious function in the Old Covenant.... Although statistically the majority of old-covenant prophets were male, the Bible refers to several prophetesses and describes them as exercising the same kind of authority in the religious sphere as their male counterparts (Miriam, Deborah, Huldah, and so on).[1]

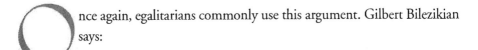 **Answer #1: While there were women prophets in the Old Testament, no women taught God's people because there were no women priests.**

The role of prophet is surely an honored role, and a vitally important one, for God speaks through a prophet to His people. But prophets and teachers have different

---

1. Gilbert Bilezikian, *Beyond Sex Roles*, 69. See also Linda Belleville, *Women Leaders and the Church*, 44–45; Judy Brown, *Women Ministers*, 83, 93, 100; J. Lee Grady, *Ten Lies the Church Tells Women*, 37–38. Belleville repeats her claims about Miriam and Deborah in "Women Leaders in the Bible," in DBE, 111–13. Contrary to the facts in Judges 4, Belleville makes the astounding claim that Deborah served as "commander-in-chief," and when the tribes of Israel were divided, Deborah "united them" and "led them to victory" (112). See Grudem, EFBT, 134.

roles in the Bible. A prophet is like a messenger who delivers a message but has no authority on his own to do more than that, such as explaining or applying the message: "Then Haggai, the *messenger* of the LORD, spoke to the people with the LORD's message, 'I am with you, declares the LORD'" (Haggai 1:13).

A prophet could not add to the message anything of his own. Even Balaam admitted, "Must I not take care to speak what the LORD puts in my mouth?" (Numbers 23:12; see also 24:13, as well as the description of false prophets as those who speak when the Lord has given them no message in Jeremiah 14:14–15; 23:16–22; Ezekiel 13:1–3).

Why then could women prophesy but not teach the people? Prophets and teachers (the priests) had different roles. The priests, not the prophets, taught God's laws to the people. God told Aaron, as instruction for himself and for the priests to follow him, "And you are to *teach* the people of Israel all the statutes that the LORD has spoken to them by Moses" (Leviticus 10:11). Later, God spoke of His covenant with Levi, from whom all the priests descended:

> *True instruction was in his mouth*, and no wrong was found on his lips. He walked with me in peace and uprightness, and he turned many from iniquity. For the lips of a priest should guard knowledge, and people should seek *instruction* from his mouth, for he is the messenger of the LORD of hosts. (Malachi 2:6–7)

The role of teaching the people was reserved for the priests.

There is a similar situation in the New Testament. Women were able to prophesy in both the Old Testament and the New (see 1 Corinthians 11:5). They could deliver messages from God to His people. But women could not assume the role of teacher over God's people in either the Old or the New Testament (see 1 Timothy 2:12; 3:2; Titus 1:6 on New Testament teachers being only men, including the elders who did most of the teaching).[2]

---

2. See the longer discussion in chapter 20, pp. 136–41, on why women could prophesy but not teach in New Testament churches, and also Grudem, EFBT, 227–32.

▬ Answer #2: Women prophets always prophesied privately or prophesied to women.

It is significant that Miriam prophesied to the women of Israel:

> Then Miriam the prophetess, the sister of Aaron, took a tambourine in her hand, and all the women went out after her with tambourines and dancing. And Miriam sang to them:
>
>> "Sing to the LORD, for he has triumphed gloriously;
>> the horse and his rider he has thrown into the sea."
>> (Exodus 15:20–21)

Rather than prophesying publicly, Deborah sent for Barak and gave a prophecy privately to him: "She sent and summoned Barak the son of Abinoam from Kedesh-naphtali and said to him, 'Has not the LORD, the God of Israel, commanded you, "Go, gather your men at Mount Tabor."'" (Judges 4:6).

And Huldah the prophetess gave her prophecy privately to a small group of five messengers from the king: "So Hilkiah the priest, and Ahikam, and Achbor, and Shaphan, and Asaiah went to Huldah the prophetess…and they talked with her" (2 Kings 22:14).

PART FOUR

EVANGELICAL FEMINIST CLAIMS FROM THE GOSPELS AND ACTS

After Genesis 1–3, the rest of the Old Testament honors godly women in many ways and shows that they, as well as men, could prophesy and could be courageous in risking their very lives to serve God by faith. But nothing in the Old Testament text indicates that women should be leaders over their husbands or lead or teach God's people.

Now we turn from the Old Testament to the New Testament. Jesus treated women with great honor and dignity. He surprised the Jewish people of His day in the way He interacted with and honored women as well as men, including several women among the group of disciples who followed Him. He even chose women to be the first witnesses to His resurrection. Don't Jesus' example and teaching show that He is overturning the patriarchal bias against women that was found in the Old Testament and in the Judaism of His day? Doesn't His example show that we should allow women and men equal access to all positions of leadership in the church?

And what about the early church? Some suggest that Jesus appointed all male

89

apostles not because that was the ideal but because that was the only thing that would have been acceptable in His day. And aren't there examples of women leaders, such as Priscilla, in the book of Acts?

It is questions like these that we consider next.

9

JESUS' TREATMENT OF WOMEN

← EGALITARIAN CLAIM: Jesus Undermined the Patriarchal Nature of First-Century Judaism Through His Positive Treatment of Women.

T he Gospels give clear testimony that Jesus treated women with dignity and respect. Egalitarians see in Jesus' interactions with women a precedent for opening all ministry positions to women. Stanley Grenz writes:

Jesus perhaps most notably departed from cultural norms by including women among his followers.... In contrast to many rabbis who considered it inappropriate to instruct women, Jesus readily taught them.... [By his response to Mary of Bethany in Luke 10:39] Jesus overturned the culturally determined priorities for women. He rejected the Jewish notion that household maintenance constituted the only appropriate role for women in society. And he defied the practice of excluding women from the study of the Torah. Our Lord set aside the customary prejudices of his day and restored the Old Testament injunction that both men and women apply themselves to learning God's law (Luke 11:27–28).[1]

---

1. Stanley Grenz, *Women in the Church*, 74–75. See also J. Lee Grady, *Ten Lies the Church Tells Women*, 32–33.

— Answer #1: It is true that Jesus undermined abuses of male leadership found in some parts of Jewish society and treated women with great respect and dignity.

There are numerous negative or demeaning statements about women in rabbinic literature, some of which stem (in oral form at least) from the time of Jesus. These are documented extensively in several studies.[2] But the picture is not entirely negative. Ben Witherington notes:

> It would be wrong to assume that a Jewish woman had no respect or *rights* in Jesus' day.... The Talmud instructs a man to love his wife as himself and to respect her more than himself.... There are even cases of women being taught the oral law and being consulted on its fine points.... Some women were able to become learned in both oral and written law and tradition.[3]

The overall picture, however, is that Jesus treated women as equals in a way that was surprising for first-century culture.

We should be thankful that Jesus honored women and treated them as persons just as He treated men. He talked openly with women, to the amazement of His disciples (John 4:1–27), taught women (Luke 10:38–42), assumed that women as well as men could talk and reason about theological truths (Luke 10:38–42; John 4:7–26; 11:21–27), had women among the band of disciples who traveled with Him (Luke 8:1–3), accepted monetary support and ministry from them (Mark 15:40–41; Luke 8:3), and used women as well as men as teaching examples (Mark 12:41–44; Luke 15:8–10; 18:1–8). Jesus thus set a pattern that should forever challenge all cultures that treat women as second-class citizens, as it no doubt challenged and rebuked the culture of Jesus' day.

---

2. For further study see the materials in Joachim Jeremias, *Jerusalem in the Time of Jesus*, 359–76; Ben Witherington, *Women and the Genesis of Christianity*, 3–9, 251–53; and Kittel and Freidrich, *Theological Dictionary of the New Testament (TDNT)* 1:781–84.
3. Witherington, *Women and the Genesis of Christianity*, 4–5, 7.

— Answer #2: But Jesus did not overthrow all male leadership because He consistently called only men to the roles of governing and teaching God's people.

Jesus appointed only men to be His twelve apostles (Matthew 10:1–4). The apostles had governing authority over the early church. When a replacement was chosen for Judas, Peter said it had to be "one of the *men* who have accompanied us" (Acts 1:21). Yes, Jesus undermined the wrongful and abusive aspects of the patriarchal culture of that time, but he did not overturn a God-given pattern of male leadership in the household and male leadership among God's people.

10

FIRST WITNESSES TO RESURRECTION

✦ EGALITARIAN CLAIM: Women Were the First Witnesses to the Resurrection (Matthew 28:1–10), Showing Their Reliability and Suitability As Messengers of the Lord. Therefore They Can Surely Be Pastors.

ida Spencer writes:

> These very women…were chosen by Jesus to be the first witnesses to his resurrection…. Jesus…wanted women to learn and to testify before others about God's actions on earth. *He wanted these women whom he had taught to go on to take authoritative leadership positions themselves.* That is why they were chosen to be the first witnesses to the resurrection.[1]

Answer #1: Yes, women were the first witnesses to Christ's resurrection, and this is a wonderful affirmation of the trustworthiness of women and their equal dignity as persons made in God's image, in contrast to some ideas in first-century culture.

We should be thankful to God for this wonderful affirmation of the trustworthiness of women as witnesses. Whereas first-century Judaism did not place confidence in

---

1. Aida Spencer, *Beyond the Curse*, 62, italics added.

the trustworthiness of women as witnesses in several kinds of legal cases, God decided that women would be the first witnesses to the most important event in all of history![2]

— Answer #2: But to give testimony as an eyewitness of a historic event is not the same as functioning as a teacher or elder in a church. Women did not do this in the New Testament.

We should not make the text say more than it says. In this case, the women ran and told the disciples, just as the angel had commanded them (Matthew 28:7–8) and as Jesus had commanded them (v. 10). But the text says nothing about teaching the assembled church or governing a local church. These same disciples did not establish these women as elders in early churches, and a few days after the resurrection, Peter specified that "one of the *men*" should replace Judas among the eleven disciples (Acts 1:21, with the male-specific term *anēr*).

---

2. After mentioning several categories of people who are not eligible to bear witness in court, the *Mishnah* then says, "This is the general rule: Any evidence that a woman is not eligible to bring, these are not eligible to bring" (*Rosh Hashanah* 1:8; quoted from Herbert Danby, *Mishnah*, 189); compare the comment in Philip Blackman, *Mishnayoth*, 2:387: "Certain kinds of evidence were accepted from a woman as for instance evidence regarding her husband's death or evidence concerning an unfaithful wife."

SERVANT LEADERSHIP IS IMPORTANT, NOT AUTHORITATIVE LEADERSHIP

⌐· EGALITARIAN CLAIM: Jesus Taught Servant Leadership, and This Is Inconsistent with a Male Leadership Pattern of Use of Power over Others.

Stanley Grenz writes:

The New Testament emphasis on facilitative leadership means that leaders of both genders best serve the church.... Many participants in the contemporary debate over women in ministry understand leadership as the exercise of power over others.... The chief flaw in this understanding of leadership, however, is that it sets aside our Lord's teaching. Jesus reveals in both word and deed that the divine way of life lies in humble servanthood.... To be a leader means above all to be a servant to others.... "Whoever wishes to be great among you must be your servant" (Mark 10:42–45).... Biblical, servant-oriented leadership...is best symbolized by men and women ministering together in this crucial dimension of church life.[1]

---

1. Stanley Grenz, *Women in the Church*, 216–18.

— Answer #1: Jesus was both a servant and a leader with great authority.

Grenz and other egalitarians wrongly pit servant leadership against authority. Jesus came to serve, yes, and to give His life for us. But He was simultaneously Lord! He said, "You call me Teacher and Lord, and you are right, for so I am" (John 13:13), and "If you love me, you will keep my commandments" (14:15).

— Answer #2: Elders should likewise use authority with a servant heart.

Similarly, the New Testament tells elders to be "examples to the flock" (1 Peter 5:3), and all elders would do well to heed Jesus' words: "Whoever would be great among you must be your servant" (Mark 10:43). But this does not negate the authority given to elders, for the New Testament also says, "Obey your leaders and submit to them, for they are keeping watch over your souls, as those who will have to give an account" (Hebrews 13:17), and "Let the elders who rule well be considered worthy of double honor" (1 Timothy 5:17). If we are faithful to the whole New Testament, we will not pit authority against servanthood, but affirm both.

12

CULTURAL REASONS FOR MALE APOSTLES

⌐· EGALITARIAN CLAIM: The Fact That Jesus Appointed Only Men to Be Apostles Was a Mere Concession to the Culture of His Time; It Is Not Normative for Us Today.

Gilbert Bilezikian says:

Because of the cultural constraints present in the Jewish world, the ministry of women apostles, or Samaritan apostles, or Gentile apostles would have been unacceptable. Therefore, the exclusion of women, Samaritans, and Gentiles was inevitable during the first phase of the fulfillment of the Great Commission. At a later date, when the gospel spread beyond the boundaries of Judaism, both men and women, Samaritans and Gentiles, became instrumental in carrying out the gospel mission.... Pragmatic considerations of accommodation determined the composition of the first apostolic group.[1]

Similarly, Aida Spencer objects that if the *maleness* of the twelve apostles requires male leadership in the church, the *Jewishness* of the twelve apostles requires Jewish leadership in the church:

---

1. Gilbert Bilezikian, *Beyond Sex Roles*, 274.

Jesus chose twelve among all his disciples to represent the original twelve tribes of Israel.... If Jesus' choice of twelve male disciples signifies that females should not be leaders in the church, then, consistently his choice also signifies that Gentiles should not be leaders in the church.[2]

➤ Answer #1: Jesus never compromised with the culture of His time in matters of moral right and wrong.

If Jesus had wanted to demonstrate that all church offices were open to women, He easily could have appointed six women and six men as apostles. That would have settled the leadership question for all time. But He did not.

It is true that Jesus' choice of twelve disciples is an evident sign that He is replacing the twelve heads of the twelve tribes of Israel and setting up new leadership for the people of God. But that did not require twelve men, for six men and six women would also have constituted a new twelve-member leadership team. The fact is that Jesus intentionally and freely chose twelve men for these leadership positions.

To say that Jesus gave in to cultural pressures on this and thus failed to model and teach what He knew was God's ideal is to call into question Jesus' integrity and courage. As James Borland writes:

Jesus was not averse to breaking social customs when He felt it necessary. He criticized Pharisees to their face in public (Matthew 23:13–36), healed on the sabbath (Mark 1:21–27; Luke 13:14; John 5:8–10), and cleansed the temple (John 2:14–17; Matthew 21:12–13). Against custom, Jesus spoke to the Samaritan woman (John 4:7–9), ate with tax collectors and sinners (Matthew 9:11), and even ate with unwashed hands (Mark 7:1–23)! The point is that when moral issues were at stake, Jesus did not bend to cultural pressure. No, it was not social custom or cultural pressure that caused Jesus to appoint an all-male group of apostles.[3]

---

2. Aida Spencer, *Beyond the Curse*, 45. Spencer repeats her argument in "Jesus' Treatment of Women in the Gospels," in DBE, 136.
3. James A. Borland, "Women in the Life and Teachings of Jesus," in Piper and Grudem, *Recovering Biblical Manhood and Womanhood*, 120.

Nor did Jesus yield to cultural expectations when appointing His disciples. Matthew was a "tax collector" (Matthew 10:3), an unpopular figure (see 18:17; 21:31), and the disciples generally were "uneducated, common men" (Acts 4:13).

So the argument that Jesus gave in to cultural pressure and gave preferential treatment to men as apostles, contrary to God's creation ideals, is not correct. To think that Jesus "accommodated" His appointment of the apostles, a foundational and eternally significant action, to what would be acceptable for the time is not consistent with the rest of Jesus' ministry and actually impugns Jesus' courage and character.

— Answer #2: The maleness of the apostles established a permanent pattern for male leadership in the church.

The highest human leadership among God's people in the New Covenant is simply not egalitarian. Even in the age to come, Jesus said, there will be a place of high authority for His twelve apostles: "Truly, I say to you, in the new world, when the Son of Man will sit on his glorious throne, you who have followed me will also sit on twelve thrones, judging the twelve tribes of Israel" (Matthew 19:28). And in the heavenly city we will see a permanent reminder of male leadership among God's people, for "the wall of the city had twelve foundations, and on them were the twelve names of the twelve apostles of the Lamb" (Revelation 21:14).

Grenz objects that the apostles are unique in their "foundational" and "temporary" role.[4] Of course they were unique. That is just the point. The most unique, foundational, authoritative leaders in the church were all men. At its very foundation, the church of Jesus Christ is not an egalitarian institution. It has 100 percent male leadership.

— Answer #3: The Jewishness of the twelve apostles was only a temporary pattern because Jesus came first to the Jews.

Bilezikian and Spencer fail to recognize that the Jewishness of the twelve apostles was because in God's sovereign plan, *there were no Gentile men* in the church when it started. God's plan was to begin with the Jews and then include Gentiles, so Jesus started His work and ministry only among the Jews. He said, "I was sent only to

---

4. Stanley Grenz, *Women in the Church*, 211.

the lost sheep of the house of Israel" (Matthew 15:24), and He told His disciples during His earthly ministry, "Go nowhere among the Gentiles and enter no town of the Samaritans, but go rather to the lost sheep of the house of Israel" (10:5–6). Even at Pentecost, the people who heard and believed were Jews (Acts 2:5). There were no Gentiles among the earliest believers. By contrast, *there were women as well as men among Jesus' followers from the beginning*, and if Jesus had wanted to appoint women, He could have done so.

Once the gospel began to spread to Gentiles, *Gentiles were immediately included among the church leaders*, in accordance with Jesus' command to make disciples of "all nations" (Matthew 28:19).[5] Luke was a Gentile and he wrote two books of the New Testament, and Paul's companions Titus and Epaphroditus have Gentile names, not Jewish names. Gentiles had leadership roles in the New Testament, but women were not included in the role of elder. The following chart shows this natural historical progression:

	Membership among God's people	Authoritative leadership over God's people
early in Acts	only Jews	Jewish men
later in Acts and epistles	Jews and Gentiles	Jewish and Gentile men

This pattern of male leadership continued throughout all periods of the New Testament.

---

5. See also Acts 1:8, and note the appointment of elders in Gentile cities in Acts 14:23; note also that the requirements for elders in Titus 1 and 1 Timothy 3 do not include being Jewish.

13

PRISCILLA TAUGHT
APOLLOS

‿· EGALITARIAN CLAIM: Since Priscilla and Aquila Both "Explained" to Apollos "The Way of God More Accurately" (Acts 18:26), Women Can Teach Men in the Church.

This argument is made by a number of egalitarian writers. Linda Belleville claims that this was the same type of teaching as done by Paul, because the same word is used:

[In Acts 18:26] Luke says that Priscilla and Aquila "expounded" (*exethento*) the way of God to Apollos, but this is the same term Luke uses for Paul's teaching. "From morning until evening," Luke reports, "Paul expounded [*exetitheto*] and testified about the kingdom of God" (Acts 28:23 AT). So to draw a distinction between private and public forms of instruction or between informal and formal types at this stage in the church's development is simply anachronistic.[1]

Gilbert Bilezikian goes even further, for on the basis of one verse that reports one private conversation, he endows Priscilla and Aquila with the status of "seminary faculty":

---

1. Linda Belleville, *Women Leaders and the Church*, 59. (The ordinary lexical form of the verb is *ektithēmi*.)

For all practical purposes, *Priscilla and Aquila acted as a seminary faculty* for a promising male pastoral student. They taught him those redemptive events of the life of Christ about which he had been left uninformed along with their theological significance.[2]

— Answer #1: Scripture encourages men and women to talk with each other about the Bible and Christian doctrine.

As I indicated in chapter 2, Acts 18:26 provides an excellent encouragement for women and men to talk with each other about the meanings of Bible passages in private discussions and in small group Bible studies, as Christians everywhere have done for centuries.[3] This has never been at issue.

— Answer #2: To say that there is no distinction between private and public teaching is to ignore the two fundamental factors of interpretation: the words of the text and the context.

When Belleville denies that there is any difference between Priscilla's conversation with Apollos and public teaching by Paul, she ignores the specific words of the text. The narrative in Acts 18 is written in such a way that it guards us against understanding that they did this publicly, for it says, "When Priscilla and Aquila heard him, *they took him* and explained to him the way of God more accurately" (v. 26). The phrase "they took him" indicates that they waited to speak to him until they could take him aside, out of public view.[4] And the context indicates that this is in contrast to the public speaking of Apollos in which "he began to speak boldly in the synagogue" (v. 26a).

Belleville's assertion that the same word (*ektithēmi*) is used to refer to Paul's public preaching in Acts 28:23 confuses the meaning of a word with its use in

---

2. Gilbert Bilezikian, *Beyond Sex Roles*, 201–02. See also Cindy Jacobs, *Women of Destiny*, 194; Judy Brown, *Women Ministers*, 177, 179; Aida Spencer, *Beyond the Curse*, 107; Stanley Grenz, *Women in the Church*, 82–83. Sarah Sumner says, "Am I the only person to be stunned by this? Priscilla taught Apollos in Ephesus!" (*Men and Women in the Church*, 241).

3. See chapter 2, pp. 44–45.

4. BDAG understand *proslambanō* in this verse to mean, "to take or lead off to oneself, *take aside*" (883).

different contexts. The word simply means "to convey information by careful elaboration, *explain, expound*,"[5] and the context shows whether that is public or private explanation. Belleville's argument is somewhat like arguing,

1. In Acts 28:23 this word is used to refer to Paul's arguing about Jesus with the Jews in Rome from morning to evening;
2. Therefore, in Acts 18:26 the same word must mean that Priscilla argued about Jesus with the Jews in Rome from morning to evening.

But this is simply false. Priscilla was not in Rome and she was not arguing with the Jews in Rome. The mistake is to think that we can import the *context* of a word used in one case into that word's use in another case. That is a fundamental error in interpretation. The word *ektithēmi* just means to "explain" and surely a person can "explain" something either in private or in public. And the different contexts show that Acts 18:26 was private and Acts 28:23 was public.

— Answer #3: Priscilla's example does not give warrant for women to teach the Bible to the assembled church.

As we also saw in chapter 2, it is specifically in situations where the whole church is assembled that Paul restricts governing and teaching activities to men (see 1 Corinthians 14:33–36; 1 Timothy 2:11–15; see also the qualifications for elders in 1 Timothy 3 and Titus 1). The example of Priscilla and Aquila instructing Apollos privately in Acts 18:26 does not contradict this.

5. Ibid., 310.

14

PRISCILLA IS NAMED FIRST

⌐· EGALITARIAN CLAIM: Since Priscilla's Name Is Put Before Aquila's Name, Especially When They Are in Ministry Situations, This Indicates That She Was the Leader in Their Ministry Team.

Linda Belleville argues:

> What is unusual, however, is that when Luke refers to their occupation as tent makers, the order is "Aquila and Priscilla" (Acts 18:2; cf. 1 Cor. 16:19), but when Luke and Paul speak from a ministry point of view, the order is always "Priscilla and Aquila." [Belleville mentions Acts 18:18, 26; Romans 16:3; 2 Timothy 4:19.] This would suggest that of the two, it was Priscilla who possessed the dominant ministry and leadership skills.[1]

▬ Answer #1: It is difficult to know what, if anything, was meant by the order of names.

There is much speculation about what might be meant by the order of the names

---

1. Linda Belleville, *Women Leaders and the Church*, 68; repeated in DBE, 122. See also Gilbert Bilezikian, *Beyond Sex Roles*, 200–01; Stanley Grenz, *Women in the Church*, 82; Cindy Jacobs, *Women of Destiny*, 194–95, quoting Ben Witherington, *Women and the Genesis of Christianity*, 220. See also Judy Brown, *Women Ministers*, 175.

Priscilla and Aquila, but very little hard evidence to go on. Was the variation merely stylistic? Were the authors at times simply trying to give honor to the woman by naming her first? Leon Morris says, "Prisca is mentioned before her husband on four occasions out of six...from which some have deduced that she came from a higher social stratum, and others that she was more able than her husband."[2] F. F. Bruce says, "Paul generally put Prisca (Priscilla) before Aquila, her husband; this may have been due to her having the more impressive personality of the two, although some have inferred that her social rank was superior to his. She may have belonged...to...a noble Roman family, while he was a Jew from Pontus in northern Asia Minor."[3] Cranfield says that the more frequent placement of Priscilla's name first is more likely "due either to her having been converted before him (and perhaps having led her husband to faith in Christ) or to her having played an even more prominent part in the life and work of the Church than Aquila had," rather than to "her having been socially superior to him."[4] The truth is that nobody is quite sure what to make of the order of names.

However, Belleville's claim that "when Luke and Paul speak from a ministry point of view, the order is always 'Priscilla and Aquila,'" is not correct. In 1 Corinthians 16:19, Paul puts Aquila first in connection with "the church in their house," which is surely a ministry connection: "Aquila and Prisca, together with the church in their house, send you hearty greetings in the Lord."[5]

In conclusion, it is difficult to say anything with certainty about the significance of the order of names. Belleville and others are simply claiming more than the text can prove.

---

2. Leon Morris, *The Epistle to the Romans*, 531.

3. F. F. Bruce, *Romans* (1973), 271.

4. C. E. B. Cranfield, *Critical and Exegetical Commentary on the Epistle to the Romans* (1979), 2:784.

5. Bilezikian again reads into the Bible things that are not there when he says that "the epistle to the Romans was intended to have been read in the congregation(s) in Rome, obviously in the presence of Aquila and Priscilla and of the home-church that met in their house *and which they co-pastored*" (*Beyond Sex Roles*, 201 [italics added]). Romans 16:3–5, to which Bilezikian refers, says, "*Greet Prisca and Aquila*, my fellow workers in Christ Jesus, who risked their necks for my life, to whom not only I give thanks but all the churches of the Gentiles give thanks as well. *Greet also the church in their house.*" Not one word is said about "co-pastoring" a church.

PART FIVE

EVANGELICAL FEMINIST CLAIMS ABOUT MARRIAGE FROM THE NEW TESTAMENT EPISTLES

The Gospels and Acts show a wonderful, remarkable pattern of treating women as well as men with full respect and honor and involving women in many crucial ministry roles for the early church. But the life of Christ and the story of the early church in Acts also show a pattern in which only men, such as Jesus' twelve apostles, were given teaching and governing roles over God's people.

As we turn to the New Testament epistles with a view first toward marriage, the question is posed: Is it really possible to determine what the New Testament epistles teach about marriage? Of course there are passages that say the husband is the "head" of the wife (Ephesians 5:23), but isn't it possible that we have misunderstood *head* and that it really means something else and does not indicate any special authority for a husband?

In addition, Galatians 3:28 says that now, in the New Covenant, "there is neither male nor female, for you are all one in Christ Jesus," and doesn't that clear principle remove all gender-based distinctions in roles and show that we no longer need to follow outmoded ideas of male headship in marriage and the church? And doesn't Ephesians 5:21 teach mutual submission in which there is no unique authority for the husband in marriage?

It is questions such as these that we now consider.

15

NO LONGER
MALE OR FEMALE

⌐· EGALITARIAN CLAIM: Galatians 3:28–"There Is
Neither Jew Nor Greek, There Is Neither Slave Nor Free, There Is
Neither Male Nor Female, for You Are All One in Christ Jesus"–
Teaches That There Is Full Gender Equality in the Kingdom of God.

This claim is one of the most common claims made by egalitarian writers.
Rebecca Groothuis is representative of many when she writes:

Of all the texts that support biblical equality, *Galatians 3:26–28 is
probably the most important.* Unlike the New Testament proof texts
traditionalists use to support hierarchical gender roles, this text is
not a specific command directed toward a specific cultural situation.
Rather, it is a broadly applicable statement of the inclusive nature
of the New Covenant, whereby all groups of people, regardless of
their previous religious status under the law, have now become one
in Christ.[1]

---

1. Rebecca Groothuis, *Good News for Women*, 25–26. See also Gilbert Bilezikian, *Beyond Sex Roles*, 126–28; Stanley Grenz, *Women in the Church*, 99–107; Klyne Snodgrass, "Galatians 3:28: Conundrum or Solution?" in Alvera Mickelsen, *Women, Authority and the Bible*, 161–81, and the responses by Susie Stanley (181–88) and W. Ward Gasque (188–92); and Judy Brown, *Women Ministers* (1996), 234–35. See also Gordon Fee's chapter "Male and Female in the New Creation: Galatians 3:26–29" in DBE, 172–85, and the response by Robert Saucy in JBMW 10:1 (Spring 2005), 29–37.

— Answer #1: Galatians 3:28 teaches unity among diverse members in the body of Christ, but it does not teach that we are all the same or have all the same roles.

Egalitarians frequently claim that if there is "neither male nor female," then distinctions in role based on our gender are abolished because we are now all "one in Christ Jesus."

The problem is that this is not what the verse says. To say that we are "one" means that we are *united*, that there should be no factions or divisions among us, and there should be no sense of pride and superiority or jealousy and inferiority between these groups that viewed themselves as so distinct in the ancient world. Jews should no longer think themselves superior to Greeks, freed men should no longer think themselves superior to slaves, and men should no longer think themselves superior to women. They are all *parts of one body* in Christ, and all share in equal value and dignity as members of one body in Christ.

But, as Richard Hove has demonstrated in detail elsewhere,[2] when the Bible says that several things are "one," it never joins things that are exactly the same. Rather, it says that things that are different, things that are diverse, share some kind of unity. So in Romans 12:4–5 we read, "For as in one body we have many members, and the members do not all have the same function, so *we*, though many, *are one body* in Christ, and individually members one of another."

Paul does not mean to say that all the members of the body are the *same*, for as anyone can see, a body has hands and feet and eyes and ears, and all the "members" are different and have different functions, though they are one body.

Similarly, Hove found that Paul, using the same construction,[3] can say, "*Now he who plants and he who waters are one*; but each will receive his own reward

2. See Richard W. Hove, "Does Galatians 3:28 Negate Gender-Specific Roles?" in Grudem, *Biblical Foundations for Manhood and Womanhood* (1991), 105–43, and also his book *Equality in Christ?* (1999).

3. Hove ran forty-five computer searches on Greek literature near the time of the New Testament. He reports finding sixteen examples of Greek expressions from the New Testament and other ancient literature that use the verb "to be" (*eimi*) plus the number "one" (Greek *heis/mia/hen*) and finds that the expression is never used to indicate unity among things that are identical, but always among things that are different and have different functions but that also share something in common that gives them a kind of unity (Hove, *Equality in Christ?* 72–76).

according to his own labor" (1 Corinthians 3:8, NASB). Now planting and watering are two different activities done by different persons in Paul's example. They are not reduced to "sameness" nor are they required to act in exactly the same way, but they are still "one" because they have a unity of purpose and goal.

And so Galatians 3:28 simply says that we have a special kind of *unity* in the body of Christ. Our differences as male and female are not obliterated by this unity, but the unity is beautiful in God's sight particularly because it is a unity of different kinds of people.

— Answer #2: Galatians 3:28 cannot teach that all role distinctions are abolished because the New Testament still gives different commands telling how men and women should obey God.

Surely this verse cannot abolish all differences between men and women, not only because Paul himself elsewhere commands husbands and wives to act differently according to their different roles, but also because marriage in Scripture from beginning to end is intended by God to be only between one man and one woman, not between one man and another man or one woman and another woman. If Galatians 3:28 truly abolished all differences between men and women, then how could anyone say that homosexual marriage was wrong? But homosexual conduct is surely forbidden by Scripture (see Romans 1:26–27; 1 Corinthians 6:9; 1 Timothy 1:10), and our egalitarian friends within the evangelical world agree that it is. Therefore Galatians 3:28 does not abolish all differences in roles between men and women.

The egalitarian objection from Galatians 3:28, therefore, is not persuasive. Galatians 3:28 tells us that we are united in Christ and that we should never be boastful or arrogant against others, and we should never feel inferior or without value in the body of Christ. But the verse does not say, as egalitarians allege, that men and women are the same or that they have to act the same.

— Answer #3: There are social implications in Galatians 3:28, but other texts in the New Testament explain what they are and are not.

Many egalitarians insist that "social implications are necessarily involved" in Galatians 3:28,[4] and I agree. This text, and others like it, taught a new oneness

4. Snodgrass, "Galatians 3:28," 177.

in the way Christians should relate to one another, different from the wrongful stereotypes and discrimination that had characterized their past. But just saying, "There are social implications of this text," does not solve any specific questions about relationships between men and women in marriage and in the church.

Therefore, we need to realize that this is not the only text in the Bible on men and women. It is a true text, and it is a wonderful text, but it is not the only text, and we should not make it say more than it does. To determine the ways men and women should relate to each other in marriage and the church, and the roles men and women should fill in marriage and the church, we need the teaching of other texts. This is why Klyne Snodgrass, writing on Galatians 3:28 in a collection of egalitarian essays, rightly says, "Galatians 3:28 does not spell out what roles and functions will look like where 'there is no male and female.'"[5]

Many other texts make clear that Paul's statement, "there is neither male nor female" does not abolish all differences in roles between men and women.

5. Ibid., 179.

16

MUTUAL SUBMISSION

↶· EGALITARIAN CLAIM: The New Testament Writers Urged the Mutual Submission of Husbands and Wives to One Another (Ephesians 5:21). Therefore There Is No Unique Leadership Role for the Husband.

Ephesians 5:21 says, "submitting to one another out of reverence for Christ."[1] Egalitarians say this verse teaches "mutual submission," and that means that just as wives have to submit to their husbands, *so husbands have to submit to their wives.* Doesn't the text say that we have to submit "to one another"? And this means that there is no unique submission that a wife owes to her husband, and no unique authority that a husband has over his wife.

Rebecca Groothuis says:

The call to mutual reciprocal submission in Eph. 5:21 establishes the framework for the instructions to wives and husbands that follow.... Wives are to submit to their husbands in the same way that all believers are to submit

---

1. I have quoted the ESV here, which rightly starts a new paragraph at verse 22 and keeps the string of Greek participles together in verses 19–21. (Verse 22 begins a new sentence in Greek, but verse 21 is the end of a long sentence running from verses 18 to 21). The question of whether to start a new paragraph with verse 21 or verse 22 is not crucial to either side's argument, however, since everyone agrees that verse 21 both modifies Paul's command to "be filled with the Spirit" in verse 18 and has implications for our understanding of the commands in 5:22–6:5. Sarah Sumner, *Men and Women in the Church,* fails to understand this and claims that the dispute turns on where the paragraph breaks (155–59). The main difference is not where the paragraph begins but what the words translated "be subject" and "one another" actually mean.

to one another. This text is not advocating a unilateral female submission to male authority. Rather, it is presenting the submission of wives as one application of the basic principle of basic submission that is to be applied by all believers within the Body of Christ.[2]

Based on the idea of "mutual submission," egalitarians will sometimes say: "Of course I believe that a wife should be subject to her husband. And *a husband should also be subject to his wife.*" Or an egalitarian woman might say, "I will be subject to my husband *as soon as he is subject to me.*" And so, as egalitarians understand Ephesians 5:21, there is no difference in roles between men and women. There is no unique leadership role, no unique authority for the husband. There is simply "mutual submission."[3]

— Answer #1: If by "mutual submission" someone means that husband and wife should love one another and be considerate of one another's needs, this is surely a biblical idea, but it is not taught in this verse.

People can mean different things by "mutual submission." There is a sense of the phrase "mutual submission" that does not nullify the husband's authority within marriage. If "mutual submission" means *being considerate of one another* and *caring for one another's needs* and *being thoughtful of one another,* then of course I agree that "mutual submission" is a good thing (unless these ideas are used to nullify all unique authority for the husband). We can get these ideas from Jesus' command to "love one another" (John 13:34) and from Paul's commands in Philippians 2:3–4: "Do nothing from rivalry or conceit, but in humility count others more significant than yourselves. Let each of you look not only to his own interests, but also to the interests of others."

But as we will see in the following discussion, it is doubtful that these ideas are taught in Ephesians 5:21. The Bible does not use the language of "being subject" to teach these things. In addition, egalitarians mean something so different by the phrase "mutual submission" and have used this phrase so often to nullify male

---

2. Rebecca Groothuis, *Good News for Women,* 164–65. See also Gilbert Bilezikian, *Beyond Sex Roles,* 154.
3. In fact, our egalitarian friends have a journal called *Mutuality,* published by Christians for Biblical Equality.

authority within marriage that I am convinced the expression "mutual submission" only leads to confusion in today's context.

— Answer #2: In the context that follows Ephesians 5:21, Paul explains what he means by "submitting to one another": He means wives should submit to husbands, children to parents, and servants to masters.

The plain sense of "submitting to one another" in Ephesians 5:21 has been clear to Christians for centuries, simply from looking at the context. Paul explains in the following context that wives are to be subject to[4] their husbands (Ephesians 5:22–23), children are to be subject to their parents (Ephesians 6:1–3), and slaves (or bondservants) are to be subject to their masters (Ephesians 6:5–8). *These relationships are never reversed.* He does not tell husbands to be subject to wives, or parents to be subject to their children (thus nullifying all parental authority), or masters to be subject to their servants.

Paul does not tell husbands and wives *generally* to be subject to each other, nor does he tell wives to be subject to *other people's husbands.* He says, "Wives, submit to *your own husbands,* as to the Lord" (Ephesians 5:22).[5]

What Paul has in mind is not a vague "mutual submission," where everybody is considerate and thoughtful of everybody else, but a specific kind of submission to an authority: The wife is subject to the authority of "her own husband." Similarly, parents and children aren't told to practice "mutual submission," but children are to be subject to (to "obey") their parents (Ephesians 6:1–3), and servants are told to be subject to (to "obey") their masters (Ephesians 6:5–8). In each case, the person in authority is not told to be subject to the one under authority, but Paul wisely gives guidelines to regulate the use of authority by husbands (who are to love their wives, Ephesians 5:25–33), by parents (who are not to provoke their children to anger, Ephesians 6:4), and by masters (who are to give up threatening their servants and remember that they too

---

4. Sometimes people have objected that the verb "be subject to" (Greek *hupotassō*) is not actually found in verse 22. This is only partly true. A few significant Greek manuscripts lack *hupotassō* in this verse (p[46], B, and some church fathers), but many include it (Sinaiticus, A, D, 1739, many church fathers, and all the early versions in other languages). Whether or not it was there explicitly makes little difference to the context, for even if it is lacking, the idea "submit to, be subject to" from verse 21 would still be required for verse 22 to make sense, and *hupotassō* does occur explicitly in verse 24, "Now as the church *submits* to Christ, so also wives should submit in everything to their husbands."

5. The Greek text has the adjective *idios*, meaning "your own."

serve Christ, Ephesians 6:9). In no case is there "mutual submission"; in each case there is submission to authority and regulated use of that authority.

And then Paul says that the kind of submission wives are to exercise is like the submission of the church to Christ: "Now as the church submits to Christ, so also wives should submit in everything to their husbands" (Ephesians 5:24). This is surely not a "mutual submission," for the church is subject to Christ's authority in a way that Christ is not, and never will be, subject to us.

— Answer #3: The egalitarian view of "mutual submission" is a novelty in the history of the church.

Throughout the history of the church, I know of no author before 1968 who thought that "submitting to one another" makes the passage mean what egalitarians understand, namely that there is no unique male headship and authority in marriage. For centuries it was understood that the passage teaches that we should all be subject to those God has put in authority over us, such as husbands, parents, or employers. Ephesians 5:21 was understood to restrain the authority of husbands, parents, and masters, but not to nullify it.

The clear meaning from the context is one reason why people didn't see "mutual submission" in Ephesians 5:21 as something that nullified a husband's authority. But feminist pressures in our culture led people to look for a way to avoid the force of Ephesians 5:22: "Wives, submit to your own husbands, as to the Lord."

In previous generations some people did speak about "mutual submission," but never in the sense in which egalitarians today understand it. In his study of the history of the interpretation of Ephesians 5:21, Daniel Doriani demonstrates that a number of earlier writers thought that there was a kind of "mutual submission" taught in the verse, but that such "submission" took very different forms for those *in authority* and for those *under authority*. They took it to mean that those in authority should govern wisely and with sacrificial concern for those under their authority. But Doriani found no author prior to the advent of feminism in the last half of the twentieth century who thought that "submitting to one another" nullified the authority of the husband within marriage.[6]

---

6. See Daniel Doriani, "The Historical Novelty of Egalitarian Interpretations of Scripture," in Grudem, *Biblical Foundations for Manhood and Womanhood*, 203–19.

— Answer #4: Husbands are never told to be subject to their wives.

There is another fact that egalitarians cannot explain well when they propose "mutual submission" as an understanding of this verse. They fail to account for the fact that, while wives are several times in the New Testament told to be subject to their husbands (Ephesians 5:22–24; Colossians 3:18; Titus 2:5; 1 Peter 3:1–6), *husbands are never told to be subject to their wives.* Why is this, if Paul wanted to teach "mutual submission"?

The command that a husband should be subject to his wife would have been startling in an ancient male-dominated culture. Therefore, if the New Testament writers thought that Christian marriage required husbands to submit to their wives, they would have had to say that very clearly—otherwise, no early Christians would have ever known that was what they should do! But nowhere do we find such a command. It is surprising that evangelical feminists claim that the New Testament teaches this when it is nowhere explicitly stated.

— Answer #5: The egalitarian position depends on giving a Greek term a meaning it has never been shown to have.

When we look at the word Paul used when he said "submitting to one another" in Ephesians 5:21, we find that this word (Greek *hupotassō*) is always used of *submission to an authority.* No one has yet produced any examples in ancient Greek literature (either inside or outside the New Testament) where *hupotassō* is applied to a relationship between persons, and where it does not carry this sense of being *subject to an authority.*[7]

Though there are abundant examples of this sense in secular Greek literature, we don't have to seek examples from non-Christian literature to demonstrate this sense.

---

7. With respect to persons, BDAG gives the meanings [active]: "to cause to be in a submissive relationship, to subject, to subordinate"; [passive]: "become subject...subject oneself, be subjected or subordinated, obey" (1042). Gilbert Bilezikian is incorrect when he claims that the meaning of the word changes when "one another" is added to it: see Grudem, EFBT, 191–92. In addition, for an excellent analysis of the interpretation of this verse, see Peter O'Brien, *The Letter to the Ephesians*, Pillar New Testament Commentary (Grand Rapids: Eerdmans, 1999), 398–405.

1. Jesus was "submissive to" the authority of His parents (Luke 2:51).
2. Demons were "subject to" the disciples (Luke 10:17). It is clear that the meaning "be considerate of, be thoughtful toward" cannot fit here, for the demons were certainly not considerate of or thoughtful toward the disciples!
3. Citizens are to be "subject to" or "in subjection" to the governing authorities (Romans 13:1, 5; Titus 3:1; 1 Peter 2:13).
4. The universe is "in subjection" to Christ (1 Corinthians 15:27; Ephesians 1:22).
5. Angels and other spiritual beings have been "subjected to" Christ (1 Peter 3:22).
6. Christ is "subjected to" God the Father (1 Corinthians 15:28).
7. Church members are to be "subject to" the elders in the church (1 Peter 5:5)[8].
8. Wives are told to be "subject to" their husbands (Ephesians 5:22, 24; Colossians 3:18; Titus 2:5; 1 Peter 3:5).
9. The church is to "submit to" Christ (Ephesians 5:24).
10. Servants are to be "submissive to" their masters (Titus 2:9; 1 Peter 2:18).
11. Christians are to be "subject to" God (Hebrews 12:9; James 4:7).

The meaning "be subject to an authority" is common, it is well attested, and it can be supported by dozens of other examples. This is the ordinary sense of the word, and Paul's readers would have understood the word in that sense.

To claim, as Linda Belleville does[9], that *hupotassō* means something in Ephesians 5:21 that it nowhere meant at any other time or place in history would require (1)

---

8. First Corinthians 16:15–16 should also be placed in this category because we know from *1 Clement* 42:4, a letter written from Clement of Rome to the church of Corinth in AD 95, that the elders in the church at Corinth came from the household of Stephanas. Therefore, when Paul tells the Corinthians to be "subject to" the household of Stephanas, he is telling them to be subject to those who were elders in Corinth.

9. Linda Belleville, "Women in Ministry," in *Two Views on Women in Ministry*, ed. James R. Beck and Craig L. Blomberg (Grand Rapids, MI: Zondervan, 2001), 131. Surprisingly, I. Howard Marshall is willing to argue that even if *hupotassō* does not have the sense of "mutual humility" anywhere else, it still takes that sense here: "All believers should place themselves under other believers in this spirit of mutual humility, even if this is the only place where the verb *hypotassomai* is so used" (DBE, 197).

that Paul wrote a word with a new, secret meaning that Greek-speaking people had never known before, (2) that Paul expected that all the Christians in all the churches to which the epistle to the Ephesians went would know this new, secret meaning and understand what he meant, (3) that they would know that he did not mean by *hupotassō* what all Greek speakers everywhere had previously meant when they used it in conversation and even what Paul himself meant by it in all his other writings, and (4) that the meaning is now suddenly so "obvious" from the context that everyone should see it. Those who invent such a definition should be honest and admit that they are believing something with no facts to support it and several relevant facts against it.

— Answer #7: The term translated "one another" often means "some to others" and not "everyone to everyone." That is the sense it has to have here.

The Greek term translated "one another" (the word *allēlōn*) can have two different meanings. Sometimes in the New Testament it means something like "everyone to everyone," as we see in verses like John 13:34: "A new commandment I give to you, that you *love one another*." Everyone agrees that this means that all Christians are to love all other Christians. It has the sense "everyone to everyone."

But egalitarians make a crucial mistake when they assume that because *allēlōn* means "everyone to everyone" in *some* verses, it must mean that in *all* verses. In many other contexts, the word doesn't mean "everyone to everyone," but "some to others."

For example, in Revelation 6:4, the rider on the red horse "was permitted to take peace from the earth, so that men should *slay one another*." This does not mean that every person first got killed and then killed the one who had murdered him! It simply means that *some* killed *others*. Here the word *allēlōn* does not mean "everyone to everyone" but "some to others."

We see a similar example in Galatians 6:2: "Bear *one another's* burdens, and so fulfill the law of Christ." Here Paul does not mean that everybody should switch burdens with everybody else, but only that some who are more able should bear the burdens of others who are less able to bear their burdens.[10] And in 1 Corinthians 11:33, Paul says, "When you come together to eat, wait for *one another*." This does not mean that those who come early should wait for those who are late and those

---

10. For a response to Sarah Sumner's objection at this point, see Grudem, EFBT, 196.

who are late should wait for those who are there early. It means that those who are early should wait for the others who are late. Here again, *allēlōn* means "some to others" (some are to wait for others). Therefore, "submitting to one another" in Ephesians 5:21 *can* take the sense "some be subject to others" if the context fits or requires this meaning. And, as we have seen above, the word translated "submitting to" (Greek *hupotassō*) requires this sense, because it is never used to speak of a reciprocal relationship between persons but always signifies one-directional submission to an authority.

Therefore we find that no idea of "mutual submission" is taught in Ephesians 5:21 and we can paraphrase the verse as follows: "Be subject to others in the church who are in positions of authority over you."[11]

— Answer #7: Colossians 3:18, Titus 2:5, and 1 Peter 3:1 do not allow the egalitarian sense of "mutual submission."

One other fact warns us that the egalitarian claim of "mutual submission" should not be used as a magic wand to wave away any claims of male leadership in marriage: There is no statement about "submitting to one another" in the context of Colossians 3:18, Titus 2:5, or 1 Peter 3:1. Yet, as we saw earlier in this chapter, those verses also explicitly teach wives to be submissive to their husbands. They say nothing about husbands being submissive to their wives.

This leaves egalitarians in a dilemma. Nothing in these letters would have even hinted to Paul's original readers in Colossae, or to Titus and the church in Crete, or to Peter's readers in hundreds of churches in Asia Minor, anything like the "mutual submission" that egalitarians advocate. *But that means (from an egalitarian standpoint) that these three letters taught a wrong idea, the idea that wives should submit to the authority of their husbands in marriage.*

Did the letters of the apostles Paul and Peter then lead the church astray? Would it have been sin for the original readers to obey the letters of Paul and Peter and teach that wives should be subject to their husbands? This would contradict our doctrine of Scripture as the inerrant, absolutely authoritative Word of God.

---

11. It is interesting that the King James Version showed an understanding of the sense of *allēlōn* in this passage. It translated the verse, "Submitting yourselves *one to another* in the fear of God." When *allēlōn* takes the sense "some to others," the King James Version often signaled that by phrases such as "one to another."

17

HEAD MEANS "SOURCE" OR "PREEMINENT ONE"

⌐· EGALITARIAN CLAIM: In Ephesians 5:23, the Word Kephalē ("Head") Does Not Mean "Person in Authority" but Rather "Source," As in "Source of a River."

I n Ephesians 5:23, Paul makes this statement:

For the husband is the *head* of the wife even as Christ is the *head* of the Church, his body, and is himself its Savior.

And in 1 Corinthians 11:3, he says:

But I want you to understand that the *head* of every man is Christ, the *head* of a wife is her husband, and the *head* of Christ is God.

The most common egalitarian interpretation of these verses is that the word translated "head" (Greek, *kephalē*) does not mean "person in authority over" but has some other meaning, especially the meaning "source." Thus, the husband is the *source* of the wife (an allusion to the creation of Eve from Adam's side in Genesis 2), as Christ is the *source* of the church.[1] It is important to realize the decisive significance of these verses, and particularly of Ephesians 5:23, for the current controversy about male-female roles in marriage. If *head* means "person in authority over," then there is a unique authority that belongs to the husband in marriage, and it is parallel to Christ's authority over the church. If this is the true meaning of *head* in these verses, then the egalitarian view of marriage is wrong. But if *head* means "source" here, then two Scripture texts significant to complementarians have been shown to have no impact on the controversy. Which view is right?

—Answer #1: A word's meaning is found by examining its use in various contexts. Kephalē is found in over fifty contexts where it refers to people who have authority over others of whom they are the "head." But it never once takes a meaning "source without authority," as egalitarians would like to make it mean.

In 1985, I looked up 2,336 examples of *kephalē* in ancient Greek literature, using texts from Homer in the eighth century BC up to some church fathers in the fourth century AD. I found that in those texts, *kephalē* was applied to many people in authority (see the list in Grudem, EFBT, Appendix 3, pp. 544–51) but it was never applied to a person without governing authority (when it was used in a metaphorical sense to say that person A was the "head" of person or persons B). This conclusion was challenged in other scholarly articles, to which I responded in two subsequent articles (my most recent study is found in Grudem, EFBT, pp. 552–99.) Interested readers can find further details in those three articles.[2]

---

1. Egalitarian writings holding that *kephalē* means "source" are numerous. Some of the most influential are: Berkeley and Alvera Mickelsen, "What Does *Kephalē* Mean in the New Testament?" in Alvera Mickelsen, *Women, Authority, and the Bible*, 97–110; Philip Payne, "Response," in Mickelsen, *Women, Authority, and the Bible*, 118–32; Gilbert Bilezikian, "A Critical Examination of Wayne Grudem's Treatment of *Kephalē* in Ancient Greek Texts," appendix to Bilezikian, *Beyond Sex Roles*, 215–52; Catherine Kroeger, "The Classical Concept of Head as 'Source,'" Appendix 3 in Gretchen Hull, *Equal to Serve*, 267–83; Gordon Fee, *First Epistle to the Corinthians*, 501–05; Catherine Kroeger, "Head," in *Dictionary of Paul and His Letters*, 375–77; and Judy Brown, *Women Ministers*, 213–15, 246. Many other egalitarian writers who have no advanced training in New Testament studies or in Greek simply quote one or more of these authors as proof of the meaning "source."

2. For details, see Grudem, "The Meaning of *kephalē* ('Head'): An Analysis of New Evidence, Real and Alleged," Appendix 4 in EFBT, 552–99. That appendix is a reprint with only slight modifications, and the addition of interaction with Anthony Thiselton's commentary, to my 2001 article, "The Meaning of *kephalē* ('Head'): An Analysis of New Evidence, Real and Alleged," *Journal of the Evangelical Theological Society* 44/1 (March 2001): 25–65.

The fact remains that more than two decades after the publication of my 1985 study, the alleged meaning "source without authority" has still not been supported with *any* citation of *any* text in ancient Greek literature that refers to person A as the "head" of person(s) B. And the meaning "person in authority over" has been supported by over fifty examples.

◄ Answer #2: Verses that refer to Christ as "head" cannot rightly be used to deny the idea of authority.

It is surprising to see Linda Belleville using four New Testament verses that refer to Christ as responses to a request for examples of *kephalē* meaning "non-authoritative source." (She cites Ephesians 4:16 and 5:22–23; Colossians 1:18 and 2:19.)[3] Does she believe that Christ has no authority over His church? This is unlikely.

These verses about Christ's role as *head* of the church support my earlier argument that wherever person A is called "head" of person (or persons) B, person A is in a position of authority over B.[4]

My 1990 study on the meaning of *kephalē* was "The Meaning of *kephalē* ('Head'): A Response to Recent Studies," *TrinJ* 11 NS (Spring 1990): 3–72 (reprinted in *Recovering Biblical Manhood and Womanhood*, 425–68).

My original 1985 study was "Does *kephalē* ('Head') Mean 'Source' or 'Authority Over' in Greek Literature? A Survey of 2,336 Examples" in George Knight, *The Role Relationship of Men and Women*, 49–80 (also printed in *TrinJ* 6 NS [Spring 1985]: 38–59). References to much other scholarly literature on *kephalē* are found in those three articles.

3. Linda Belleville, "Women in Ministry," 138. Similarly, I. Howard Marshall insists that the dispute over the meaning of *kephalē* can only be decided by considering how Paul uses the word in various contexts (DBE, 198), but he likewise places emphasis on verses that refer to Christ as "head." The fact remains that one cannot divorce Christ's authoritative lordship over the church from verses that refer to him as head of the church, or use verses about Christ and the church to prove that the idea of a "head" carried no sense of authority over the church!

4. Belleville notes that Christ "feeds and cares for" the church (Ephesians 5:29), which is surely true. In every relationship of authority between persons, the person in authority gives or provides some benefit to the person or group under authority (such as leadership, care, protection, example, teaching, love, or nourishment, depending on the nature of the relationship). But that does not mean that person A is the *source* of person B. Nor does it mean that *head* means "source" when applied to that relationship.

To take a similar example from English, it makes sense to say that a school principal is the "head" of the school, since he or she has authority over the school. The principal also provides students with many things, such as leadership, discipline, and protection, so we could say that the principal is the "source" of leadership, discipline, and protection for the students. But we cannot say that the principal is the "source" of the students. They do not spring out of the principal! The principal is the "head" of the school only in the sense of being the "person in authority over" the school.

— Answer #3: A listing of several ancient texts where one person is the "head" of another makes clear the meaning "person in authority over another."

Here are several examples where *kephalē* is used to say that one person is the "head" of another, and the person who is called head is the one in authority:[5]

1. David as king of Israel is called the "head" of the people he conquered (2 Samuel [LXX 2 Kings] 22:44): "You kept me as the *head* of the nations; people whom I had not known served me"; similarly, Psalm 18 (LXX 17):43

2. The leaders of the tribes of Israel are called "heads" of the tribes (1 Kings [LXX 3 Kings] 8:1, Alexandrinus text): "Then Solomon assembled the elders of Israel and all the *heads* of the tribes" (similar statements in the second-century AD Greek translation of Aquila, Deuteronomy 5:23; 29:9 (English verse 10); 1 Kings [LXX 3 Kings] 8:1)

3. Jephthah becomes the "head" of the people of Gilead (Judges 11:11: "the people made him *head* and leader over them"; also stated in 10:18; 11:8, 9)

4. Pekah the son of Remaliah is the "head" of Samaria (Isaiah 7:9: "The *head* of Samaria is the son of Remaliah")

5. The father is the "head" of the family (Hermas, *Similitudes* 7.3; the man is called "the *head* of the house")

6. The husband is the "head" of the wife (Ephesians 5:23: "The husband is *head* of the wife even as Christ is *head* of the church")

7. Christ is the "head" of the church (Colossians 1:18: "He is the *head* of the body, the church"; also in Ephesians 5:23)

8. Christ is the "head" of all things (Ephesians 1:22: "He put all things under his feet and gave him as *head* over all things to the church")

9. God the Father is the "head" of Christ (1 Corinthians 11:3: "the *head* of Christ is God")

---

5. See Grudem, EFBT, Appendix 3, pp. 544–51, for additional references like the ones cited here. These texts are discussed in my 1985 and 1990 articles on *kephalē* (mentioned above, footnote 2).

— Answer #4: The meaning "source" makes no sense in key passages like Ephesians 5:23: "The husband is the head of the wife."

I am not the source of my wife in any meaningful sense of the word "source." And so it is with all husbands and wives. It is just not true to say, "The husband is the *source* of the wife as Christ is the source of the church." It makes the verse into nonsense.

— Answer #5: All the recognized lexicons (dictionaries) for ancient Greek, or their editors, now give kephalē the meaning "person in authority over" or something similar, but none give the meaning "source."

- Bauer-Danker-Arndt-Gingrich *Greek-English Lexicon* (BDAG): "in the case of living beings, to denote superior rank" (542).
- Louw-Nida *Greek English Lexicon of the New Testament Based on Semantic Domains*[6]: "One who is of supreme or preeminent status, in view of authority to order or command—'one who is the head of, one who is superior to, one who is supreme over'" (vol. 1, p. 739).
- Geoffrey Lampe's *Patristic Greek Lexicon*:

  > B. of persons; 1. head of the house, Herm. *sim.* 7.3; 2. chief, head-man... 3. religious superior... 4. of bishops, *kephalai ekklēsiōn* [other examples include "of the bishop of the city of Rome, being head of all the churches"]... 5. *kephalē einai* c. genit. [to be head, with genitive] take precedence of (p. 749).

- The standard lexicon for all of ancient Greek, the Liddell-Scott *Greek-English Lexicon*,[7] does have an entry in which it mentioned the sense "source" of a river for *kephalē* (in plural, but "mouth" of a river for *kephalē* singular). But this sense does not apply to persons, because it is listed under the general heading "of things, extremity," and simply meant that

---

6. Johannes P. Louw and Eugene E. Nida, eds., *Greek-English Lexicon of the New Testament Based on Semantic Domains*, two vols. (New York: United Bible Societies, 1988).

7. LS, *Greek-English Lexicon*, 945.

the "source" and the "mouth" of a river were at the two "end points" of the river, and *kephalē* was taking an established meaning, "end point, extremity."[8]

In conclusion, the question for egalitarians is this: Why should we give *kephalē* in the New Testament a sense that it is nowhere attested to have, and that, when applied to persons, no Greek lexicon gives it?[9] The term "head" in "the husband is the head of the wife" (Ephesians 5:23) means "person in authority over."

---

8. For further clarification on the LS entry for *kephalē,* see the personal letter from editor P. G. W. Glare to Wayne Grudem in Grudem, EFBT, p. 207.

9. For responses to an alternative proposal from Anthony Thiselton and others, that the meaning "preeminent one" is the best for *kephalē* in these contexts, see my detailed response in Grudem, EFBT, 209–11 and 590–97.

PART SIX

EVANGELICAL FEMINIST CLAIMS ABOUT THE CHURCH FROM THE NEW TESTAMENT EPISTLES

In part 5 we considered several major egalitarian objections to a complementarian view of marriage based on claims about the New Testament epistles—and all were found to be unpersuasive, not representing the meaning of Scripture accurately.

When we turn to the teachings about church leadership in the New Testament epistles, egalitarians propose many claims that would undermine the idea of restricting some leadership roles to men. For instance, aren't there women such as Phoebe and Junia who hold leading positions in the church? In addition, in 1 Corinthians 11, Paul clearly says that women could prophesy, and isn't that a leading role that indicates much influence in the church? Paul also had women as his coworkers in a number of cases, and perhaps there are indications of other women in leadership roles, such as deacons. In short, egalitarians claim that there are abundant evidences of women in leadership roles in the epistles.

In this part, we consider such egalitarian claims regarding the New Testament epistles' teaching about women in the church. However, the material on 1 Timothy 2:11–15 is so extensive that I have put it in a separate section, which follows this one.

18

PHOEBE AS LEADER

⌐· EGALITARIAN CLAIM: Romans 16:2 Says That Phoebe Was a "Leader" or "Ruler" of Many People, and Even of Paul Himself.

Romans 16:2 says that Phoebe "has been a *patron* (Greek *prostatis*) of many and of myself as well." Other translations say that Phoebe was a "helper": The NASB says, "She herself has also been a *helper* of many, and of myself as well," and the NIV says, "For she has been a great *help* to many people, including me."

But Aida Spencer and several other egalitarians dispute this translation. Spencer says the verse means that Phoebe was a leader and ruler over Paul:

The verb form of *prostatis*, which is *proistēmi*, literally signifies "to stand, place before or over".... Phoebe...is "a woman set over others" or "one who stands before." No other person is called a *prostatis* in the New Testament.... *She has been a leader over many and even over Paul!*... The verb form *proistēmi*...with the genitive signifies "I am set over, I am the head of"..."I govern, direct," and "I stand before so as to guard".... The noun *prostatis* takes the genitive case of "many" and "me" to indicate these are the persons over whom Phoebe has been set. Phoebe is an explicit, commendable example of *a woman set in authority over a man*, in this case, the great apostle Paul.[1]

---

1. Aida Spencer, *Beyond the Curse*, 115–16 (italics added). Spencer is quoted with approval by Ruth Tucker, *Women in the Maze*, 100. See also Judy Brown, *Women Ministers*, 167; and Cindy Jacobs, *Women of Destiny*, 181–82, who quotes, in support of the idea that Phoebe was a leader, a book by Charles Trombley, *Who Said Women Can't Teach?* 194–95.

— Answer #1: We should be hesitant to accept an interpretation that is found in no English translation.

When an author claims a meaning for a word that is found in no English translation, and in fact is not even close to any meaning given in the text or margin of any English translation, we should require extensive evidence for such a meaning. That is the case here, for Spencer's translation "leader" is significantly different from "helper," "patron," "benefactor," and similar terms used in the common English Bible translations.[2]

In addition, when the interpretation creates an apparent conflict with other things found in the New Testament, it becomes even more doubtful. In this case, we recall that the apostle Paul did not think that even the Jerusalem apostles ruled over him. His apostleship, as did his message, came "not from men nor through man, but through Jesus Christ and God the Father, who raised him from the dead" (Galatians 1:1, 11–12). The status of "those who seemed to be influential" in the Jerusalem church was not greater than Paul, for he says, "What they were makes no difference to me; God shows no partiality" (2:6), and he goes on to tell of how he rebuked Peter publicly (2:11–14).

Spencer's argument therefore is inconsistent with the clear New Testament evidence that the apostle Paul did not consider himself subject to any human leader but to Jesus Christ alone.

— Answer #2: Recent Greek lexicons show the meaning "patron" or "helper" to be most likely.

The two most recent Greek lexicons do not give the meaning "leader" for *prostatis*, which is the actual word used in Romans 16:2. The BDAG lexicon defines it as "woman in a supportive role, *patron, benefactor*" (885) and similarly defines the related masculine noun *prostatēs* as "one who looks out for the interest of others, *defender, guardian, benefactor*" (885). The Louw-Nida lexicon defines *prostatis* as "a woman who is active in helping—'helper, patroness...'" (1.459). While the older lexicon by Thayer did give the entry, "properly *a woman set over others*,"[3] that is

---

2. The archaic KJV word *succourer* has a similar sense to these other translations. The other common English translations have "patron" (ESV), "helper" (NASB, RSV, NKJV), "help" (NIV), "has helped" (NLT), and "benefactor" (NRSV).

3. Thayer, *Greek-English Lexicon of the New Testament* (Edinburgh: T. & T. Clark, 1901), 549.

apparently just an explanation of the word's connection to the masculine form *prostatēs*, and no actual examples are given. But the next meaning explains in what sense this is intended, because with specific reference to Romans 16:2 it says, "*a female guardian, protectress, patroness,* caring for the affairs of others and aiding them with her resources" (549).[4]

—Answer #3: Spencer has constructed a lexical "sleight of hand" argument, because she is not defining the noun prostatis but the related verb proistēmi and words don't take all the meanings of all the other words that are related to them.

It is not legitimate to say, "Word A is related to word B, and word B has a certain meaning, therefore, word A has this meaning as well."

Words just don't take all the meanings of related words. This is a simple fact of human language. For example, the word *butterfly* is related to *butter* and *fly*, but that does not mean that *butterfly* means "a pound of butter that has learned to fly." Relationships among words are extremely complex, and we should put primary emphasis on *uses of a word itself,* not on related words.

Of course, words are often related in meaning to other words formed from the same root, but that is not always the case. *Autograph, automatic, automobile,* and *autopsy* do not mean the same thing, nor is an autopsy something one does on oneself! We cannot just take the meaning of one word and import it into another related word (which is exactly what this argument does).

But if the noun *prostatis* is related to the verb *proistēmi,* then shouldn't we expect that their meanings will be at least somehow related? While it is not certain, we would expect that a noun and related verb will often have similar meanings. But even if we grant this, what Spencer (like others who use this argument) does not reveal to readers is that the related verb *proistēmi* can also mean "to have an interest in, *show concern for, care for, give aid*" (BDAG, 870). And this seems to be the sense in which the noun *prostatis* is used in Romans 16:2. So even if we expect a related meaning, Spencer incorrectly depends on a selective citation of meaning for the verb *proistēmi* to explain the noun *prostatis.*

---

4. The LS *Lexicon* defines *prostatis* as "feminine of *prostatēs*" (1527), but *prostatēs* takes a range of meanings, including not only "leader, ruler" but also "patron" (1527), and LS gives no discussion of which senses of *prostatēs* are also taken by the feminine form.

Romans 16:2 has another word built on the same *histēmi* root as *prostatis*, and Paul is probably making a play on words, for he says that the church should "help (*paristēmi*) her in whatever way she may require from you, for she has been a helper (*prostatis*) of many and of myself as well" (Romans 16:2, RSV).

19

JUNIA

↶· EGALITARIAN CLAIM: There Was Even a Woman Apostle, Junia (Romans 16:7). If a Woman Can Be an Apostle, She Can Hold Any Other Church Office As Well.

In Romans 16:7, Paul writes, "Greet Andronicus and Junias [or *Junia*], my kinsmen and my fellow prisoners, who are outstanding among the apostles, who also were in Christ before me" (NASB).

Egalitarians regularly claim that this refers to a woman named Junia, who was an apostle. Aida Spencer writes:

Junia (and her male colleague Andronicus) would be Paul's counterpart in Rome. As an apostle, sent by God as an eyewitness to the resurrection of Jesus, Paul would lay the foundation for a church. Certainly authoritative preaching would have to be part of such a testimony. Junia, along with Andronicus, apparently laid the foundation for the churches at Rome.[1]

Similarly, Gilbert Bilezikian writes:

Paul sends greetings in Rome to Andronicus and Junias, probably a husband-and-wife team of veteran missionaries, who are told to be "outstanding among the apostles" (Rom. 16:7).... The term apostle connoted the highest level of leadership and authority in the early church.... Even in its broader, more general use, it was an appellation of the highest distinction. Apparently, the openness of the early church to women in positions

---

1. Aida Spencer, *Beyond the Curse*, 102.

of leadership was such that their identification as "apostles" was received without difficulty.[2]

—Answer #1: The name that is spelled ιουνιαν in the Greek text of Romans 16:7 could be either a man's name or a woman's name simply according to the spelling.

Just as in English there are some names (such as Chris or Pat) that could be either a man's name or a woman's name, so in Greek, this name could be either masculine or feminine, and we cannot tell from the spelling alone.[3] Some translations have taken it as Junias (NIV, NASB, RSV, ASV), and some have taken it as Junia (KJV, NKJV, NRSV, NLT, ESV), usually indicating the alternative in the margin. (The ESV translation committee, of which I was a member, decided in light of Latin evidence that the name "Junia" was more likely, and put "Or Junias" in the margin.)

— Answer #2: In light of recent research in Greek grammar, the verse means, "Greet Andronicus and Junia(s)...well-known to the apostles."

The verse is best understood to say not that Andronicus and Junia(s) were "well-known *among* the apostles" but "well known *to* the apostles" (so ESV, *NET Bible*). Therefore it does not make much difference if this is a man's or a woman's name because it does not say that Junia(s) was an apostle.

Prior to 2001, scholars had not done any significant computer-assisted research on the Greek construction (*episēmos* + dative) that is found in this verse, and therefore writings and translations before 2001 usually assumed that the meaning "well known *among*" was correct. But then in 2001, in an extensively researched technical article, the meaning "well known *to*" received strong support, with significant evidence from extra-biblical Greek.[4] A note to the *NET Bible* (in which Dan

---

2. Gilbert Bilezikian, *Beyond Sex Roles*, 198. See also Craig Keener, *Paul, Women and Wives*, 241–42; Rebecca Groothuis, *Good News for Women*, 194–96; Judy Brown, *Women Ministers*, 183; Cindy Jacobs, *Women of Destiny*, 184–86; J. Lee Grady, *Ten Lies the Church Tells Women*, 41; and Andrew Perriman, *Speaking of Women*, 68–70. However, Linda Belleville, *Women Leaders and the Church*, 54–56, thinks that "apostle" here is not used in the same sense as it was with Paul and the Twelve, but in the sense of "church planter."

3. The ending *-an* is the accusative singular ending for a first declension masculine name ending in *-as* (*Iounias*) or for a first declension feminine name (*Iounia*) ending in *-a*. For an extended discussion of how this name has been translated historically, as well as a look at the bearing of Latin on the translation, see EFBT pp. 225–226

4. M. H. Burer and D. B. Wallace, "Was Junia Really an Apostle? A Reexamination of Romans 16:7,"

Wallace had significant influence after his research was underway, but prior to the publication of his article) explains, "in collocation with words of perception, (*en* plus) dative personal nouns are often used to show the recipients."[5]

The ESV (published in the fall of 2001) therefore translates the verse:

Greet Andronicus and Junia [or *Junias*], my kinsmen and my fellow prisoners. They are *well known to the apostles* [or *messengers*], and they were in Christ before me.

This means that the verse does not even name Junia (Junias) as an apostle. It just says that the apostles know her (or him) well, and also Andronicus.

— Answer #3: The word translated "apostles" could just mean "church messengers" here as it does elsewhere in Paul's writings.

A further uncertainty about this verse is the word translated "apostles." This same term (Greek *apostolos*) is used elsewhere in the New Testament to mean "messenger, one who is sent" when it refers to people who were not apostles in the sense of the Twelve or Paul: We see this use in John 13:16: "Nor is a *messenger* greater than the one who sent him"; also 2 Corinthians 8:23, referring to the men who were accompanying Paul in bringing money to Jerusalem: "They are *messengers* of the churches"; and Paul tells the Philippians that Epaphroditus, who came to him, is "your *messenger* and minister to my need" (Philippians 2:25). Since Andronicus and Junia(s) are otherwise unknown as apostles, even if someone wanted to translate "well known *among*," the sense "well known among the messengers" would be more appropriate.[6]

New Testament Studies 47 (2001): 76–91. Linda Belleville differed with their conclusion in DBE, 117–20, but only by providing her own idiosyncratic translation of one parallel text (Psalms of Solomon 2:6), claiming that another one is too early to count (Euripides *Hippolytus*, 103), and simply ignoring Burer and Wallace's other literary evidence and evidence from inscriptions. She wrongly says they claim that "every known instance" of this construction bears the sense they claim, whereas they only claim that most show this sense, not all. (Burer and Wallace are preparing a more detailed response to Belleville and other critics, but even before that appears it should still be evident from their article that many convincing examples of the sense "well known to" have been demonstrated by their research.)

5. *NET Bible*, note to Romans 16:7.
6. Another alternative meaning, with a broader sense of "apostle," is "traveling missionaries," which Moo favors (see Grudem, EFBT, p. 226, fn. 16).

WOMEN COULD PROPHESY

EGALITARIAN CLAIM: Women Could Prophesy in the New Testament (1 Corinthians 11:5), and This Implies That They Could Also Teach God's Word and Be Pastors or Elders.

Aida Spencer says:

> The prophet functioned in the service as does a contemporary preacher.... The New Testament provides clear examples of women who are called prophets and described as prophesying. Prophets come second in Paul's list of the priority of gifts and second in his list of persons given to the church.[1]

Answer #1: Prophecy and teaching are not the same. They are always viewed as separate gifts in the New Testament.

People who claim that "prophesying was the same as preaching and teaching," or "if women can prophesy they can teach the Bible," fail to understand how clearly the New Testament distinguishes prophecy and teaching. They are always viewed as separate gifts:

---

1. Aida Spencer, *Beyond the Curse*, 103, 106. See also Gilbert Bilezikian, *Beyond Sex Roles*, 199; Linda Belleville, *Women Leaders and the Church*, 59. Judy Brown, *Women Ministers*, 247; J. Lee Grady, *Ten Lies the Church Tells Women*, 44; Andrew Perriman, *Speaking of Women*, 73, 83.

136

Romans 12:6–7: "Having gifts that differ according to the grace given to us, let us use them: if *prophecy*, in proportion to our faith; if service, in our serving; the one who *teaches*, in his teaching."

1 Corinthians 12:28–29: "And God has appointed in the church first apostles, second *prophets*, third *teachers*, then miracles, then gifts of healing, helping, administrating, and various kinds of tongues. Are all apostles? Are all *prophets*? Are all *teachers*? Do all work miracles?"

Ephesians 4:11: "And he gave the apostles, the *prophets*, the evangelists, the pastors and *teachers*."

— Answer #2: Prophecy in the New Testament is reporting something God spontaneously brings to mind, while teaching is explaining and applying Scripture or the teachings of the apostles.

The authority of a prophet is unlike the authority of a teacher. Prophecy is always "reporting something God spontaneously brings to mind,"[2] as in 1 Corinthians 14:30–31, where Paul pictures one prophet speaking and then says, "If a *revelation* is made to another sitting there, let the first be silent. For you can all *prophesy* one by one." God suddenly brought something to someone's mind.

Or in 1 Corinthians 14:25, if a stranger comes in and all prophesy, "the secrets of his heart are disclosed; and so, falling on his face, he will worship God and declare that God is really among you." God had suddenly brought to people's minds things they would not otherwise know.

As far as I can tell from the relevant passages, all New Testament prophecy was based on this kind of spontaneous prompting from the Holy Spirit. Agabus's prophecy of a famine had to be based on such a revelation (Acts 11:28), and so did his prediction of Paul's imprisonment in Jerusalem (21:10–11). The disciples at Tyre apparently had some kind of indication from God about the dangers Paul

---

2. See my defense of this view of prophecy in Grudem, *Gift of Prophecy*. A brief summary of my position is found in Grudem, *Systematic Theology*, 1049–61. (The difference between prophecy and teaching is also maintained by those who differ with my understanding of the gift of prophecy in the New Testament; see answer #6 below, p. 141.)

would encounter in Jerusalem (21:4). And even in John 11:51, when Caiaphas spoke unknowingly of Jesus' death for the people, he "prophesied." By contrast, no prophecy in New Testament churches is ever said to consist of the interpretation and application of texts of Scripture.

But teaching is different. In contrast to the gift of prophecy, no human speech called "teaching" (*didaskalia, didachē*) or an act done by a "teacher" (*didaskalos*), or described by the verb "teach" (*didaskō*), is ever said to be based on a "revelation" in the New Testament. Rather, teaching is usually an explanation and application of Scripture.

In Acts 15:35, Paul and Barnabas and "many others" are in Antioch "*teaching* and preaching *the word of the Lord.*" At Corinth, Paul stayed one and a half years "*teaching* the *word of God* among them" (Acts 18:11). And the author of Hebrews tells his readers, "you need someone to teach you again the basic principles of the oracles of God" (Hebrews 5:12). Paul tells Timothy that "all *Scripture*" is "profitable for *teaching*" (2 Timothy 3:16). Since the apostles' writings had equal authority to the written Old Testament Scripture (see 2 Peter 3:2, 15–16), it is not surprising that Paul told Timothy to "command and teach" (1 Timothy 4:11) and to "teach and urge" (6:2) Paul's instructions to the Ephesian church.

The difference with prophecy is quite clear here: Timothy wasn't to *prophesy* Paul's instructions; he was to *teach* them. Paul didn't prophesy his ways in every church; he taught them. The Thessalonians were not told to hold firm to the traditions that were "prophesied" to them but to the traditions they were "taught."

It was not prophecy but teaching that provided the doctrinal and ethical norms by which the church was regulated. An elder was to be "able to *teach*" (1 Timothy 3:2; cf. Titus 1:9), not "able to prophesy"! Timothy was to take heed to himself and to his "teaching" (1 Timothy 4:16), but he is never told to take heed to his prophesying. James warned that those who *teach*, not those who *prophesy*, "will be judged with greater strictness" (James 3:1).

So teaching in the New Testament epistles consisted of explaining and applying the words of Scripture or the equally authoritative teachings of Jesus and of the apostles. In the New Testament epistles, "teaching" was very much like what we call "Bible teaching" today. Many charismatic and Pentecostal churches today understand this difference quite well: Prophecy, like other miraculous gifts, is subject to the governing authority of the elders or pastors of the church. There are many people in these church who are allowed to give "prophecies" (reporting words or thoughts that they believe God has brought to mind), but very few of these people would be allowed to preach the sermon on Sunday morning! Prophecy and teaching are different gifts.

— Answer #3: Therefore it makes sense to say that women could prophesy but not teach in the church.

Prophesying did not carry the same authority as teaching. Therefore it makes sense that Paul would allow women to prophesy but not to teach. It was those who taught, particularly the elders, who governed the church.

It also makes sense, therefore, for Paul to say that women could prophesy but could not speak out and judge prophecies in the church, for the judging of prophecies was assuming governing authority over the assembled congregation. (See chapter 21 on 1 Corinthians 14:34–35.)

In the early church, the church father Tertullian (ca. 160/170–ca. 215/220) taught that women could prophesy but not teach in the church:

> In precisely the same manner, when enjoining on women silence in the church, that they speak not for the mere sake of learning (although that even they have the right of prophesying, he has already shown when he covers the woman that prophesies with a veil), he goes to the law for his sanction that woman should be under obedience.[3]

He also wrote:

> It is not permitted to a woman to speak in the church; but neither [is it permitted her] to teach, nor to baptize.[4]

This means that from a very early period in the history of the church, at least some recognized that women had a right to prophesy, but they were not allowed to teach in the church.

---

3. Tertullian, "Against Marcion," 5.8.11, cited from *ANF* 3:446, col. 2.
4. Tertullian, "On the Veiling of Virgins" 9.1, cited from *ANF* 4:33, col. 1.

— Answer #4: The fact that people can learn from prophecies does not mean that prophets were the same as teachers.

It is true that people learn from prophecies, as is seen in 1 Corinthians 14:31: "For you can all prophesy one by one, so that all may *learn* and all be encouraged." But that does not mean that prophets are doing Bible teaching in the church. People can *learn* from many things—from a song, from a personal testimony, from someone's confession of sin, from someone's joy in the midst of trials, and so forth. But this does not mean that any of these activities, including prophecy, *is the same activity* as Bible teaching. The numerous verses above that clearly distinguish prophecy from teaching should make that clear.

Along this same line, Linda Belleville argues that the word "instruct" (*katecheō*) in 1 Corinthians 14:19 shows that prophets carried out a teaching function in the church.[5] But this is a sleight of hand argument, because in her repeated references to this verse as a proof that prophets could "instruct" or "teach,"[6] Belleville fails to tell her readers that this verse *does not mention prophecy!* She never actually quotes 1 Corinthians 14:19 so that readers would see this for themselves: "Nevertheless, in church I would rather speak five words with my mind in order to *instruct* (*katecheō*) others, than ten thousand words in a tongue."

Paul says nothing about prophecy in this verse. He is contrasting intelligible speech in the church with speaking in tongues. "Teaching" has already been mentioned in the context (v. 6), and that is most likely what Paul has in mind when he talks about speaking to "instruct others."

— Answer #5: Prophecy, like other spiritual gifts, was to be subject to the teaching authority of the elders.

The New Testament says, "Obey your leaders and *submit to them*" (Hebrews 13:17), and "You who are younger, *be subject to the elders*" (1 Peter 5:5), and "Let the elders who *rule well* be considered worthy of double honor, especially those who labor in preaching and teaching" (1 Timothy 5:17). Elders had governing authority in the early churches, and teaching authority belonged to the elders.

---

5. Belleville, "Women in Ministry," 97, 99–100.

6. Ibid., 87, 97, 100.

But prophecies had to be subject to the governing authority of the churches. Paul says, "Do not despise prophecies, but *test everything*; hold fast what is good" (1 Thessalonians 5:20–21). He says, "Let two or three prophets speak, and let the others weigh what is said" (1 Corinthians 14:29).

So the gift of prophecy did not involve either teaching authority or governing authority over the church. That is why women can prophesy but not teach in the assembled church.

— Answer #6: Those who believe that the New Testament gift of prophecy was the same as fully inspired prophecy in the Old Testament still see a difference between prophecy and Bible teaching.

Not all evangelicals agree with the understanding of the gift of prophecy that I presented above. Some claim that the gift of prophecy in the New Testament always involved declaring the very words of God, which had absolute authority and were never in error.[7] Those who hold this view still insist on a distinction between prophecy and teaching. The prophet would be like an ambassador who can deliver a message from the president but cannot add to or subtract from it. The teacher, on the other hand, brings much explanation and application *based on* the message, but does not deliver the original message. Another analogy is the difference between someone reading a Scripture passage in the church service and someone teaching on the basis of that passage. Most churches from time to time allow anyone—men or women, sometimes even children—to read Scripture aloud to the congregation. But they do not allow all of those people to bring the sermon to the congregation. They recognize a difference between simply repeating a message that God has given in His own words and teaching the church on the basis of that message.

---

7. For example, this is the view of Richard Gaffin in his essays in *Are Miraculous Gifts for Today: Four Views*, ed. Wayne Grudem (Grand Rapids: Zondervan, 1996), esp. 41–60.

21

NOBODY OBEYS
1 CORINTHIANS 14:34

↶ · EGALITARIAN CLAIM: Complementarians Can't Be Consistent; 1 Corinthians 14:34 Requires That Women Be Silent in Church, But Everybody Disobeys That Command Today Because Women Can Sing, Pray, Read Scripture, and So Forth. Similarly, Other New Testament Restrictions on Women Were for a Particular Circumstance, Not for All Time.

P aul wrote in 1 Corinthians:

> As in all the churches of the saints, *the women should keep silent in the churches*. For they are not permitted to speak, but should be in submission, as the Law also says. If there is anything they desire to learn, let them ask their husbands at home. For it is shameful for a woman to speak in church. (14:33b–35)

Although the argument that "nobody obeys 1 Corinthians 14:34 today" may not be explicitly made by any egalitarian writer, it is implicit in the thinking of many readers of the Bible who realize that no evangelical churches require complete silence of women today. So readers think, *This passage must be talking about a different situation than what we find in our modern church services. Maybe more of the Bible's commands concerning women in church are intended only for a specific situation as well.* The expectation of course is that people will decide that this verse is not in force for us today.

— Answer #1: The passage does not require women to be completely silent.

The passage never did require complete silence of women, even when Paul wrote it. This is evident because Paul says in 1 Corinthians 11, just three chapters earlier, that women who pray and prophesy should have their heads covered, which assumes that they could pray and prophesy aloud in church services. That passage says:

> Every man who prays or prophesies with his head covered dishonors his head, but every wife who prays or prophesies with her head uncovered dishonors her head—it is the same as if her head were shaven. (1 Corinthians 11:4–5)

Therefore the question is, what kind of "silence" does Paul mean in 1 Corinthians 14:34?

As I suggest below, speech that involves judging prophecies fits this description, for it involves assuming the possession of superior authority in matters of doctrinal or ethical instruction.

A similar example of "silence" not meaning total silence but silence in one kind of speech, is found in this same context, where Paul says about those who speak in tongues, "But if there is no one to interpret, *let each of them keep silent in church* and speak to himself and to God" (1 Corinthians 14:28, just six verses before 14:34). Does Paul mean that people who had the gift of tongues could never say anything in church, never pray (in a known language) or read Scripture or sing aloud? Of course not. What Paul means is, "Let each of them *keep silent* in church *with respect to the topic I am discussing,* that is, do not speak in tongues." Speaking in tongues is what he is discussing in 1 Corinthians 14:27–28, but starting at verse 29, he turns to prophecies and the judging of prophecies.

— Answer #2: This passage requires women to be silent with respect to the activity under discussion, which is the judging of prophecies.[1]

What is the topic under discussion in the context 1 Corinthians 14:34? The topic in verses 29–33 has been prophecies and judging prophecies, beginning with verse 29: "Let two or three prophets speak, and let the others weigh what is said." In fact, verse 29 is a general principle about prophesying that divides itself into two halves, with (a) the first half talking about *prophesying* ("Let two or three prophets speak") and (b) the second half talking about *judging those prophecies* ("and let the others weigh what is said").

After giving this general principle in verse 29, Paul goes on to explain it: In verses 30–33a, he explains how to proceed with (a) "let two or three prophets speak," telling the Corinthians they should prophesy in turn, not all at once! Then in verses 33b–35, he explains how to proceed with (b) "let the others weigh what is said" and tells the Corinthians that women cannot speak aloud to pass judgment on the prophecies: "As in all the churches of the saints, let the women keep silent in the churches."

If someone gave a prophecy, for example, that Jesus was coming back "five days from now," there would need to be a correction given before the congregation because Jesus Himself taught that people can know "neither the day nor the hour" of His return (Matthew 25:13). But Paul says men should give such a correction, for in such a case, as is done "in all the churches of the saints,"[2] the women are to "keep silent in the churches" during that time. They are not to pass judgment out loud on the prophecies.

---

1. The interpretation followed here, that Paul is prohibiting women from passing spoken judgment on the prophecies given in church, was advocated by James Hurley, *Man and Woman in Biblical Perspective*, 188–94. It was defended by Grudem, *Gift of Prophecy*, 185–92, and defended in considerable detail by D. A. Carson, "'Silent in the Churches': On the Role of Women in 1 Corinthians 14:33b–36," in Piper and Grudem, *Recovering Biblical Manhood and Womanhood*, 140–53. The most recent, and most lengthy, defense of this view is Anthony Thiselton, *First Epistle to the Corinthians*, 1146–61, with extensive interaction with other literature.

2. Grammatically it is possible to make "as in all the churches of the saints" modify the preceding clause, and thus the passage would read, "For God is not a God of confusion but of peace, as in all the churches of the saints." However, this division of the sentences does not fit the sense of the passage. After saying something about the character of God, which is always the same, it would be pointless for Paul to add "as in all the churches of the saints," as if the Corinthians would have imagined that God would be a God of peace in some churches but not in others.

The rest of the passage gives further explanation. When Paul says, "For they are not permitted to speak, but should be in submission, as the Law also says," (v. 34b), he views speaking aloud to judge prophecies as a "governing" or "ruling" function in the congregation, the opposite of being submissive to male leadership in the church. (Paul is not quoting any specific Old Testament passage, but seems to be referring to the Old Testament generally as "the Law," probably especially the creation order in Genesis 2, and understanding it as teaching a principle of male leadership among God's people.)

Then in verse 35, Paul adds, "If there is anything they desire to learn, let them ask their husbands at home. For it is shameful for a woman to speak in church." Here Paul anticipates an evasion of his teaching. He expects that there might be some women in Corinth who would say, "Okay, Paul, we won't stand up and pass judgment on any prophecies. But we just want to ask a few questions. What's wrong with that?" And Paul realizes that for some women, the questions would become a springboard for judgments, such as, "Your prophecy just said that Jesus would come back in five days. My question is, didn't Jesus Himself say that we can know neither the day nor the hour?"

In this way the question is really a judgment against the prophecy. So Paul rules out that evasion by saying, "If there is anything they desire to learn, let them ask their husbands at home." (He gives the general case, since most women would be married, and he assumes that the Corinthians can make appropriate applications for single women, who would no doubt know some men they could talk to after the service.)

— Answer #3: This passage is consistent with other New Testament passages that reserve the task of teaching and governing the whole congregation to men.

It is not surprising that Paul would say only men can give spoken corrections to prophecies. Such correction is part of the task of "teaching and having authority" over the congregation, the task that Paul reserves for men in 1 Timothy 2:12. For Paul to restrict this "doctrinal guardianship" job to men is entirely consistent with what he does in 1 Timothy 2, and also consistent with his expectation that elders are men ("husband of one wife" in 1 Timothy 3:2; Titus 1:6; compare "men" in Acts 20:30).

22

WOMEN AS PAUL'S COWORKERS

⌐· EGALITARIAN CLAIM: Women Such As Euodia and Syntyche (Philippians 4:2–3) Were Paul's "Coworkers" and Therefore Had Significant Leadership Roles in the New Testament.

Linda Belleville writes:

Women were actively engaged in evangelism during the early years of the church. Paul commends Priscilla and Aquila as "coworkers" (Rom. 16:3) and Tryphena, Tryphosa, and Persis as "those who work hard in the Lord" (Rom. 16:12). This is the language of missionary activity. In fact, *Paul uses exactly the same language of his own and other male colleagues' missionary labors....* Euodia and Syntyche are the only women explicitly named as evangelists. They were Paul's coworkers, "who have contended 'by' his side in the cause of the gospel" (Phil. 4:2–3). Some would say these women did nothing more than provide hospitality, but the language does not in the least suggest this. For one, the term Paul uses of their role is a strong one.... Also, Paul says that they labored side by side with him and names them as partners.... There is more. The broader context shows that *these women were not only co-evangelists but key leaders of the Philippian church*. Why else would Paul publicly appeal to a third party (the enigmatic "yokefellow") to help these women work out their differences?[1]

---

1. Linda Belleville, *Women Leaders and the Church*, 60.

Aida Spencer says:

> A "coworker" and possibly "worker" is someone whom Paul considers a colleague placed in a position of authority similar to his own position. Women certainly were called "coworkers."[2]

—Answer #1: It is true that women were Paul's coworkers, but the title "coworker" does not imply that they had equal authority to Paul, or that they had the office of elder, or that they taught or governed in any New Testament churches.

The Greek term translated "coworker" is *sunergos*. It means someone who worked with Paul, who helped him in his ministry. But to be a "fellow worker" or "coworker" does not mean that this person had governing or teaching authority in the churches. Paul calls many people "fellow workers," such as Prisca and Aquila (Romans 16:3); Urbanus (Romans 16:9); Epaphroditus (Philippians 2:25); Aristarchus, Mark, and Jesus who is called Justus (Colossians 4:10–11); Philemon (Philemon 1:1); Mark, Artistarchus, Demas, and Luke (Philemon 1:24); and others who are better known such as Titus (2 Corinthians 8:23) and Timothy (1 Thessalonians 3:2). John even applies the term *sunergos* to anyone who supports traveling missionaries or evangelists, for he writes, "Therefore we ought to support people like these, that we may be *fellow workers* (plural of Greek *sunergos*) for the truth" (3 John 1:8). But this surely does not mean that everyone who supported a traveling missionary had ruling authority over the churches!

— Answer #2: Some coworkers do things that other coworkers do not do.

It is true that some people who are called coworkers, such as Timothy and Titus, have considerable authority. But that does not mean that everyone who is called a coworker has similar authority or does the same thing.

Those who claim this are making an elementary mistake in logic:

1. Some coworkers had governing authority over churches.
2. Therefore all coworkers had governing authority over churches.

---

2. Aida Spencer, *Beyond the Curse*, 118–19. See also Gilbert Bilezikian, *Beyond Sex Roles*, 198; Stanley Grenz, *Women in the Church*, 84; Judy Brown, *Women Ministers*, 176.

But it may not be true, for other people may be coworkers by helping in other ways (such as giving money in 3 John 1:8). The activity of *one* does not have to be duplicated in the activity of *all* unless it can be shown that such activities belonged to the essence of what it meant to be a coworker (and it cannot, for their activities are too diverse). It is doubtful that Paul even thought of *coworker* as a technical term or a special category of person. He seemed generally willing to apply it to all who helped and worked with him to spread the gospel and build up the churches. (A similar form of argument could be made by reasoning: (1) Some coworkers are women; (2) therefore, all coworkers are women. But surely this is incorrect, and it shows the mistake of egalitarian reasoning at this point.)

Egalitarians are trying to make more out of a term than the term will bear. Paul's coworkers were simply those who worked with him in various ways, just as he called himself a coworker (*sunergos*) with all the Christians at Corinth (2 Corinthians 1:24) and also called himself a coworker (*sunergos*) with God (1 Corinthians 3:9). The term is not a technical term for any specific kind of responsibility in the early church.

—Answer #3: 1 Corinthians 16:16 does not tell Christians to be subject to every coworker.

Stanley Grenz and others make much of 1 Corinthians 16:15–16:

> Now I urge you, brothers—you know that the household of Stephanas were the first converts in Achaia, and that they have devoted themselves to the service of the saints—*be subject to such as these, and to every fellow worker and laborer.*

Grenz writes about this verse:

> Whatever their actual functions, Paul esteemed the labors of his female associates. In 1 Corinthians 16:16 (NIV) Paul instructs his readers "to submit…to everyone who joins in the work [*sunergounti*], and labors at it [*kopiōnti*]." The apostle employs these same words to describe the work of his male and female friends. All believers—including men—were to honor these women as leaders and submit to their authority.[3]

---

3. Grenz, ibid., 86.

But Grenz is mistaken when he says the apostle uses "these same words" to describe the work of his male and female friends. Paul does not use the same words, for this verse does not even use the noun "fellow worker" or "coworker" (Greek *sunergos*). Instead this verse has a related verb, *sunergeō*, which only occurs three other times in the New Testament and never elsewhere refers to those who work for the gospel:

Romans 8:28: "And we know that for those who love God all things *work together* for good, for those who are called according to his purpose."

2 Corinthians 6:1: "*Working together* with him, then, we appeal to you not to receive the grace of God in vain."

James 2:22: "You see that faith *was active along with* his works, and faith was completed by his works."[4]

Grenz does not tell his readers that 1 Corinthians 16:16 does not even have the noun *sunergos*, but a participle from the verb *sunergeō*. Though the words are related, it is no more true to say that everyone who "works together with" someone else (*sunergeō*) is a "coworker" (*sunergos*) than it is to say that everyone who is "sent" (*apostellō*) somewhere by someone is an "apostle" (*apostolos*). This verse cannot rightly be used to draw any conclusions about what is meant by "coworker" where it does occur in Paul's writings.

What does this verse mean then? In 1 Corinthians 16:16, Paul must be referring to a more limited group whom the Corinthians would recognize as elders or leaders in the church, as indicated by the earlier phrases in these two verses. The passage specifically mentions "the household of Stephanas" and calls them the "first converts" (Greek *aparchē*, "firstfruits") of Achaia. It is likely that Stephanas and some others in his household were appointed elders in the church at Corinth, not only because Paul tells the church to be subject to them, but also because in AD 95 the epistle of 1 Clement (written *to Corinth* to encourage the church not to

---

4. The term is also used in Mark 16:20, a verse not in the oldest and best manuscripts: "And they went out and preached everywhere, while the Lord *worked with* them and confirmed the message by accompanying signs."

remove the elders whom the apostles had set in place) has a probable allusion to this verse. It says that the apostles "appointed their first converts [Greek *aparchē*, the same word used in 1 Corinthians 16:15]...to be bishops and deacons of the future believers" (1 Clement 42:4).[5]

Another reason for taking this passage in a restrictive sense is that Paul also tells them to be "subject to...every fellow worker *and laborer* [participle of Greek *kopiaō*]" (1 Corinthians 16:16). But surely Paul cannot mean they were to be subject to everyone referred to with the verb *kopiaō* in his epistles. For example, he uses the same word to say, "Let the thief no longer steal, but rather let him *labor*, doing honest work with his own hands, so that he may have something to share with anyone in need" (Ephesians 4:28).

Surely Paul cannot be saying that the Corinthians should be subject to every thief who stops stealing and starts earning a living! But on the same logic as Grenz uses for "fellow worker" (*sunergeō*) in 1 Corinthians 16:16, we would also have to say Christians have to be subject to everyone whom Paul says is "laboring." It is far better to think that in 1 Corinthians 16:16 "every fellow worker and laborer" means "everyone who works and labors with Stephanus and his household in the leadership of the church."

Such an understanding is confirmed by the fact that the prefix *sun-* on the verb *sunergeō* implies that there is someone in the context *with whom* the worker would be working. Translating the participles very literally, we would render this verse, "be subject to such as these, and to everyone *working with* and laboring."

The expression "working with" (the participle *sunergounti*, from *sunergeō*) causes the reader instinctively to ask, "Working with whom?" and to conclude, "Working with Stephanus and those like him who have leadership in the church." Readers would naturally read it as, "be subject to such as these, and to everyone *working with them* and laboring."

---

5. Cited from *The Apostolic Fathers*, trans. Kirsopp Lake, (Loeb Classical Library; Cambridge: Harvard University Press, 1970), vol. 1, p. 81. There are several quotations from 1 Corinthians in 1 Clement (see, for example, 1 Clement 13.1; 24.1; 34.8; 37.5; 49.5), and at one point the author even says, "Take up the epistle of the blessed Paul the apostle. What did he first write to you at the beginning of his preaching? With true inspiration he charged you concerning himself and Cephas and Apollos, because even then you had made yourselves partisans" (1 Clement 47:1–3). Therefore, the readers in Corinth would likely have understood 1 Clement 42:4 as a reference to 1 Corinthians 16:15.

This means that Paul is referring in 1 Corinthians 16:15–16 to people whom the Corinthians would know as elders (and perhaps other church leaders), and this is consistent with his encouragement to be subject to "such as these." The verse does not even contain the term Paul uses elsewhere for coworker, and it is a mistake for Grenz to claim this verse as evidence that women had leadership or governing roles in the church.

AUTHOR OF HEBREWS

⌐· EGALITARIAN CLAIM: It Is Very Possible That a Woman Was the Author of the Book of Hebrews.

This argument is made by Gilbert Bilezikian, who writes:

> It is not inconceivable that Priscilla had been commissioned by some church leaders to address the issue of the relation of the two covenants.... Because of the anti-female bias of the Judeo-Christian congregations, she may have been requested to write anonymously.[1]

━ Answer #1: The author's identity as a man is revealed in Hebrews 11:32.

In Hebrews 11:32, the author says, "And what more shall I say? For time would fail *me to tell* of Gideon, Barak, Samson, Jephthah, of David and Samuel and the prophets."

In English not much can be told about the author from this verse. But in Greek, the expression "to tell" is a participle (*diēgoumenon*) that modifies "me," and the participle is masculine (the feminine form would be *diēgoumenēn*). So the author identifies himself as male. Someone could respond, "Well, that's just part of the disguise so that people won't know she is a woman." The problem with that argument is that it involves the author in dishonesty, saying something that she *intends* all Greek readers to take as an indication that she is a man. But in fact that is false. This would be outright dishonesty, and would be unworthy of an author of Scripture. Therefore the author of Hebrews identifies himself as a man.

---

1. Gilbert Bilezikian, *Beyond Sex Roles*, 302. Bilezikian gives several reasons why this theory seems plausible, but concludes that it is still a "very tentative theory" (305).

WOMEN DEACONS

⌐· EGALITARIAN CLAIM: Women Such as Phoebe (Romans 16:1) Were Deacons in the Early Church, and This Shows That All Leadership Roles Should Be Open to Women.

Linda Belleville says that in Romans 16:1, "Paul explicitly salutes Phoebe as a deacon of the church at Cenchrea."[1] And she says, "The Ephesian church most certainly had female deacons" (1 Timothy 3:11) since the qualifications for these women "are the exact duplicates of those listed for male deacons in 1 Timothy 3:8–10."[2]

---

1. Linda Belleville, "Women in Ministry," in *Two Views on Women in Ministry*, ed. James R. Beck and Craig L. Blomberg (Grand Rapids, MI: Zondervan, 2001), 100. Craig Keener, *Paul, Women and Wives*, 237–40 has an extensive discussion of Phoebe as a deacon, claiming that Paul applies the term diakonos "generally to a minister of the word" (238). But Keener has made a mistake in logic here, for the fact that some ministers of the word are called "deacons" or "servants" (*diakonoi*) does not mean that all "servants" (*diakonoi*) are ministers of the word. (To take another example showing the error of such logic, all the women in a certain church may be called Christians, but that does not mean that all who are called Christians in that church are women.)

2. Linda Belleville, "Women in Ministry," 102. See also Judy Brown, *Women Ministers*, 167. Whether or not we see women as deacons in 1 Timothy 3:11, Belleville's claim that the qualifications are the same is not the whole story, because verse 11 does not include some of the qualifications Paul mentions for men in verses 8–10, such as "not addicted to much wine," "not greedy for dishonest gain," and "they must hold the mystery of the faith with a clear conscience." In addition, in verse 12 Paul adds a qualification that could not be true of women: "Let deacons each be the husband of one wife, managing their children and their own households well," for a woman could not be a "husband," and the NT never uses *proistēmi* to speak of women "managing" or governing a household, but only of men. (BDAG, 870: "to exercise a position of leadership, *rule, direct, be at the head [of]*.")

— Answer #1: Many people think there were women deacons in the New Testament, while many others think there were not. But in either case, the office of deacon in the New Testament does not include the governing and teaching authority that is reserved for elders.

The two passages in question are Romans 16:1–2 and 1 Timothy 3:11. Romans 16:1–2 says:

> I commend to you our sister Phoebe, a servant of the church at Cenchreae, that you may welcome her in the Lord in a way worthy of the saints, and help her in whatever she may need from you, for she has been a patron of many and of myself as well.

Some translations of this verse refer to Phoebe as a "deacon" instead of a "servant" (NRSV, TNIV, NLT), while others use the term "deaconess" (RSV, NIV margin). Other translations use "servant" (ESV, NIV, NASB, KJV, NKJV).

The Greek word *diakonos* can take both meanings. In Romans 13:4, it is translated "servant" (referring to the civil authority as the "*servant* of God"), and in Romans 15:8 Christ is called a "*servant* to the circumcised to show God's truthfulness." The same word is used to refer to Apollos and Paul as "*servants* through whom you believed" in 1 Corinthians 3:5. But the term is also used to refer to the office of "deacon" in Philippians 1:1 and 1 Timothy 3:8, 12. And then it is translated "servant" again when referring to Timothy in 1 Timothy 4:6. In addition, the same term is translated "minister" in other verses (2 Corinthians 3:6; Ephesians 3:7; 6:21; Colossians 1:7, 23, 25; 4:7).[3]

With such a range of meaning, how are we to decide if Phoebe should be called "deacon" or "servant" in Romans 16:1? The question is whether Paul has a church office in view ("deacon") or is simply honoring Phoebe for her service to the church, and particularly (as most interpreters believe) for her work in carrying Paul's epistle to the church at Rome.

It does not matter very much to the argument of this book whether Phoebe is

---

3. In the foregoing examples I am using the English Standard Version as a basis for comparison and to show the range of meanings of *diakonos*, but other translations would show similar variety in translating the word.

called a faithful "servant" or a "deacon" in Romans 16:1. In neither case does this passage show that she had any teaching or governing authority in the church. Teaching and governing the whole church are functions given to "elders," not deacons, in the New Testament (see 1 Timothy 3:2, 5; 5:17; Titus 1:9; also Acts 20:17, 28).

Sarah Sumner shows no knowledge of the differences in responsibilities between deacons and apostles in the New Testament when she argues that Phoebe was a *deacon* (*diakonos*, Romans 16:1), and Paul was also called a *diakonos*, and therefore Phoebe was a minister of the Word of God like Paul was. The flaw in reasoning is twofold. First, she is making the same mistake in logic as those who say that *some* coworkers had governing authority over the churches, therefore *all* coworkers had governing authority over the churches (see chapter 22). Here Sumner's reasoning is as follows:

1. Some people who are called *diakonos* were ministers of God's Word.
2. Therefore all people who are called *diakonos* were ministers of God's Word.

Of course the reasoning does not follow, because the term *diakonos* with the sense *servant* is applied very broadly in the New Testament, and not all who are called a *diakonos* have the same responsibilities.

The second flaw in Sumner's argument is more serious. Sumner presumably has enough knowledge of Greek to know that the common word *diakonos* (which appears twenty-nine times in the New Testament) can mean either "servant" or "deacon" (LS, 398) and is translated both ways in most English translations, depending on whether a church office is indicated in the context or not. However, she does not let her readers know this alternative sense of the word but merely quotes a number of verses that call Paul, Apollos, and others a *diakonos* and says, "The word is exactly the same."[4] She does not quote Romans 13:4, for example, which says the civil magistrate is "God's *servant* for your good." Nor does she quote John 2:5: "His mother said to the *servants*, 'Do whatever he tells you,'" or other verses where the meaning *servant* and not *deacon* is required (such as Matthew 20:26; 22:13; Romans 15:8; 2 Corinthians 11:5; Galatians 2:17). She gives her readers no clue that a meaning other than "deacon" is possible, but just asserts:

4. Sarah Sumner, *Men and Women in the Church*, 242–43.

Some might argue that Phoebe was a deaconness, not a deacon. But the Bible says in Greek she was a deacon (*diakonos*). As a *diakonos*, Phoebe was a minister like Paul (Col. 1:23).... A *diakonos* is a leader who acts as a minister of God's Word.... Phoebe was a *diakonos* like Apollos (1 Cor. 3:5).... The word is exactly the same.[5]

The other passage at issue regarding whether women had the office of deacon is 1 Timothy 3:11. In the middle of a discussion about the qualifications and responsibilities of deacons, Paul says:

Their wives [or "wives," or "women"; Greek, *gunaikas,* plural of *gune*] likewise must be dignified, not slanderers, but sober-minded, faithful in all things.

Is Paul here giving qualifications for women who serve as deacons? Or is he talking about the qualifications for the wives of deacons? The question is complex, and both viewpoints are represented in *Recovering Biblical Manhood and Womanhood.* Tom Schreiner writes:

With respect to women deacons, we need not come to a firm decision, for even if women were deacons this does not refute our thesis regarding male governance in the church. Even if women were appointed as deacons, they were not appointed as elders (1 Tim. 3:1–7; Titus 1:5–9). Two qualities demanded of elders—being apt to teach (1 Tim. 3:2) and governing of the church (1 Tim. 3:5)—are not part of the responsibility of deacons (cf. also 1 Tim. 5:17; Titus 1:9; Acts 20:17, 28 ff.). The deacon's tasks consisted mainly in practical service to the needs of the congregation. This is sug-

---

5. Ibid. At this point, rather than giving her readers any indication of responsible complementarian understandings of Phoebe, she trivializes any opposing view, saying, "How are we conservatives going to choose to respond to that? Are we going to tell ourselves, 'Well, it appears we have another exception on our hands'?... I can't do that anymore in good conscience" (243). If she is aware that complementarians point out different responsibilities for deacons and argue that *diakonos* could mean *servant* in Romans 16:1, then she is not being honest with her readers in failing to mention these alternatives. If she is not aware of these common alternatives, how can her book be taken as a responsible treatment of the issue?

gested by Acts 6:1–6, where the apostles devote themselves to prayer and the ministry of the Word (6:4), while the seven are selected to care for the practical concern of the daily distribution to widows. Elders were given the responsibility to lead and teach the congregation.[6]

━ Answer #2: If the people who govern local churches are called "deacons," then women should not be deacons today.

In some churches today, the deacons are the main governing board of the church. In that case, the deacons are functioning like elders functioned in the New Testament, and it is not appropriate for women to fill that role. But in other churches, deacons are simply what the Greek term first suggests, "servants" who carry out various activities in ministry to others, such as helping the needy (compare Acts 6:1–6), caring for the sick, or overseeing church activities such as youth work, finances, or prayer. In such cases, these activities do not involve teaching or governing activity over the whole church, and it seems appropriate for women as well as men to fill those roles.

There is room for legitimate differences of opinion over whether women could or could not be deacons in the early church, but in either case the office of deacon did not include the teaching and governing responsibilities that Paul reserves for men in 1 Timothy 2:12.

---

6. Schreiner, "Valuable Ministries of Women," 220. Schreiner gives the argument in favor of women deacons on 213–14 and summarizes the arguments against women as deacons in 505–13.

PART SEVEN

EVANGELICAL FEMINIST CLAIMS ABOUT THE CHURCH FROM 1 TIMOTHY 2

W e have considered several egalitarian arguments regarding women's roles in the church according to the New Testament epistles. Egalitarian authors have claimed that women prophets were the same as teachers, that Paul's coworkers were elders, that women deacons governed the churches, and that specific women such as Phoebe and Junia had governing authority over the churches. But none of these claims have turned out to be persuasive.

Even before we look at 1 Timothy 2:11–15 in detail, the egalitarian claims from the rest of the New Testament epistles are not consistent with what the New Testament actually says: Certain teaching and governing roles in the church are reserved for men.

Yet whenever we say this we must remember that Jesus and the New Testament apostles gave much more affirmation to women's ministries and to women's value in the church than many churches have done historically. Several of these egalitarian objections have shown us that very clearly. These teachings of Scripture show us that in the midst of this controversy, we must continue to affirm and encourage multiple kinds of ministries by women throughout every aspect of the church's life. *Both* men and women are given spiritual gifts to be used for the common good, as the Holy Spirit intends.

Nevertheless, Paul says clearly in 1 Timothy 2:12, "I do not permit a woman to teach or to exercise authority over a man." Here, as elsewhere in the New Testament, egalitarians must propose several alternative explanations for the passage.

They suggest that perhaps there was a unique situation in Ephesus in which women were teaching false doctrine, and Paul's command was relevant for that particular situation only. Others suggest that women were not well educated in the ancient world, and that is why Paul does not let them teach. Still others suggest that this command was restricted only to husbands and wives, or that it was a temporary command Paul gave only until women could be trained more fully.

Egalitarians also propose several alternative meanings to the word translated "exercise authority." Perhaps it means "domineer" or "misuse authority." Or perhaps it means "not commit violence" or some other negative idea.

In this part, we consider several of these and other egalitarian objections.

WOMEN WERE TEACHING FALSE DOCTRINE

← EGALITARIAN CLAIM: Women in Ephesus Were Teaching False Doctrine, and This Is the Reason Paul Prohibits Women from Teaching in 1 Timothy 2:11–15. But That Was a Specific Command for That Particular Situation, and Therefore It Is Not Universally Binding on Us Today.

This view is commonly argued by egalitarians. Richard and Catherine Kroeger argue that women were teaching false doctrine, and they specifically suggest it was connected either to Gnosticism or to proto-Gnosticism:

> Our hypothesis will deal with the possibility that the false teachers were indeed Gnostics, proto-Gnostics, or some group with a mythology remarkably like that of the Gnostics.... We maintain that those involved with the false doctrines included both men and women, and that the women were involved in telling stories which contradicted the Scriptures.[1]

---

1. R. and C. Kroeger, *I Suffer Not a Woman*, 65–66. Cindy Jacobs, *Women of Destiny*, 240–41, shows sympathy for this "Gnostic heresy" view, depending only on the Kroegers for support. Gnosticism was an early Christian heresy (from the second century AD) that taught that salvation came through special hidden knowledge (Greek *gnōsis*), and that created matter was evil. Gnostics denied that Jesus had a human nature.

Craig Keener says, "Much of the false teaching in Ephesus was being spread through women in the congregation.... Presumably, Paul wants them to learn so that they could *teach*."[2] Gordon Fee writes (regarding 1 Timothy 2:12):

> It is probably because some of them have been so terribly deceived by the false teachers, who are specifically abusing the OT.... The word translated **authority**, which occurs only here in the NT, has the connotation "to domineer." In context it probably reflects again on the role the women were playing in advancing the errors—or speculations—of the false teachers and therefore is to be understood very closely with the prohibition against teaching.[3]

— Answer #1: The only false teachers named at Ephesus are men, not women.

We have three passages that speak of false teachers in the church at Ephesus, and they all speak of men, not women, as doing the false teaching:

1. 1 Timothy 1:19–20: "Some have made shipwreck of their faith, among whom are *Hymenaeus and Alexander*, whom I have handed over to Satan that they may learn not to blaspheme."
2. 2 Timothy 2:17–18: "Among them are *Hymenaeus and Philetus*, who have swerved from the truth, saying that the resurrection has already happened."
3. Acts 20:30: Paul warns the Ephesian elders that in the future, "from among your own selves will arise *men* speaking twisted things, to draw away the disciples after them." Here Paul specifically uses the term *anēr* (plural *andres*), which refers to male human beings, not to people generally. And he is speaking to the elders of the church at Ephesus, who were only men. He tells them that these false teachers will arise "from among your own selves."

---

2. Craig Keener, *Paul, Women and Wives*, 111–12.
3. Gordon Fee, *1 and 2 Timothy, Titus*, 73. For others who say women were promoting false teaching at Ephesus, see J. Lee Grady, *Ten Lies the Church Tells Women*, 57; Don Williams, *The Apostle Paul and Women in the Church*, 111; and Andrew Perriman, *Speaking of Women*, 141–42. I. Howard Marshall also thinks that behind 1 Timothy 2:12 "lies some particular false teaching by some women" (Marshall, *A Critical and Exegetical Commentary on the Pastoral Epistles*, ICC [Edinburgh: T & T Clark, 1999], 458).

So we have three passages that specify who the false teachers were (or would be in the future) at Ephesus, and in all three cases, the false teachers who are named are men, not women.

— Answer #2: No clear proof of women teaching false doctrine at Ephesus has been found either inside the Bible or outside the Bible.

Sometimes egalitarians claim that various verses in 1 and 2 Timothy prove that women were teaching false doctrine, but the verses simply do not demonstrate that.

First Timothy 5:13 warns that younger women who do not marry again will become "gossips and busybodies, *saying what they should not.*" But this does not indicate that any women were teaching false doctrine. To "gossip" means to spread "intimate or private rumors or facts,"[4] not the same as teaching false doctrine. Most of us can probably think of people in our local churches or communities who gossip, but they are not teachers of false doctrine! The two speech activities are quite distinct.

When Paul says in 1 Timothy 5:13 that such young women will become "*gossips* and busybodies, *saying what they should not*," the natural interpretation of "saying what they should not," is to take it as an expansion of what Paul means by "gossips." These younger widows who go from house to house will be saying things they should not say, spreading rumors and misinformation about other people. But this does not mean they are spreading false doctrine, such as denying the resurrection of Christ, or saying that the Resurrection is past already, or uttering blasphemies as Hymenaeus and Alexander did (1 Timothy 1:20), or speaking twisted things to gain a following as Paul predicted false teachers would do in Acts 20:30. There is good evidence that Paul was concerned about *gossip* becoming a problem among some women at Ephesus, but the needed evidence for women *teaching false doctrine* at Ephesus simply cannot be found in 1 Timothy 5:13.

However, my friend Rich Nathan depends on 1 Timothy 5:13 for his view that the most convincing solution regarding 1 Timothy 2 is that "the women in the Ephesian church had become the carriers of this false teaching," and he says that Gordon Fee's definition "to talk foolishness" or "to communicate false teaching" is

---

4. *American Heritage Dictionary*, 3rd ed. (Boston: Houghton Mifflin, 1996), 783. The Greek term *phluaros* is an adjective meaning "gossipy" (BDAG, 1060).

a better translation than "gossips" for the word *phluaros* in 1 Timothy 5:13.[5] The reference he gives to Fee does not mention *phluaros*, so it is unclear what evidence Nathan is using to propose this new definition for the word.[6] The standard lexicons do not mention the sense "to communicate false teaching," and such a verbal idea would be surprising to find for a definition of an adjective in any case. The BDAG definition is simply "*gossipy*,"[7] and LS says, "*silly talk, foolery, nonsense; tattler, babbler.*"[8] No English translation known to me gives the sense "to communicate false teaching," and the sense "gossips" is the near-unanimous sense in modern translations (NASB, NIV, ESV, RSV, NRSV, NLT, NKJV). Thus, no nuance of "communicating false teaching" in 1 Timothy 5:13 has been proven by Fee or Nathan, and Nathan's claim that women were teaching false doctrine in Ephesus remains an assertion with no evidence to support it.[9]

Second Timothy 3:6–7 is another passage egalitarians sometimes use to claim there were women teaching false doctrine at Ephesus:

> For among them are those who creep into households and capture weak women, burdened with sins and led astray by various passions, always learning and never able to arrive at a knowledge of the truth.

This passage indicates that some women were *led astray* by false teachers. That is not surprising, for when false teaching comes into a church, some men and some women will be led astray—God does not give immunity from wrong belief to either men or women in general. But the passage does not say that the women were *doing the false teaching*; it simply says they were being led astray.

---

5. Rich Nathan, *Who Is My Enemy?* 151.
6. Page 151–16 refers to p. 278, where Nathan cites Gordon Fee and Douglas Stewart, *How to Read the Bible for All Its Worth*, 72–76. But this page says nothing about the word *phluaros*! Though Nathan does not mention it, Gordon Fee's commentary on 1 Timothy does claim that *phluaros* is used of "speaking something foolish or absurd in comparison to truth" (Gordon Fee, *1 and 2 Timothy, Titus*, 122), but it is unclear on what basis Nathan or Fee can claim that the word means specifically to communicate false teaching. (Fee gives no evidence for his claim either.)
7. BDAG, 1060.
8. LS, 1946.
9. I am surprised to see Nathan, who is a careful thinker, advocate this position. It is kind of him to write, "My friend Wayne Grudem, a theologian, suggests that no external evidence exists of a feminist cult operating in Ephesus at the time of the writing of 1 Timothy, so how do we know that the apostle Paul was linking his prohibition to that particular problem?" (*Who Is My Enemy?* 150). Nathan offers no answer to this question. His interpretation is without basis in fact.

There is no proof that any woman or any group of women were engaged in teaching false doctrine at Ephesus. But even if that could be established, the egalitarian claim is not persuasive because it does not show that women were *primarily* responsible for spreading the false teaching—of which the only named proponents are men. And unless women were *primarily* responsible for spreading the false teaching, Paul's silencing of the women (in the egalitarian view) would not make sense.

Is there any other proof? Some have mentioned the passage about Jezebel in Revelation 2, where Jesus says to the church in Thyatira,

> "But I have this against you, that you tolerate that woman Jezebel, who calls herself a prophetess and is teaching and seducing my servants to practice sexual immorality and to eat food sacrificed to idols." (v. 20)

Does this prove there were women teaching false doctrine at Ephesus? It does prove there was one woman in the church at Thyatira, a different church, teaching false doctrine and claiming to be a prophetess. And I do not deny that there have been women who taught false doctrine at various points in the history of the church. But *one woman teaching false doctrine at Thyatira* does not prove that there were *any women teaching false doctrine at Ephesus!* There may or may not have been women teaching false doctrine at Ephesus.

My point is simply that there is *no evidence* that women were teaching false doctrine at Ephesus. And so the claim turns out to be speculation without any hard evidence to support it. *Should we base our interpretation of a passage on a claim with no clear supporting evidence and with substantial contrary evidence?*

— Answer #3: Richard and Catherine Kroegers' claim of a Gnostic heresy that Eve was created before Adam has no persuasive historical basis.

Richard and Catherine Kroeger argue at great length for the presence of a Gnostic or proto-Gnostic heresy in Ephesus that taught that Eve was created before Adam and taught Adam spiritual knowledge.[10] To construct their case, they have no proof

---

10. See especially R. and C. Kroeger, *I Suffer Not a Woman*, especially 59–66 and 119–25, with other additional historical material supposedly supporting this idea in the next several chapters. (For an analysis of the Kroegers' claim that *authenteō* in 1 Timothy 2:12 means "proclaim oneself author of a man," in accordance with this alleged Gnostic heresy, see egalitarian claim 8.10, below.)

from any first-century material outside the New Testament but use *later sources* in such a way that has opened their work to significant criticism.

New Testament scholars with expertise in this area have not been positively impressed with the Kroegers' work.[11] Thomas Schreiner summarizes much of the academic rejection of the Kroegers' speculative work in the following statement:

> Unfortunately, the Kroegers' reconstruction is riddled with methodological errors. They nod in the direction of saying that the heresy is *"proto-gnostic,"* but consistently appeal to later sources to establish the contours of the heresy. The lack of historical rigor, if I can say this kindly, is nothing less than astonishing. They have clearly not grasped how one should apply the historical method in discerning the nature of false teaching in the Pauline letters.[12]

— Answer #4: If the fact that some people were teaching false doctrine disqualified everyone of the same gender, then all men would have been disqualified from teaching.

The egalitarian argument (whether depending on the Kroegers' claim of a Gnostic myth, or on other claims that women were teaching false doctrine) simply is not consistent. Even if *some* women were teaching false doctrine at Ephesus, why would that lead Paul to prohibit *all* women from teaching? It would not be fair or consistent to do so. As we saw above, the only false teachers we know about with certainty at Ephesus are men, not women. Therefore if the egalitarian argument were consistent, it would have Paul prohibiting *all men* from teaching, just because some men were teaching false doctrine! But Paul does not do that, and this shows the inconsistency of the egalitarian argument.

---

11. For a more extensive analysis of reviews of the Kroegers' work by New Testament experts see EFBT, pp. 284–287.

12. Thomas Schreiner, "Interpretation of 1 Timothy 2:9–15," in Köstenberger, *Women in the Church*, 109–10. Schreiner adds, "For three devastating reviews of the Kroegers' work, see Robert W. Yarbrough, '*I Suffer Not a Woman: A Review Essay*,' *Presbyterion* 18 (1992): 25–33; Albert Wolters, 'Review: *I Suffer Not a Woman*,' *Calvin Theological Journal* 28 (1993): 208–13; S. M. Baugh, 'The Apostle Among the Amazons,' *Westminster Theological Journal* 56 (1994): 153–71." (See Appendix 6 of EFBT for these reviews, 646–74.)

— Answer #5: Paul gives the reason for his command, and it is the creation order (1 Timothy 2:13–14), not any false teaching by women. It is precarious to substitute a reason Paul does not give for what he does give.

Paul does not mention false teaching by women as a reason for his command. He does not say, "I do not permit a woman to teach or to exercise authority over a man; rather, she is to remain quiet *for some women are teaching false doctrine there at Ephesus.*" Rather, Paul's reason is the creation order: "*For Adam was formed first, then Eve.*"

We should be reluctant to accept a position based on a reason Paul does not give, especially when it minimizes, ignores, or presents an eccentric interpretation of the reason Paul actually does give (as several egalitarian positions do).

— Answer #6: The argument that no men were even present with the women fails to consider the actual wording of this text.

Sarah Sumner proposes another explanation of why Paul said that only women, not men, should be silent: Perhaps there were no men present. She writes:

> The women in Ephesus were talking when they should have been listening. Whether or not the men were present with them we do not know. If they weren't, that would constitute one plausible explanation of why Paul commanded women, not men, to be silent.[13]

This is indeed a novel proposal. The reason no one has proposed this before may be the difficulty of explaining why Paul commands absent men to "pray, lifting holy hands without anger or quarreling" (1 Timothy 2:8), or why Paul would waste time telling women not to teach people who weren't even there (v. 12)! Sumner's argument is unsupported speculation.

---

13. Sumner, *Men and Women in the Church*, 250.

WOMEN NOT EDUCATED

⌐• EGALITARIAN CLAIM: The Reference to Eve's Deception
in 1 Timothy 2:14 Shows That Eve Was Less Educated than Adam,
Just As the Women in Ephesus Were Less Educated than the Men.
But Women Today Have As Much Education As Men;
Therefore, 1 Timothy 2:11–15 Does Not Apply to Us Today.

Gilbert Bilezikian says:

In the fateful story of the fall, it was Eve, the lesser informed person,
who initiated a mistaken course of action and who led herself into
error. Eve was not created first or at the same time as Adam. She was
the late-comer on the scene. Of the two, she was the one bereft of the
first hand experience of God's giving the prohibition relative to the
tree. She should have deferred the matter to Adam, who was better
prepared to deal with it since he had received the command directly
from God.... Her mistake was to exercise an authoritative function
for which she was not prepared....

Paul's teaching in this passage has an absolute and universal relevance. The principle he lays down to protect the teaching ministry
and the exercise-of-authority functions from incompetent persons is
valid for all times and for all churches. Christian communities should

always remain watchful to authorize in positions of leadership only those persons who have received adequate training.... According to Paul's principle, neither men nor women should be appointed to positions of leadership in the church until they can show evidence of maturity and competency.[1]

Craig Keener also thinks that the most likely reason for Paul's prohibition in 1 Timothy 2 against women teaching is their inadequate education:

> The third possibility [which Keener thinks most likely] is that Paul intends to connect Eve's later creation to why she was deceived: She was not present when God gave the commandment, and thus was dependent on Adam for the teaching. In other words, she was inadequately educated—like the women in the Ephesian church.[2]

— Answer #1: Many men and many women had basic literacy skills in the first century, and very few men or women had education beyond this.

Steven Baugh, an expert in the history of ancient Ephesus, says about cultures like that of ancient Ephesus, "Few people in antiquity advanced in their formal

---

1. Gilbert Bilezikian, *Beyond Sex Roles*, 180–81. He elaborates on this on page 297: "Paul's understanding of the primacy of Adam as a safeguard against deception shows that he is concerned with competency. The reference to Eve...provides further evidence that Paul is establishing a principle based not on chronology but on competency." See also Cindy Jacobs, *Women of Destiny*, 230; Judy Brown, *Women Ministers*, 297–98; Andres Perriman, *Speaking of Women*, 165–68; Rich Nathan, *Who Is My Enemy?* 150, 153.

   Craig Keener, "Learning in the Assemblies: 1 Corinthians 14:34–35," in DBE 161–71 claims that "women on average were less educated than men" (169), and he sees this as a reason why they may have been asking some disruptive questions that provided the background for 1 Corinthians 14:34–35. But there is no evidence inside or outside the Bible showing that women in Corinth were asking disruptive questions: See Grudem, EFBT, 242–47, and the response by David P. Nelson in JBMW 10:1 (Spring 2005): 22–28.

2. Keener, *Paul, Women and Wives*, 116. In a similar way, Cindy Jacobs says (in her discussion of 1 Corinthians 14:34–35), "Also, at that time, most women were illiterate and hadn't had the privilege of an education" (Jacobs, *Women of Destiny*, 230). J. Lee Grady agrees, claiming, "The women in Ephesus needed more instruction.... Women in this culture had been denied all educational opportunities. Except for some Roman women in the upper class, women in the Middle East and Asia Minor were sequestered at home and kept away from books and learning" (*Twenty-Five Tough Questions*, 141).

education beyond today's elementary school levels, including men like Socrates, Sophocles, and Herodotus."[3] However, there is considerable evidence that *many women received basic literacy skills in the ancient world.* Baugh continues:

> Because women's education in antiquity usually took place privately, we get only a glimpse of it here and there. As for women's literacy, daughters of the upper classes needed some level of education for their duties in managing large households. And though they were not commonly found in fields like philosophy, women did read and write literature and poetry during this period.[4]

Baugh mentions that from Ephesus we have several examples of writing by women, including some poems and prayers.[5]

Other sources indicate that in Greek culture, the "Hellenistic school" form of education "endured with but slight changes to the end of the ancient world," and "girls, too, were educated at all age levels. In some cases they came under the control of the same officials as the boys and shared the same teachers.... In other cases separate state officials were responsible for them."[6]

In Roman society, one of the factors of Roman schools was "the inclusion of girls in the benefits of education."[7] The *Oxford Classical Dictionary* notes that both Plato and Aristotle "believed that men and women should have the same education and training."[8] And, with regard to women in earlier Greek society, "Papyri (private letters, etc.) show widespread literacy among the Greeks of Egypt" while in Rome, "upper-class Roman women were influential...many women were educated and witty."[9]

---

3. S. M. Baugh, "A Foreign World: Ephesus in the First Century," in Köstenberger, *Women in the Church*, 46, with reference to H. I. Marrou, *Education in Antiquity*, trans. George Lamb (New York: Sheed and Ward, 1956).

4. Ibid., 46.

5. Ibid., 47, footnote 140; additional evidence from several other sources is given on 46, notes 136, 138–39.

6. F. A. G. Beck, "Education" (1970), in the *Oxford Classical Dictionary*, 2nd ed., ed. N. G. L. Hammond and H. H. Scullard (Oxford: Clarendon Press, 1970), 371.

7. Ibid., 372.

8. Walter K. Lacey, "Women", in the OCD, 2nd ed., 1139.

9. Ibid.

In *Women and Men in Ministry: A Complementary Perspective,* Clinton Arnold and Robert Saucy report further evidence of the significant educational achievements of women in ancient Ephesus:

> There is now inscriptional evidence that women served in some of the cities in a position that would be a close functional equivalent of our "superintendent of schools," that is, in the capacity of a gymnasiarch (*gymnasiarchos*). The "gymnasium" was the center for education in a Greek city.... The "gymnasiarch" had oversight of the intellectual training of the citizens and for the general management of the facility. Inscriptions dating from the first to the third centuries attest to forty-eight women who served as gymnasiarchs in twenty-three cities of Asia Minor and the coastal islands. This suggests that women not only had access to education, but also that in many places they were leading the educational system.[10]

— Answer #2: The Bible never requires advanced degrees for people who teach God's Word or have governing authority in the church.

The fact that many women as well as men had basic literacy skills in Greek, Roman, and Jewish cultures is enough by itself to disprove the egalitarian claims about 1 Timothy 2. If absolutely *no* women and *only* men could read and write in ancient Ephesus, and if that practice had carried over into the church so that no Christian women learned the Bible, then the egalitarian claim would deserve some consideration. But that is simply not the case. Both women and men could read and write.

Formal academic training in Scripture (as in a modern seminary or an ancient school for rabbis) was not required for leaders in the New Testament church. We even see that several of the apostles did not have formal biblical training or schooling as the rabbis did (see Acts 4:13). The ability to read and study Scripture was available to both men and women alike, and *both men and women learned and studied Scripture in the ancient church* (note Acts 18:26, where Priscilla and Aquila

---

10. Arnold, Clinton and Robert Saucy. "The Ephesian Background of Paul's Teaching on Women's Ministry," in *Women and Men in Ministry: A Complementary Perspective,* ed. Robert L. Saucy and Judith K. TenElshof (Chicago: Moody Press, 2001), 281–83 (italics added). See Grudem, EFBT, 290–91 for more information.

together instruct Apollos; also 1 Timothy 2:11, which encourages women to "learn"; and Titus 2:3–4, where older women are to "teach what is good, and so train the young women"). This would have certainly been true in a major metropolitan center like Ephesus, where there would have been many literate, educated women in the church.

▬ Answer #3: It simply is not true that no women in the first-century churches were well enough educated to be teachers or rulers in the church, and therefore lack of education cannot be the reason for Paul's statement.

The New Testament shows several women who had a considerable level of understanding Scripture. Many women accompanied Jesus and learned from Him during His earthly ministry. (See Luke 8:1–3; 10:38–41; also John 4:1–27; 11:21–27). In this very passage in 1 Timothy, Paul says that women should "learn" (v. 11).

Perhaps the best example of a woman well trained in knowledge of the Bible is Priscilla. When Paul went to Corinth, he stayed with Aquila and Priscilla: "Because he was of the same trade he stayed with them and worked, for they were tentmakers by trade" (Acts 18:3). Paul stayed a year and six months at Corinth (v. 11), and we may ponder just how much Bible and theology Priscilla would have learned while having the apostle Paul as a houseguest and business partner during that time! Then Priscilla and Aquila went with Paul to Ephesus (vv. 18–19). It was at Ephesus in AD 51 that Priscilla and Aquila together "explained" to Apollos "the way of God more accurately" (v. 26). So in AD 51, Priscilla knew Scripture well enough to help instruct Apollos.

After that, Priscilla probably learned from Paul for another three years while he stayed at Ephesus teaching "the whole counsel of God" (Acts 20:27; compare 1 Corinthians 16:19, where Priscilla is called Prisca, and Paul sends greeting to Corinth from Aquila and Prisca and the church that meets "in their house"). By the end of Paul's three-year stay in Ephesus, Priscilla had probably received four and a half years of teaching directly from the apostle Paul. No doubt many other women in Ephesus also learned from Paul—and from Priscilla!

Aquila and Priscilla went to Rome sometime later (Romans 16:3, perhaps around AD 58), but they returned to Ephesus, for they were in Ephesus again at the end of Paul's life (in 2 Timothy 4:19, Paul writes to Timothy at Ephesus, "Greet Prisca and Aquila"). Now 2 Timothy was probably written in AD 66 or 67

(Eusebius says that Paul died in AD 67), and 1 Timothy a short time before that, in perhaps AD 65. In addition, before he wrote 1 Timothy, Paul seems to have been in Ephesus, and it seems he told Timothy to remain there when he left for Macedonia (see 1 Timothy 1:3: "As I urged you when I was going to Macedonia, remain at Ephesus…").

Therefore, both because 1 Timothy is near in time to 2 Timothy, and because Paul had last been in Ephesus to know who was there before he wrote 1 Timothy or 2 Timothy, it seems likely that Priscilla and Aquila were back in Ephesus by the time Paul wrote 1 Timothy, about AD 65.

What is the point of this? Not even well-educated Priscilla nor any other well-educated women of Ephesus who followed her example and listened to Paul's teaching for several years were allowed to teach men in the public assembly of the church. Writing to a church where many women had received significant training in the Bible from Paul himself for over three years, Paul said, "I do not permit a woman to teach or to exercise authority over a man" (1 Timothy 2:12). Paul's reason was certainly not lack of education.

— Answer #4: Lack of education is not the reason Paul gives for restricting teaching and governing roles to men. We should not deny the reason Paul gives and substitute a reason he does not give.

Paul does not say, "I do not permit a woman to teach or to exercise authority over a man; rather, she is to remain quiet, *for women are not as well-educated as men.*" That is not the reason Paul gives. The reason he gives is the order that God established when He created Adam and Eve: "*For Adam was formed first, then Eve; and Adam was not deceived, but the woman was deceived and became a transgressor*" (1 Timothy 2:13–14).

— Answer #5: If lack of education were the reason, it would be unfair and inconsistent for Paul not to prohibit teaching by uneducated men.

Moreover, if lack of training was the reason that Paul prohibited women from teaching, then why did he not also prohibit untrained men from teaching? Surely there were untrained men in the congregations at Ephesus, including new converts and perhaps some poorly educated and illiterate slaves or day laborers. But Paul does not mention them. Why does he focus on women?

The egalitarian position is inconsistent at this point, for it cannot explain why Paul excludes all women (even the well-educated ones) and does not exclude any men (even the poorly educated ones). Lack of education is not the reason for Paul's command.

But could Paul have meant that Eve's creation after Adam led to her misunderstanding the command not to eat from the tree of the knowledge of good and evil? Was Paul referring to Eve's lack of training? Deficient education cannot be the meaning because the prohibition was so simple. How many years of education does one need in order to understand the meaning of "but of the tree of the knowledge of good and evil you shall not eat, for in the day that you eat of it you shall surely die" (Genesis 2:17)? These are not difficult words in English or in Hebrew. There is no hint that any formal education or advanced training would have been necessary to understand that when God said they should not eat of that tree, He meant they should not eat of that tree.

Therefore, the claim that "For Adam was formed first, then Eve" refers to lack of education ignores the plain force of the words and the meaning they have in the text that Paul is quoting and is an interpretation that would have seemed foreign to the text and clearly wrong to Paul's original readers.

27

RESTRICTED TO HUSBANDS AND WIVES

↶·EGALITARIAN CLAIM: 1 Timothy 2:11–15 Applies Only to Husbands and Wives, Meaning Essentially, "I Do Not Permit a Woman to Teach or Have Authority over Her Husband."

This position was advocated by my friend Gordon Hugenberger in a 1992 article.[1] Hugenberger notes that the Greek word *anēr* can mean either "man" or "husband," and *gunē* can mean either "woman" or "wife." (To this point, Hugenberger is correct.) He then argues that in eleven other passages in Paul's writings, where the words *anēr* and *gunē* occur closely together, they mean "husband" and "wife." And then he says that the parallels between 1 Timothy 2 and 1 Peter 3:1–7 are "so impressive" that they "must be determinative for our exegesis of 1 Timothy 2."[2] Since 1 Peter 3:1–7 is discussing husbands and wives, Hugenberger argues, it is evident that 1 Timothy 2:8–15 must also be discussing husbands and wives. He argues that 1 Timothy 2 should be translated as follows:

> Therefore I want *husbands* everywhere to pray, lifting up holy hands without anger or disputing [with their wives]. Likewise I want *wives* to adorn themselves with proper dress, with decency and propriety.… A wife should

---

1. Gordon Hugenberger, "Women in Church Office: Hermeneutics or Exegesis? A Survey of Approaches to 1 Timothy 2:8–15," in *Journal of the Evangelical Theological Society* 35:3 (September 1992): 341–60.
2. Ibid., 354–55.

learn in quietness and full submission. I do not permit a *wife* to teach—that is, to boss her *husband*; she must be quiet. For Adam was formed first, then Eve. And Adam was not deceived but *his wife* was deceived and became a sinner. But she will be saved even through [the seemingly mundane work of] child rearing—that is, if they continue in faith, love, and holiness with propriety.[3]

However, several considerations argue against the idea that 1 Timothy 2:8–15 applies only to husbands and wives.

— Answer #1: It is true that the Greek words used here can mean either "man" or "husband" and either "woman" or "wife" according to the context. But all the other New Testament passages where the words mean "husband" or "wife" are different from this passage, because in those passages, the meanings "husband" and "wife" are made very clear from decisive clues in the context.

If we look at the other eleven passages that Hugenberger appeals to claim that *anēr* and *gunē* mean "husband" and "wife" when they occur together, it is evident in every case that *the subject under discussion is marriage*, and there are decisive clues that require that meaning in those other contexts. Here are some examples:

Romans 7:2: "A *married* (*hupandros*) woman"

1 Corinthians 7:2: "Each man should have his *own* (*heautou*) wife and each woman her *own* (*idion*) husband"

1 Corinthians 7:12: "If any brother *has* (*echei*) a wife" (and the entire context of 1 Corinthians 7 is a discussion about marriage)

1 Corinthians 7:39: "A wife is bound to *her* (*autēs*) husband as long as he lives"

---

3. Ibid., 355–56. Hugenberger's rendering of this passage inserts the Greek words at various points in order to show verbal parallels with 1 Peter 3, but these Greek words have been removed in order to give his English translation of the text itself.

Ephesians 5:22: "Wives submit to your *own* (*idiois*) husband." (Some translations, such as the NIV, RSV, NRSV, and NLT, omit the word "own," but in doing so they fail to translate the Greek word *idiois*; in any case, everyone agrees that Ephesians 5 is talking about marriage.)[4]

Therefore, when Hugenberger mentions all these other contexts where *anēr* and *gunē* mean "husband" and "wife," he fails to recognize that this is nothing remarkable because those contexts are talking about marriage! But those contexts do not prove that marriage is in view in 1 Timothy 2, unless similar decisive clues are found there.

Hugenberger's claim that the parallels with 1 Peter 3:1–7 are especially important, even "determinative for our exegesis of 1 Timothy 2," is likewise unpersuasive. Peter starts out by saying, "Likewise, wives, be subject to your *own* (*idiois*) husbands." Immediately the context tells readers that marriage is in view.

In addition, 1 Peter 3:1–7 includes instructions on how husbands should act toward their wives (v. 7), something that is present whenever the New Testament authors discuss relationships between husbands and wives. But that is not the case in 1 Timothy 2. So Hugenberger's supposedly parallel passages are all significantly different in subject matter and in significant linguistic markers within those texts.

— Answer #2: No decisive clues from the context of 1 Timothy 2 would cause the original Greek readers to think that husbands and wives were meant here, and several clues would make them think of men and women in general.

If we look at the full passage in 1 Timothy 2, it is unlikely that Paul could mean that only "*husbands* should pray, lifting holy hands without anger or quarreling," or that only "*wives* should adorn themselves in respectable apparel, with modesty and self-control" (1 Timothy 2:8–9). Should not *single* men pray without anger or quarreling? Should not *single* women dress modestly? Paul's original readers would certainly have taken these directions to apply to *all* men and women, not just to husbands and wives, but that means that *in this very context*, their minds are already set on understanding *anēr* to mean "man" and *gunē* to mean "woman." Therefore

---

4. More examples are given by Schreiner, "An Interpretation of 1 Timothy 2:9–15," in Köstenberger, *Women in the Church*, 116.

it would take strong indications in the wording if the author wanted his readers to change their minds and begin thinking that the same words in this same context suddenly meant wives and husbands.

But nothing in the context gives such an indication.

Paul simply says, "Let a woman learn quietly with all submissiveness." He does not say (as he could easily have said), "Let a *married* woman learn quietly with all submissiveness." And he does not say, "I do not permit a woman to teach or exercise authority over *her own* husband" (as he could easily have done). He simply says, "I do not permit a woman to teach or exercise authority over a man."

So the needed linguistic clues for a shift in meaning are absent, and other strong clues pointing to women and men generally are present.

In short, the view that 1 Timothy 2:12 talks about a "wife" and a "husband" is not persuasive because all the other New Testament passages that use these words for wives and husbands have different contexts and different wording, and this context and this wording in 1 Timothy 2 contain several factors indicating that men and women generally are in view.

28

TEMPORARY COMMAND

↳· EGALITARIAN CLAIM: Paul's Statement in 1 Timothy 2:12, "I Do Not Permit" Uses a Present Tense Verb That Shows It to Be a Temporary Command. It Could Be Translated, "I Am Not Now Permitting a Woman to Teach or to Exercise Authority over a Man."

This egalitarian argument claims that Paul's command is temporary because there was an unusual situation in the church at Ephesus, probably one in which a number of women were taking the lead in teaching false doctrine. Because of that unusual situation, Paul *temporarily* said that women should not teach or have authority over a man, but that command, by its temporary nature, does not apply today. Gilbert Bilezikian represents this view:

> Scholars have already pointed out that the present tense of Paul's "I do not permit…" has the force of "I do not permit *now* a woman to teach." But when these women will have learned sufficiently by sitting quietly and receptively under authorized teachers and when they "continue in faith, love, sanctification and discretion," there would remain no hindrance for them to serve as teachers.[1]

---

1. Gilbert Bilezikian, *Beyond Sex Roles*, 180. This position was apparently first stated by Don Williams in *The Apostle Paul and Women in the Church*, 112. It is also held by Sarah Sumner, *Men and Women in the Church*, 240, and R. and C. Kroeger, *I Suffer Not a Woman*, 83. See also Judy Brown, *Women Ministers*, 296.

Similarly, Gordon Fee says that verse 12 is best translated, "I am not permitting," which, according to Fee, implies, "specific instructions to this situation."[2]

— Answer #1: This argument misunderstands how Paul uses the present tense in commands.

Craig Blomberg rightly says about Paul's use of the present tense for "permit": "The present tense does not suggest Paul is making only a temporary ban; it is regularly used in a gnomic or timeless sense for proverbial instruction."[3]

Thomas Schreiner has done a helpful study of Paul's commands, showing how this egalitarian position cannot be defended in light of the pattern of Paul's other commands where he uses present tense verbs (actually, present indicatives that correspond to the present indicative *epitrepō*, "permit," in the phrase "I do not permit" (1 Timothy 2:12):[4]

1 Timothy 2:1: "I urge (*parakalō*, present indicative) that supplications, prayers, intercessions, and thanksgivings be made for all people." (This does not mean, "I temporarily urge that you pray, but this command has no relevance for future situations or future generations.")

Romans 12:1: "I appeal (*parakalō*, present indicative) to you therefore, brothers, by the mercies of God, to present your bodies as a living sacrifice, holy and acceptable to God, which is your spiritual worship." (This does not mean, "I appeal temporarily to you readers in Rome in a special situation to present your bodies as a living sacrifice, but this command is not relevant for future years or future generations.")

Ephesians 4:1: "I therefore, a prisoner for the Lord, urge (*parakalō*, present indicative) you to walk in a manner worthy of the calling to which you have been called." (This is not a temporary command.)

---

2. Gordon Fee, *1 and 2 Timothy, Titus*, 72.
3. Craig Blomberg, "Neither Hierarchicalist nor Egalitarian: Gender Roles in Paul," in Beck and Blomberg, *Two Views on Women in Ministry*, 361.
4. Schreiner, "Interpretation of 1 Timothy 2:9–15," in Köstenberger, *Women in the Church*, 125–27.

Schreiner gives several other examples,[5] but the point should be clear. Appealing to the present tense or to Paul's use of first person "I do not permit" cannot be used to argue that this is a temporary command. Such a claim misunderstands the force of the Greek present in Paul's commands. Of course, Paul is writing to specific situations, but Christians who believe Scripture to be the Word of God have rightly understood these to be *commands that are applicable for all Christians for all times.*[6] If we deny this, once again we end up denying a large number of the commands of the New Testament.

— **Answer #2: This argument would soon lead people to avoid many of the commands of the New Testament. Here as elsewhere, egalitarians use a process of interpreting Scripture that will quickly nullify the authority of Scripture in the lives of Christians today.**

Perhaps the danger of this egalitarian claim is not immediately evident. But when we realize that the New Testament epistles were written as *personal* correspondence to *specific churches* (in most cases), then we realize how much of the New Testament is threatened by any procedure that says, "This is just Paul's temporary command for that situation," or "This is just Paul's personal preference, not an abiding command for us today." In Paul's epistles alone, he uses the word "I" approximately 760 times.[7] To argue that the personal nature of these commands makes them temporary or invalidates their authority for us calls into question the authority of much of Paul's writings.

Similarly, Peter refers to his whole epistle by saying, "I have written briefly to you, exhorting and declaring [both of his verbs are present participles, explaining what Peter is doing in the epistle] that this is the true grace of God" (1 Peter 5:12). Surely we cannot make all of the epistle of 1 Peter a temporary command

---

5. See ibid., 126.

6. See EFBT chapter 9, 397–402, for a discussion of how we can know when some commands have specific applications that are culturally relative.

7. This is not an exact count because it is based on a search of one English translation, the *English Standard Version*, using Bible Works. In Greek, the personal pronoun "I" (Greek *egō*) is often unexpressed because its meaning is conveyed by the form of the verb. In addition, Paul uses the word *me* another 183 times (again merely using the ESV translation to give a rough idea of the frequency). And he sometimes refers to himself as "we."

that applies only to a specific ancient situation! But the same procedure used by egalitarians in this objection could lead quickly to such a denial. And in this way the authority of much of the New Testament would be undermined.

If we compiled a long list of the commands given by the apostles in the New Testament, and crossed out all of those written in the first person with a present tense verb that said something like "I command," or "I exhort," or "I do not permit," we would end up deleting large numbers of the commands in the New Testament. Once again, this egalitarian argument uses a procedure which not only leads to the wrong conclusion regarding the role of men and women in the church, but also threatens to undermine the authority of Scripture itself in our lives.

29

"EXERCISE AUTHORITY" MEANS SOMETHING ELSE

↶· EGALITARIAN CLAIMS: "Not Exercise Authority"
in 1 Timothy 2:12 Means "Not Misuse Authority,"
"Not Domineer," "Not Murder," "Not Commit Violence,"
or "Not Proclaim Oneself Author of a Man."

I have listed these egalitarian claims together because the answers to them will involve much of the same material. Each of these claims argues that 1 Timothy 2:12 does not mean simply, "I do not permit a woman to teach or *to exercise authority* over a man," but rather has *some wrongful practice, some abuse of authority,* in view. The argument has to do with the specific word Paul used, the Greek verb *authenteō*. What did that verb mean?[1]

The most common alternative interpretation is that Paul is prohibiting some kind of *misuse* of authority. Thus David Scholer wrote:

---

1. Regarding Paul's use of the verb *authenteō* rather than the noun *exousia* ("authority"), see chapter 30.

I am convinced that the evidence is in and that it clearly establishes *authentein*[2] as a negative term, indicating violence and inappropriate behavior. Thus, what Paul does not allow for women in 1 Timothy 2 is this type of behavior.... 1 Timothy 2 is opposing the negative behavior of women, probably the women mentioned in 1 Timothy 5:15 who follow and represent the false teachers 1 and 2 Timothy are dedicated to opposing.[3]

A second possible interpretation, related to the idea of violence, has been proposed by Richard and Catherine Kroeger:

Authentēs is applied on several occasions to those who perform ritual murder.... Such material does not allow us to rule out the possibility that 1 Timothy 2:12 prohibits cultic action involving actual or representational murder.... More likely than actual murder is the "voluntary death" or sham murder which played a significant part in mystery initiations.... It is at least possible that some sort of ritual murder, probably of a simulated nature, could be involved.[4]

And yet a third alternative has also been proposed by Richard and Catherine Kroeger. They argue that Paul here uses the word *authenteō* to mean, "proclaim oneself author of a man." The Kroegers then translate 1 Timothy 2 as, "I do not allow a woman to teach nor to proclaim herself author of man." The Kroegers understand this to be Paul's rejection of "a Gnostic notion of Eve as creator of Adam."[5]

But are these alternative meanings correct? Is Paul prohibiting the *misuse* of

2. Throughout this book I normally cite Greek words with their lexical form (the form in which they occur in a Greek dictionary or lexicon) which in this case is *authenteō*. Some of the writers I quote cite this same word by using the infinitive form *authentein*. In both cases, the same word is being referred to.

3. David M. Scholer, "The Evangelical Debate over Biblical 'Headship,'" in Kroeger and Beck, *Women, Abuse, and the Bible*, 50. Scholer says in his final footnote that this essay is a paper given at a conference on April 16, 1994, and his footnotes indicate interaction with literature up to 1993.

4. R. and C. Kroeger, *I Suffer Not a Woman*, 185–88.

5. Ibid., 103. See also Cindy Jacobs, *Women of Destiny*, 240–41, who finds the Kroegers' proposal persuasive. (For analysis of the Kroegers' claims that false teachers were promoting a Gnostic heresy about Eve being created first, see chapter 25, answer #3 above, pp. 165–66.)

authority, or some other wrongful act, due to some problem unique to Ephesus at that time? If so, then someone might argue that 1 Timothy 2 applies only to that special situation and in ordinary situations women are free to teach and exercise authority over men. On the other hand, if *authenteō* has an ordinary, neutral meaning such as "have authority," then it is more likely that Paul is making a general statement for all churches for all times. Rebecca Groothuis understands this, for she says, "All traditionalist interpretations, of course, require that *authentein* be defined in the sense of the normal, neutral exercise of authority."[6]

— Answer #1: The most complete study of this word shows that its meaning is primarily neutral, "to exercise authority over."

In 1995, H. Scott Baldwin published the most thorough study of the verb *authenteō* that had ever been done. Several earlier studies had looked at a number of occurrences of this verb, but no one had ever looked at *all* the examples that exist from ancient literature and ancient papyrus manuscripts.[7] Baldwin found eighty-two occurrences of *authenteō* in ancient writings, and he listed them all with the Greek text and English translation in a long appendix.[8] (Because such a list is not available anywhere else, I have reproduced Baldwin's list in an appendix to my book *Evangelical Feminism and Biblical Truth*).[9]

Baldwin found that in all uses of this verb, "the one unifying concept is that of *authority.*"[10] Baldwin summarized his findings on the range of possible meaning for *authenteō* in the following table.[11]

---

6. Rebecca Groothuis, *Good News for Women*, 216. See also Judy Brown, *Women Ministers*, 301.

7. H. Scott Baldwin, "A Difficult Word: *Authenteō* in 1 Timothy 2:12," in Köstenberger, *Women in the Church*, 65–80, 269–305. Baldwin explains, however, that he did not include in his list citations from the early church fathers where they just quoted 1 Timothy 2:12, since he did not think those quotations would add additional information that would help us understand the word.

8. See Baldwin's entire list of eighty-two examples of *authenteō* in Grudem, EFBT, Appendix 7, pp. 675–702.

9. I have listed only the English translation of Baldwin's examples. Full Greek texts can be found at www.EFBT100.com.

10. Baldwin, "A Difficult Word," 72–73.

11. Ibid., 73.

THE MEANING OF *AUTHENTEŌ:*

1. To rule, to reign sovereignly
2. To control, to dominate[12]
    a. to compel, to influence someone/thing
    b. middle voice: to be in effect, to have legal standing
    c. hyperbolically: to domineer/play the tyrant (one example
        in Chrysostom, about 390 AD)
    d. to grant authorization
3. To act independently
    a. to assume authority over
    b. to exercise one's own jurisdiction
    c. to flout the authority of (two examples, one from 690 AD
        and one from tenth century AD)
4. To be primarily responsible for or to instigate something
5. To commit a murder (unattested before the tenth century AD)

What should be evident from this chart is that there are no negative examples of the word *authenteō* at or around the time of the New Testament. Because language changes and meanings of words change over time, even the Chrysostom quotation from AD 390, coming more than three hundred years after Paul wrote 1 Timothy, is of limited value in understanding the meaning of what Paul wrote.[13]

Baldwin's essay is especially helpful because he provides the full citation (usually in paragraph length) for each of these eighty-two examples, both in Greek and in English translation. Therefore anyone who questions his conclusions can simply read the examples in context to see if his reasoning is persuasive.

What is most striking about Baldwin's exhaustive study is *the complete absence of some of the other meanings that have been proposed,* meanings that are unrelated to the idea of using authority. I have included all eighty-two of Baldwin's examples in an appendix to my book *Evangelical Feminism and Biblical Truth* so that readers can

---

12. Baldwin cautions readers that in accordance with standard English usage, he uses "dominate" as a *neutral* term, not as a negative or pejorative term. By contrast, he uses "domineer" as a *negative* term meaning "to rule or govern arbitrarily or despotically…to exercise authority in an overbearing manner" (ibid). Sarah Sumner, *Men and Women in the Church,* ignores this distinction and quotes Baldwin's definition "dominate" on p. 252 but changes it to "domineer" in her conclusion on p. 253.

13. Even that Chrysostom quote is capable of more than one interpretation: see Grudem, EFBT, 308–87.

see for themselves how foreign to the general use of the word some of these egalitarian claims are.[14] To my knowledge, since Baldwin's study, no additional examples of *authenteō* from ancient sources have been found or published by egalitarians, and one additional example confirming Baldwin has been found by David Huttar (see answer #2 below), and two additional confirming examples have been found by Albert Wolters (see answer #6 below). Therefore if egalitarians are going to find support for their argument in any ancient examples of *authenteō*, they will have to find it in the examples cited by Baldwin. And the evidence is simply not there.

—Answer #2: The meaning "to murder" is not supported by the ancient evidence.

Baldwin shows that there is no example of the verb *authenteō* with the meaning "to murder" until the tenth century AD! But this is nine hundred years after the time of the New Testament and hardly counts as evidence of the meaning of a word in New Testament times. Baldwin writes, "The sometimes asserted meaning, 'to murder' (5), is not substantiated for any period even remotely close to the period of the writing of the New Testament."[15]

Now more recently David Huttar has argued, on the basis of careful examination of the manuscript tradition of Aeschylus, that the meaning "murder" even in this one late example was the result of a conjectural reading by an editor of a fragmentary manuscript. He thinks the supposed instance of *authenteō* meaning "murder" actually has the meaning "initiate an action" and does not mean murder. He now finds the meaning "murder" only in one linguistically erroneous manuscript from the thirteenth century.[16]

---

14. See Grudem, EFBT, Appendix 7, 675–702, for all eighty-two examples of *authenteō*.
15. Baldwin, "A Difficult Word," 76. The tenth-century quotation he refers to is in a marginal note (a "scholion") added to Aeschylus's play *Eumenides*, line 42a; see Greek text and English translation in Baldwin, p. 302; I have quoted the English text in EFBT, 700.

    In light of the extensive discussion of this text in the literature dealing with *authenteō* it is surprising and disappointing to see Linda Belleville claim (with no documentation) that this tenth-century AD scholion is from "the fifth to first centuries B.C." (DBE, 214). This is the first and only text Belleville quotes for this verb with the meaning "to commit an act of violence," and yet ordinary readers of DBE will have no way of knowing that her pre–New Testament date for the text is simply untrue.
16. David Huttar, "AUTHENTEIN in the Aeschylus Scholium," *Journal of the Evangelical Theological Society* 44 (2001): 625.

    A similar conclusion was stated by Albert Wolters in a private letter to H. Scott Baldwin, which Baldwin quotes: "The verb *authenteō* is attested only once in the meaning 'to murder,' and this anomalous use is best explained as a case of hypercorrection by an Atticist pedant, based on the noun *authentēs* meaning 'murderer' in Attic usage" (Baldwin, "A Difficult Word," 77n31).

But if the meaning "to murder" does not occur until twelve hundred years after the time of the New Testament, why have people claimed this meaning for the word? Apparently because they confused this verb with a noun that had a similar spelling but a vastly different meaning.[17]

— Answer #3: The meaning "to instigate violence" is not supported by the ancient evidence.

What we said about the meaning "to murder" can also be said about the suggestion from Leland Wilshire that the meaning "instigating violence" was the best sense of *authenteō* at the time of the New Testament. Wilshire depended on other words, particularly the noun *authentēs*, but no Greek lexicon and no example of the verb *authenteō* from around the time of the New Testament gives support to his claim. We may safely reject it as a claim without persuasive evidence.[18]

— Answer #4: Richard and Catherine Kroegers' claim that *authenteō* means "to proclaim oneself author of a man" (related to a Gnostic heresy that Eve was created first) is not supported by the ancient evidence.

In 1992, Richard and Catherine Kroeger argued that *authenteō* in 1 Timothy 2:12 means "proclaim oneself author of man" and that we should translate 1 Timothy 2:12, "I do not allow a woman to teach nor *to proclaim herself author of man*."[19] The Kroegers say their translation would then answer a Gnostic heresy circulating at Ephesus, the idea that Eve was the creator of Adam. But several factors make this an impossible translation.

1. Not one of the eighty-two examples of *authenteō* quoted by Baldwin show the meaning "proclaim oneself to be the author of" (something).[20] Baldwin does give some examples where the verb means "to be

---

17. For a more extensive treatment of this linguistic issue, see EFBT, pp. 309–10.

18. Leland Wilshire's claim for the meaning "instigating violence" is in the article "1 Timothy 2:12 Revisited," in *Evangelical Quarterly* 65:1 (1993), 43–55. Except for the ninth- or tenth-century AD citation from the scholion to Aeschylus, none of his unambiguous examples with the meaning "murder" are instances with the verb *authenteō*, but rely instead on the noun *authentēs* (see list on his pp. 46–47).

19. R. and C. Kroeger, *I Suffer Not a Woman*, 103.

20. See all of Baldwin's eighty-two examples in Grudem, EFBT, 675–702.

primarily responsible for or to instigate something"[21]), but no text shows the meaning, "to proclaim oneself the author of something"— there is nothing about proclaiming anything for that matter.

2. The examples of the recognized sense, "to be primarily responsible for or to instigate something," all refer to being responsible for actions or activities (such as instigating a judgment), but none take the sense of *creating a person*, as in, "to proclaim oneself author of man." Therefore there are no actual quotations from any literature of any period that support the Kroegers' meaning, and in fact those who have looked at the Kroegers' evidence find numerous examples of misquoting ancient literature in their argument.[22]

3. No modern lexicon even hints a meaning such as "to proclaim oneself to be the author of."[23]

— Answer #5: The grammatical structure of the sentence rules out any negative meaning (such as, "to misuse authority, to domineer, or to murder") and shows that the verb must have a positive meaning (such as "to exercise authority").

Another recent study of one hundred parallel examples to the sentence structure in 1 Timothy 2 has produced some important conclusions. Andreas Köstenberger found in the New Testament fifty-two other examples of the construction that is found in 1 Timothy 2:12, which we can summarize as: Neither [verb A] nor [verb B].[24]

The important point of Köstenberger's study is this: All of the examples fell into only two patterns:

Pattern 1: Two activities or concepts are viewed positively in and of them selves.

Pattern 2: Two activities or concepts are viewed negatively.

---

21. Baldwin, "A Difficult Word," 73; see specific examples at 274, sec. 4.

22. See Grudem, EFBT, 311–13, and the reviews cited there. Baldwin also refers to the highly critical review of the Kroegers' claim for such a meaning by Albert Wolters in *Calvin Theological Journal* 28 (1993): 208–19.

23. See the list of nine modern lexicons in Baldwin's article, 66–67.

24. Andreas Köstenberger, "A Complex Sentence Structure in 1 Timothy 2:12," in Köstenberger, *Women in the Church*, 81–103.

Köstenberger found no exceptions to these patterns.

Some examples of pattern 1 are Matthew 6:28 (they neither labor nor spin); Matthew 13:13 (they neither hear nor understand, but both hearing and understanding are viewed as desirable activities); Luke 12:24 (they neither sow nor harvest); or Acts 4:18 (neither speak nor teach). These activities are all viewed positively in their contexts. Examples of pattern 2, where both activities are viewed negatively, are Matthew 6:20 (neither break in nor steal); John 14:27 (neither be troubled nor be afraid); Philippians 2:16 (neither run in vain nor labor in vain), and Hebrews 13:5 (neither leave nor forsake).

Köstenberger then considered forty-eight other examples of this kind of construction in literature outside the New Testament, from the third century BC to the end of the first century AD, and for all of these he lists both the Greek text and the English translation as well.[25] Again, the same pattern is found: Either both activities are viewed positively (and negated for some other reason in the context), or both activities are viewed negatively. No exceptions were found.[26]

The importance for 1 Timothy 2:12 is this: One hundred other examples of the construction found in 1 Timothy 2:12 show that in ancient Greek writing, both activities in this construction must be viewed positively, or else both activities must be viewed negatively. No exceptions were found. This means that if the activity of "teaching" is viewed positively in the context of 1 Timothy, then the activity of "having authority" must also be viewed positively.

Which is it? Köstenberger notes several cases where "teaching" is viewed positively in 1 and 2 Timothy, such as 1 Timothy 4:11, where Paul tells Timothy, "Command and *teach* these things"; 1 Timothy 6:2, where Paul says, "*Teach* and urge these things"; and 2 Timothy 2:2, where Paul says pass on these things to faithful individuals "who will be able to *teach* others also." Certainly in 1 and 2 Timothy, the activity of Bible teaching is viewed as a positive one.[27]

But this means that "to have authority" must also be viewed as a positive activity

---

25. Ibid., 91–99.

26. Dan Doriani notes that when an activity that is viewed positively is joined with another viewed negatively, a different construction is used, for such activities are joined by *kai mē* ("and not"): He cites Matthew 17:7; John 20:27; Romans 12:14; 1 Timothy 5:16 (Doriani, *Women and Ministry*, 179).

27. For a response to the objections of Alan Padgett and Sarah Sumner, see Grudem, EFBT, 315.

in 1 Timothy 2:12. If 1 Timothy 2:12 follows the uniform pattern of one hundred other examples, then the verb *authenteō* in this verse cannot take any negative meaning such as "usurp authority,"[28] or "domineer," or "misuse authority."[29]

One further objection to Köstenberger comes from I. Howard Marshall. When Köstenberger says Paul would have used a negative term like *heterodidaskalein* if he had intended a negative action such as teaching false doctrine, Marshall responds that this "overlooks the fact that to say 'But I do not permit women to give false teaching' in this context would imply 'But I do allow men to do so'; in short, *heterodidaskalein* would be an inappropriate choice of word."[30]

But Marshall himself argues that *authenteō* has a negative nuance of "exercising autocratic power."[31] Marshall's argument essentially says, "Paul used negative word *A* because it would have been inappropriate for him to use *B*, since it was a negative word."

Marshall's same objection could be made against his own view in this way: to say, "But I do not permit women to exercise autocratic power" would imply, "But I do allow men to do so." But this is surely not Paul's meaning! By Marshall's own reasoning, therefore, his argument for a negative sense of *authenteō* is disproved.

---

28. The King James Version in 1611 actually translated 1 Timothy 2:12 as "usurp authority," but this meaning has not been followed by any modern version, so far as I can tell. (The NKJV translates it "have authority.")

29. Köstenberger also demonstrates the inadequacy of a 1986 argument by Philip Barton Payne, in an unpublished paper, "*Oude* in 1 Timothy 2:12," read at the 1986 annual meeting of the Evangelical Theological Society. Payne argued that the two verbs "convey a single coherent idea" and that the passage should be translated, "I do not permit a woman to teach in a domineering manner." But, as Köstenberger demonstrates (82–84), Payne's argument is seriously flawed because it assumes without proof that *authenteō* has the negative meaning "domineer," and Köstenberger's one hundred examples demonstrate that the verbs in such construction do not simply convey one "coherent idea," but refer to two activities that are related yet distinct.

30. I. Howard Marshall, *Pastoral Epistles*, 458. Linda Belleville raised several objections to Andreas Köstenberger's syntactical argument in DBE, 217–19, which he answered extensively in his article "Teaching and Usurping Authority: 1 Timothy 2:11–15 (Ch 12) by Linda L. Belleville," in JBMW 10:1 (Spring 2005): 44–46. He also responds to objections from I. Howard Marshall and Craig Blomberg in that same essay (47–51).

31. Ibid.

— Answer #6: An extensive study of cognate words now confirms that the meaning of *authenteō* is primarily positive or neutral.

In addition to these earlier studies of *authenteō*, a massive, erudite study of the entire *authenteō* word group by Al Wolters has now appeared, encompassing and now surpassing all earlier studies in its scope.[32] After a detailed survey of all extant examples, not just of the verb *authenteō* but of several cognate words as well, Wolters concludes,

> First, the verb *authenteō* should not be interpreted in the light of *authentēs* "murderer," or the muddled definitions of it given in the Atticistic lexica. Instead, it should be understood, like all the other Hellenistic derivatives of *authentēs*, in the light of the meaning which that word had in the living Greek of the day, namely "master." Secondly, there seems to be no basis for the claim that *authenteō* in 1 Tim. 2:12 has a pejorative connotation, as in "usurp authority" or "domineer." Although it is possible to identify isolated cases of a pejorative use for both *authenteō* and *authentia*, these are not found before the fourth century AD. Overwhelmingly, the authority to which *authentēs* "master" and all its derivatives refer is a positive or neutral concept.[33]

---

32. Albert Wolters, "A Semantic Study of *authentēs* and Its Derivatives," *Journal for Biblical Manhood and Womanhood* 11/1 (Spring, 2006), 45–65. This article was previously published in an online journal, *Journal of Greco-Roman Christianity and Judaism* 1 (2000): 145–75. see http://divinity.mcmaster.ca/pages/jgrchj/index.html).

33. Ibid., 54.

30

UNCOMMON
WORD

⌐· EGALITARIAN CLAIM: In 1 Timothy 2:12,
Paul Does Not Use the Common Word for Authority (Exousia),
but Uses a Relatively Uncommon Word, Authenteō. Since the
Word Is Rare, Its Meaning Cannot Be Known with Any Certainty,
and We Should Not Put Much Weight on This Verse.

Some egalitarian writers point out that in 1 Timothy 2:12 Paul uses the verb *authenteō* rather than the more common word for authority, *exousia*. They argue that *authenteō* occurs only one time in the New Testament and claim that its meaning is uncertain or unknown. Rebecca Groothuis says:

It isn't even entirely clear what Paul was prohibiting. The word in verse 12 that is translated "authority" (*authentein*) is not the word used elsewhere in the New Testament to denote the positive or legitimate use of authority (*exousia*); in fact, this word occurs nowhere else in the New Testament. Moreover, it had a variety of meanings in ancient Greek usage, many of which were much stronger than mere authority, even to the point of denoting violence. Given that there is so much uncertainty concerning the word's intended meaning in this text, any definitive statement that Paul was forbidding women to exercise authority per se seems unwarranted.[1]

— Answer #1: Paul's use of a less common word does not mean that the word's meaning is uncertain or unknown.

Someone might think that if a word is uncommon in the New Testament, it is difficult to be sure what the word means. But that is not usually true. Because so much other Greek literature exists from the ancient world, a word that is uncommon in the New Testament may be quite common outside the New Testament. It is simply not the case that we have to be uncertain about words that occur only once in the New Testament. In fact, there are 1,934 words that occur only once,[2] and for the great majority of these, there are multiple examples of the word used in literature outside the New Testament so that discovery of the meaning of the word is a process well grounded in hard evidence. In 1 Timothy alone, there are sixty-five words that occur only once in the whole New Testament,[3] including the following:

dioktēs, "persecutor" (1 Timothy 1:13)
antilutron, "ransom" (1 Timothy 2:6)

---

1. Rebecca Groothuis, *Good News for Women*, 215, with reference to David Scholer, "The Evangelical Debate over Biblical 'Headship,'" in *Women, Abuse, and the Bible*, ed. Catherine Kroeger and James R. Beck, 46. See also Craig Keener, *Paul, Women and Wives*, 109.

   Rich Nathan, *Who Is My Enemy?* writes, "The problem is that the connotation of the word *authentein* changed from classical Greek usage (where it meant to 'domineer over') to the time of the church fathers (where it meant merely 'to have authority over'). We simply don't have enough information regarding what Paul meant, based on the word's contemporary usage in the New Testament era, to conclusively state what the plain meaning of *authentein* is" (143). Nathan gives no support for his claim that *authentein* meant "to domineer over" in Greek usage before the time of the New Testament, nor does he show any awareness of the 1995 studies of this word by Baldwin and Köstenberger, so it is not clear what he bases his statement on. In actual fact, in Baldwin's exhaustive list of eighty-two examples of *authentein,* there is no example of the meaning "domineer" from classical Greek usage or anywhere near the time of the New Testament (see the list of examples in Grudem, EFBT, 675–702).

2. Robert Morgenthaler, *Statistik des Neutestamentlichen Wortschatzes* (Zurich: Gotthelf, 1958), 165.

3. See Andreas Köstenberger and Raymond Bouchoc, *The Book Study Concordance of the Greek New Testament* (Nashville: Broadman and Holman, 2003), 1172. The following list of words is taken from that page.

neophutos, "recent convert" (1 Timothy 3:6)

xenodocheō, "show hospitality" (1 Timothy 5:10)

hudropoteō, "drink water" (1 Timothy 5:23)

philarguria, "love of money" (1 Timothy 6:10)

That these and other terms are "rare in the New Testament" does not make their meanings uncertain.

In the case of *authenteō*, we now have eighty-two other examples of this verb from Baldwin's study, which is a large base of information from which to draw fairly certain conclusions. In addition, we have evidence from several cognate words, and although I have argued above that such related words do not always accurately indicate a word's meaning, they often do, and in this case most of the evidence from related words also points to the idea of "authority" in some form, such as the noun *authentēs* in the sense of "master," and the noun *authentia*, meaning "absolute sway, authority."[4]

Of course, when the New Testament authors were writing, they had no way of knowing whether a word that seemed ordinary to them and to their readers would appear once or twice or five or ten times in the New Testament. They simply used words that conveyed clearly the meaning they intended, and they assumed their readers would understand that meaning. It is our task today to use all the available data we have to understand the meaning of those words as precisely as we can.

Does it make any difference that Paul used *authenteō* rather than *exousia*? It is difficult to say much one way or the other. To begin with, *exousia* is a *noun* meaning "authority," but Paul used a verb *authenteō*, which means "to have or exercise authority." A simple reason for using *authenteō* may be that as Paul wrote he wanted a verb, not a noun, to express his meaning. There is a verb *exousiazō*, which means "to have the right of control, have the right/power for something or over someone," but it is not very common in the New Testament either, since it is used only four times (Luke 22:25; 1 Corinthians 6:12; 7:4 [twice]).

The noun *exousia* is quite common (102 times in the New Testament), but I see no reason why Paul had to be limited to using only common words or why any-

---

4. LS, 275.

one should say he should have used a noun in this verse. Nor can I see any reason why he should not be able to use words that were approximately synonymous, but had different nuances of meaning. There may have been nuances of *exousia* that he wanted to avoid, or nuances of *authenteō* that he wanted to include, but it is difficult for us to say what those might be. In any case, the verb he did use means "to have authority over," and that meaning now, in the light of much scholarly research, is established beyond reasonable doubt.

One more confirmation of the rightness of this understanding of *authenteō* is found in the very context in 1 Timothy 2. Paul says, "Let a woman learn quietly *with all submissiveness.* I do not permit a woman to teach or to exercise authority over a man; rather, she is to remain quiet" (1 Timothy 2:11–12). Here the activities of teaching and having authority are set in contrast to learning "with all submissiveness," and submissiveness is a fitting contrast to having authority.

EVANGELICAL FEMINIST CLAIMS ABOUT HOW TO INTERPRET AND APPLY THE BIBLE

It should be clear after our examination of many of the common egalitarian claims thus far that much of the controversy over men's and women's roles in marriage and the church has to do with how one interprets the Bible. There are significant differences over methods of interpretation in this controversy.

Egalitarians object that we don't follow the prohibitions about jewelry or braided hair for women today, nor do churches generally require head coverings for women. So why should we say that other restrictive verses about women's roles in the church are to be followed today? In addition, haven't we discovered that some other teachings of the New Testament are culturally relative and not to be followed today? We don't teach that slavery is right today, so why should we teach that women's submission is required? Some egalitarians argue that the New Testament's ethical commands are not the final ethical standard God wants us to follow; they were simply one point in a "trajectory," and we can now see that the

New Testament authors were taking significant steps toward a much higher ethic, an ethic that we can discern today but that the New Testament authors did not reach in their lifetimes.

Other evangelicals today say it is acceptable for women to teach the Bible to both sexes if the woman is "under the authority of the pastor and elders."

Are these objections persuasive? They all have to do with questions about how the Bible should be interpreted and applied today.

31

NOBODY FORBIDS JEWELRY OR BRAIDS

↶· EGALITARIAN CLAIM: Complementarians Are Inconsistent Because They Don't Prohibit Women from Wearing Jewelry or Braided Hair, but That Prohibition Is Found in the Very Same Paragraph in the Bible As the Command About Women Not Teaching or Having Authority over Men (1 Timothy 2:9). We Should Realize That the Whole Section Was Binding Only for That Situation and Culture.

Paul says in 1 Timothy 2 that "women should adorn themselves in respectable apparel, with modesty and self-control, not with braided hair and gold or pearls or costly attire, but with what is proper for women who profess godliness—with good works" (vv. 9–10).

Alvera Mickelsen comments on this passage:

Those who believe that verse 12 forever bars all women of all time from teaching or having authority over men usually ignore the commands in the other six verses in this section. This is a classic case of "selective literalism."

If this passage is universal for all Christian women of all time, then no woman should ever wear pearls or gold (including wedding rings) or have braided hair or expensive clothing.[1]

— Answer #1: This passage does not prohibit jewelry or braided hair; it prohibits ostentation or excessive emphasis on jewelry or braided hair as a woman's source of beauty. Christian women should still obey that understanding of this passage today.

Thomas Schreiner points to a parallel passage in 1 Peter 3:3, where Peter says, "Do not let your adorning be external—the braiding of hair, the wearing of gold, or the putting on of clothing," and certainly Peter cannot be prohibiting all wearing of clothing in church![2] So Schreiner rightly says, "The proscription is not against all wearing of clothing, but luxurious adornment, an excessive devotion to beautiful and splendid attire." With regard to braided hair and gold and pearls, Schreiner says, "Paul's purpose is probably not to ban these altogether, but to warn against expensive and extravagant preoccupation with one's appearance.... In conclusion, the text does not rule out all wearing of jewelry by women, but forbids ostentation and luxury in adornment."[3]

Therefore complementarians are consistent, because they say (with most of the evangelical world) that these passages *are still relevant for us* and *must still be obeyed* today in largely the same sense that Paul and Peter intended 1 Timothy 2:9–10 and 1 Peter 3:3 to be obeyed by churches in their day. They were not legalistically prohibiting all use of jewelry, but were teaching the churches that women should exercise modesty and restraint rather than ostentation in their clothing.

---

1. Alvera Mickelsen, "An Egalitarian View: There Is Neither Male nor Female in Christ," in Bonnidell and Robert G. Clouse, *Women in Ministry: Four Views*, 201.
2. The NASB and KJV, along with the ESV, which is quoted here, correctly translate *himation* simply as "clothing" or "apparel" or "dresses." The NIV, as well as the RSV, NRSV, and NKJV insert the word "fine" before "clothes," but that is an interpretative addition because such a qualification is not represented in the Greek text.
3. Schreiner, "Interpretation of 1 Timothy 2:9–15," in Köstenberger, *Women in the Church*, 119.

— Answer #2: This egalitarian claim again comes dangerously close to denying the authority of Scripture.

It is troubling to read the claims of some egalitarians who seem eager to find passages that they say we must disobey! Their reasoning goes as follows:

1. Of course we must disobey 1 Timothy 2:9 (about jewelry).
2. Therefore we should also disobey 1 Timothy 2:12 (about women teaching and having authority).

Such reasoning doubly rejects the authority of Scripture! Even if people say we should not follow 1 Timothy 2:9 in exactly the sense people followed it in the first century, our doctrine of Scripture as the Word of God requires us to obey 1 Timothy 2:9 *in some way or with some parallel application today*. And, similarly, we should have a way to understand 1 Timothy 2:12 that enables us to obey it in a similar way. But the egalitarian position argument as represented in this section encourages disobedience to both passages. That practice could rapidly lead to a broader disintegration of the authority of the New Testament epistles in our lives today.

32

HEAD COVERINGS

⌐· EGALITARIAN CLAIM: Just As the Church
Has Now Learned That Women Do Not Have to Wear Head Coverings
As Commanded in 1 Corinthians 11, So It Needs to Learn That
Women Do Not Have to Submit to Their Husbands or to Give Up
Leadership Roles in the Church to Men. All of These Were
Simply Traditions Paul Was Following in That Culture.

Rich Nathan writes:

> Paul commands women in the church at Corinth to wear head coverings. Yet, most churches today (even the most traditional ones) don't require women to wear head coverings.... It is very rare, especially in America, for men to follow the explicit teaching of Scripture by kissing each other. We must admit that we all read the Bible with the understanding that the New Testament culture is different from ours.[1]

Such reasoning sounds plausible enough on first reading. When lay persons read that Paul required head coverings, and when they realize that few churches

---

1. Rich Nathan, *Who Is My Enemy?* 146. In this present section I deal only with the objection about head coverings, since it is used more often. Regarding the question of a holy kiss (Romans 16:16; 1 Corinthians 16:20; 2 Corinthians 13:12; 1 Thessalonians 5:26; 1 Peter 5:14), see Grudem, EFBT, 397–402.

require head coverings for women today, it is easy to reason from (1) we don't require women to cover their heads as they did in the ancient world to (2) we don't need to exclude women from Bible teaching to the church, as they did in the ancient world.

The passage under discussion is as follows:

> Every man who prays or prophesies with his head covered dishonors his head, but every wife who prays or prophesies with her head uncovered dishonors her head—it is the same as if her head were shaven. For if a wife will not cover her head, then she should cut her hair short. But since it is disgraceful for a wife to cut off her hair or shave her head, let her cover her head. (1 Corinthians 11:4–6; see also vv. 10, 13)

(Some translations render the Greek word *gunē* in this passage as "woman" rather than "wife," and both meanings are possible for this word.)

— Answer #1: Paul is concerned about head covering because it is an outward symbol of something else. But the meaning of such a symbol will vary according to how people in a given culture understand it. It would be wrong to require the same symbol today if it carried a completely different meaning.

No matter what people think about requiring head coverings for women today, all interpreters agree that head covering was a symbol for something else and that Paul was concerned about it because of what that symbol meant. People have thought that head covering for women in the first century was a symbol of (a) a woman being in submission to her husband (or perhaps to the elders of the church), (b) being a woman rather than a man, (c) being a wife rather than an unmarried woman, or (d) having authority to pray and prophesy publicly in the church.

There may be other explanations of the symbolism, but everyone agrees that Paul's concern is what wearing a head covering *symbolized* to people in Corinth and what, if anything, wearing a head covering symbolizes today.

Whatever we think a head covering symbolized in first-century Corinth, it does not symbolize the same thing today. And that means if Paul's concern was over what a head covering symbolized, then he would not want women to wear a head covering in a situation where a head covering did not carry the same symbolic meaning. Therefore, even if we cannot be sure what the head coverings symbolized for women in the first century (for interpreters differ on this), the very fact that it does not symbolize much of anything to people today, even to Christians, is a strong argument that Paul would not have wanted us to follow it as sort of a meaningless symbol. I think it also means that God Himself does not intend us to follow this practice today, in a society and culture where it carries no symbolic meaning.

In fact, the response most people today are likely to have when they see a woman wearing a head covering in church is, "I suppose she's trying to be old fashioned. Well, she is free to do that if she wants, but it certainly looks strange."

That is surely *not* the symbolic meaning that people attached to a woman's head covering in the first century.

— Answer #2: The most likely meaning of a woman wearing a head covering in first-century Corinth was to indicate that she was married. But no such meaning would be understood from a woman's head covering today.

The translators of the English Standard Version (quoted above) understood a woman's head covering in the first century to indicate that she was married. Therefore in every verse in which head covering is mentioned, the ESV translates *gunē* as "wife." But the other verses it translates *gunē* as "woman," because these verses have more general statements about womanhood that Paul was using in order to discuss this specific application.

Evidence that head covering for a woman indicated that she was married is found both in literary sources and in archaeological discoveries of artwork portraying wedding scenes. Bruce Winter writes:

> The very mention of the word "veil" by Paul would automatically indicate to the Corinthians that the females under discussion in this passage were married.... The marriage ceremony involved what was called in Greek "veiling the bride" (*tēn numphēn katakalupsantes*). Both Tacitus and Juvenal describe the taking of "the veil of a bride" as one of the essential components of marriage. It was the social indicator by which the marital status of a woman was made clear to everyone.[2]

2. Bruce W. Winter, *After Paul Left Corinth*, 127. See further evidence, including a photo of a statue in the British Museum, in Grudem, EFBT, 334-36.

Bruce Winter appears to be correct in concluding, with regard to 1 Corinthians 11,

> Because any reference connecting a woman and a veil would immediately alert a first century reader to the fact that she was a married woman, there are secure grounds for concluding that the issue here was married women praying and prophesying without their veil in the Christian meeting.[3]

— Answer #3: Today we obey the head covering commands for women in 1 Corinthians 11 by encouraging married women to wear whatever symbolizes being married in their own cultures.

In modern American society, a married woman wears a wedding ring to give public evidence that she is married. Just as Paul was concerned that women in Corinth not throw off their veils and thereby dishonor their husbands by not acting like married women in the church services, so married women today should not hide their wedding rings or otherwise publicly dishonor their marriage when they come to church. (There are probably a number of other symbols of being married in other cultures around the world, and the application of 1 Corinthians 11 to churches in those cultures is that married women [and men!] should not discard those symbols.)[4]

Notice that I am *not* saying that "we no longer have to obey 1 Corinthians 11." I am saying, rather, that the *outward form* in which we obey the passage may vary from culture to culture, just as the physical sign that symbolizes marriage varies from culture to culture. This is similar to the way that "you shall not covet your neighbor's...ox" (Exodus 20:17) applies today to not coveting our neighbor's car (or, in an agricultural society, his tractor).

Our approach here is very different from any egalitarian argument that says,

---

3. Winter, *After Paul Left Corinth,* 127. For an analysis of the claim that *exousia* in 1 Corinthians 11:10 ("symbol of authority" or "authority") implies that women have the authority to speak or teach in the church, see Grudem, EFBT, 338-339.
4. It is likely that a head covering symbolized not only being married but also being under the authority of one's husband in the ancient world. There may be no specific modern counterpart to this aspect of the symbolism other than a submissive demeanor and public words and actions that hint at the nature of the husband-wife relationship.

"We don't have to obey the passage on head coverings, and we don't have to obey the passage on holy kisses, and we don't have to obey the passage on foot washing, so we probably don't have to obey the passages on male headship in marriage either." That form of argument is particularly dangerous because it accumulates more and more sections of Scripture that "we don't have to obey today." But our submission to the authority of God as He speaks in His Word means that we have to obey *all* of these passages, though the *specific form* that obedience takes will vary from culture to culture, because the thing that God was concerned about in each case was not the outward form but the meaning conveyed by that form.[5]

— Answer #4: The situation is far different with male headship in marriage and the church. These are not just outward symbols that can vary from culture to culture, but they are the reality itself.

It is easy enough to understand that a *physical object* can be a symbol of something else, such as a wedding ring or a head covering being a symbol of being married. (Similar physical symbols are a policeman's hat or badge as a symbol of his authority, or a crown as a symbol of royalty, or a chef's hat being a symbol of a preparer of fine foods, or a general's stars being a symbol of holding the rank of general in the army, or the black and white striped shirt of a referee being the symbol of the status of being a referee at a football game. These symbols could all change from culture to culture, but the underlying status that they represent would be the same.)

Similarly, we can understand how a *physical action* can be a symbol for an underlying reality. A kiss or a handshake or a hug can be a physical symbol for the reality of a warm greeting. But a similar kind of greeting might be conveyed by bowing in a Japanese culture. Sticking one's fingers in one's ears can be a symbol for not wanting to listen to something. (That symbol might be nearly universal.) And we understand quite well how the physical actions of baptism and partaking of the Lord's Supper are physical symbols of deeper spiritual realities.

But "Wives, submit to your own husbands," and "Husbands, love your wives" (Ephesians 5:22, 25) are not mere symbols of some deeper reality. *They are the reality itself!* These commands are not physical items of clothing or momentary

5. For further discussion of the general question of how to know which commands of the Bible are culturally relative and which apply today, see Grudem, EFBT, 397–402.

actions like a holy kiss, but they are fundamental, ongoing attitudes that should characterize the marriage relationship every hour of every day throughout one's married life. Similarly, leadership of the church by male elders (1 Timothy 2:12; 3:2) is not a temporary *symbol* of some deeper reality, *but is the reality itself.* It characterizes the ongoing leadership pattern of the church throughout all of its days.

33

SLAVERY

↜ EGALITARIAN CLAIM: Just As the Church Finally Recognized That Slavery Was Wrong, So It Should Now Recognize That Male Headship in Marriage and the Church Is Wrong.

This claim is frequently mentioned by egalitarian authors. Craig Keener says:

Modern writers who argue that Paul's charge to wives to submit to their husbands "as to Christ" is binding in all cultures must come to grips with the fact that Paul even more plainly tells slaves to "obey" their masters "as they would Christ" (Eph 6:5). *If one is binding in all cultures, so is the other.*[1]

— Answer #1: Slavery is very different from marriage and from the church. Marriage was part of God's original creation, but slavery was not. The church is a wonderful creation of God, but slavery was not.

Egalitarians fail to realize the full implications of the wonderful differences between marriage and the church, on the one hand, and slavery on the other hand. Marriage and the church are good gifts from God. Slavery is not. It was right to abolish slavery. It is not right to attempt to abolish marriage or the church.

Slavery did not exist in God's original creation in the Garden of Eden, but marriage did, and male headship did. It is something good and noble and right, something that God established before the Fall.[2]

---

1. Craig Keener, *Paul, Women and Wives*, 184 (italics added).
2. See chapter 1, above.

Therefore, people who abolished slavery, *based on an appeal to biblical principles* (such as William Wilberforce in England and many Christians in the abolitionist movement in the United States), were abolishing something evil that God did not create. But Christians who oppose male headship in marriage and the church are attempting to abolish something good, something that God did create. The examples are simply not parallel.

— Answer #2: The New Testament never commanded slavery, but gave principles that regulated it and ultimately led to its abolition.

Paul says to slaves, "If you can gain your freedom, avail yourself of the opportunity" (1 Corinthians 7:21). And he tells Philemon that he should welcome his slave Onesimus back "no longer as a slave but more than a slave, as a beloved brother" (Philemon 1:16), and that he should "receive him as you would receive me" (v. 17). Paul tells Philemon that if Onesimus owes him anything, Paul would pay it himself (vv. 18–19). Finally he says, "Confident of your obedience, I write to you, knowing that you will do *even more than I say*" (v. 21). This is a strong and not very subtle hint that Philemon should grant freedom to Onesimus.

More explicitly, Paul condemns "enslavers" in 1 Timothy 1:10 in the same list as "murderers" and "the sexually immoral" and "liars." This shows that the Bible explicitly condemns any forcible enslavement of any other person. (The King James Version rendered this "menstealers," and the application to slavery was not as directly seen.) Exodus 21:16 even declares, "Whoever steals a man and sells him, and anyone found in possession of him, shall be put to death," and abolitionists who argued against American slavery in the nineteenth century used this verse to argue powerfully against the practice of slavery in the United States (see below on Theodore Weld).

When we couple those verses with the realization that every human being is created in the image of God (see Genesis 1:27; 9:6; James 3:9), we see that the Bible, especially in the New Testament, contains powerful principles that would lead to an abolition of slavery. The New Testament never commands people to practice slavery or to own slaves; rather, it regulates the existing institution with statements such as, "masters, treat your slaves justly and fairly, knowing that you also have a Master in heaven" (Colossians 4:1). Similarly, even the Old Testament laws give regulations restricting the practice of slavery but do not endorse it, as egalitarian author Ronald Pierce also argues.[3]

When the Bible tells slaves to be submissive to their masters, it does not mean that the Bible supports or commands slavery, but only that it tells people who are slaves how they should respond. The evangelical, Bible-believing Christians who ultimately brought about the abolition of slavery *did not modify or nullify any biblical teaching*, but that is what egalitarians want us to do with the teachings about men and women in marriage and in the church.

— Answer #3: The fact that some Christians used the Bible to defend slavery in the past does not mean the Bible supports slavery.

Sometimes egalitarians seem to assume that if they can show that Christians used the Bible to defend slavery, that proves the Bible supported slavery, and this provides them a basis for arguing that we should "move beyond" other things the New Testament teaches as well.

William Webb sometimes appeals to the fact that proponents of slavery or proponents of monarchy in the past appealed to the Bible to prove their case. He says, "Slavery proponents frequently argued from theological and christological analogies in the text,"[4] and that "in the past, the submission texts cited above were used by Christians to support monarchy as the only appropriate, God-honoring form of government."[5]

But the fact of the matter is that the Bible was used by more Christians to *oppose* slavery than to defend it, and eventually their arguments won and slavery was abolished. No churches or denominations today support slavery. The people who tried to use the Bible to defend slavery lost the argument! Shall we now reverse history and say that their losing argument was correct?

One example of antislavery arguments based on the Bible is found in Theodore Weld's *The Bible Against Slavery* (1837), which was widely distributed by aboli-

---

3. Ronald Pierce, in a helpful chapter in the recent egalitarian book *Discovering Biblical Equality*, writes the following about Old Testament slavery: "The law of Moses does not endorse slavery (economic or personal) any more than it does patriarchy, but works within these frameworks and regulates them, providing a degree of care and protection for slaves and women" (DBE, p. 101).

4. William Webb, *Slaves, Women and Homosexuals*, 186.

5. Ibid., 107.

tionists and frequently reprinted. Weld argues strongly against American slavery from Exodus 21:16: "He that stealeth a man, and selleth him, or if he be found in his hand, he shall surely be put to death" (KJV) (pp. 13–15), as well as from the fact that men are in the image of God and therefore it is morally wrong to treat any human being as property (pp. 8–9, 15–17). He argues that ownership of another person breaks the eighth commandment, "Thou shalt not steal," as follows: "The eighth commandment forbids the taking of any part of that which belongs to another. Slavery takes the whole. Does the same Bible which prohibits the taking of any thing from him, sanction the taking of every thing? Does it thunder wrath against the man who robs his neighbor of a cent, yet commission him to rob his neighbor of himself? Slaveholding is the highest possible violation of the eighth commandment" (pp. 10–11). In the rest of the book he answers detailed objections about various verses used by slavery proponents. The whole basis of his book is that the moral standards taught in the Bible are right, and there is no hint that we have to move beyond the Bible's ethics as Webb would have us do.[6]

— Answer #4: The horrible abuses of human beings that occurred in American slavery made it an institution that was different in character from the first century institution of being a "slave" or "bondservant" (Greek *doulos*).

When we hear the word "slavery" today, what comes to mind is what we have read in books, or seen in movies or on television, concerning the horrible abuses that occurred in American slavery during the nineteenth century and earlier. But if that is the picture that comes to mind when we read the word "slave" in the Bible, it is a distorted picture.

The Greek word *doulos*, which is translated "slave" or "servant" in many translations, is translated in the NASB and NKJV as "bond-servant" or "bondservant," and this helps signal to readers that it was a different institution than anything we know today. The person referred to as a "slave" or "bondservant" in the New Testament (Greek *doulos*) was legally "bound" to a certain master, almost always for a limited period of time until he could obtain his freedom. A detailed article in *The International Standard Bible Encyclopedia* explains:

---

6. Theodore Weld, *The Bible Against Slavery* (New York: American Anti-Slavery Society, 1838; first published 1837), 8–17. See also several essays in *Against Slavery: An Abolitionist Reader*, ed. Mason Lowance (New York: Penguin, 2000).

Persons in slavery under Roman law in the 1st cent. AD could generally count on being set free by age thirty.... Pertinent inscriptions indicate, however, that large numbers, approaching 50 percent, were set free prior to their thirtieth birthdays.[7]

Slaves in this sense had a higher social status and better economic situation than free day laborers who had to search for employment each day (see Matthew 20:1–7, where the master of a house goes into the marketplace to hire day laborers at different times during the day). By contrast, those who were "bondservants" (or "slaves") had greater economic security with a continuing job and steady income.[8]

Such "slaves" or "bondservants" (in the first-century sense of "bondservants") worked in a variety of occupations:

In Greco-Roman households slaves served not only as cooks, cleaners, and personal attendants, but also as tutors of persons of all ages, physicians, nurses, close companions, and managers of the household. In the business world, slaves were not only janitors and delivery boys; they were managers of estates, shops, and ships, as well as salesmen and contracting agents. In the civil service, slaves were not only used in street-paving and sewer-cleaning gangs, but also as administrators of funds and personnel and as executives with decision making powers.[9]

How then did people become slaves? While many were born into slavery, and while in earlier years up to the time of Caesar Augustus (63 BC to AD 14), the Romans had obtained slaves through conquest in war, by the time of the New Testament,

---

7. S. S. Bartchy, "Slavery," in *The International Standard Bible Encyclopedia*, ed. Geoffrey W. Bromiley, 4:545.

8. Ibid., 546: "To have turned all the slaves into free day laborers would have been to create an economy in which those at the bottom would have suffered even more insecurity and potential poverty than before." A. A. Ruprecht says, "Eighty-five to 90 percent of the inhabitants of Rome and peninsula Italy were slaves or of slave origin in the first and second centuries" ("Slave, Slavery," *DPL*, 881).

9. Bartchy, "Slavery," 544. A. A. Ruprecht agrees: see "Slave, Slavery," *DPL* 881–83.

Large numbers of people sold themselves into slavery for various reasons, above all to enter a life that was easier and more secure than existence as a poor, freeborn person, to obtain special jobs, and to climb socially....

Many non-Romans sold themselves to Roman citizens with the justified expectation, carefully regulated by Roman law, of becoming Roman citizens themselves when manumitted....

Certainly, capable slaves had an advantage over their free counterparts in that they were often given an excellent education at their owner's expense. Famous philosophers (Epictetus), teachers...grammarians... administrators (M. A. Felix, the procurator who was Paul's judge in Acts 23:24–24:27), artists, physicians, and writers were the result of this practice. These slaves and former slaves formed the broad "class" of intellectuals in the 1st century. Such slaves did not have to wait until manumission before they were capable of establishing friendships with their owners and other free persons as human beings....

For many, self-sale into slavery with anticipation of manumission was regarded as the most direct means to be integrated into Greek and Roman society. As such, in stark contrast to New World slavery in the 17th–19th cents, Greco-Roman slavery functioned as a process rather than a permanent condition.[10]

This is not to say that slavery was an ideal condition, for slaves looked forward to the time when they could purchase their freedom. They were still regarded by the law as things rather than persons according to their legal status. However,

It was, of course, recognized that those in slavery, as many as one-third of the population in the large cities such as Rome, Ephesus, Antioch, and Corinth, were human beings if not "legal persons." As such they were protected by law against severe cruelty from their owners or others....

A slave's property was entirely under the control of the slave, who could

---

10. Bartchy, "Slavery," 543–44. (In Matthew 25:15, slaves are entrusted with "talents"—immense amounts of money equal to twenty years' wges for a laborer, so one tallent = about $400,000.00 (US) in 2006 terms.)

seek to increase it for use in purchasing legal freedom and in establishing a comfortable life as a freed person.[11]

So we must realize that first century "slavery" was for the most part much different in character from the horrible abuses that we commonly picture as "slavery" from our knowledge of American history. And yet we must recognize that the New Testament (a) never commanded this practice, (b) gave principles that regulated it while it was in existence, and (c) gave principles that ultimately led to the abolition of slavery itself.

11. Ibid., 544. It should be noted that some scholars differ with Bartchy and portray ancient slavery more negatively. While they may debate for a long time exactly how evil first-century slavery was, I am not willing to say that the first century institution of a *doulos* ("bondservant") was so inherently and pervasively evil that the New Testament authors should have condemned it entirely, but they didn't, and therefore we can see that the New Testament's moral standards are inadequate. This would be to say that the New Testament actually teaches a defective moral standard, and I do not think that option is open for Christians who take the Bible as the flawless, pure Word of God. I believe the slave trade and slavery in America in the 19th century were that evil, but I cannot say the same for the different institution of being a "bondservant" (*doulos*) in the first century.

34

TRAJECTORY

⌐· EGALITARIAN CLAIM: Paul and Other New Testament
Authors Were Moving in a Trajectory Toward Full Inclusion
of Women in Leadership, but They Didn't Quite Reach That Goal
by the Time the New Testament Was Completed. Today We
Can See the Direction They Were Heading and Affirm the
Egalitarian Conclusions They Were Heading Toward.

R. T. France, in his book *Women in the Church's Ministry: A Test Case for Biblical Interpretation*, takes this position. He argues that the Old Testament and Judaism in the time of Jesus were male-dominated and biased against women, but that Jesus began to overturn this system and that the New Testament churches continued the process. We can now follow this "trajectory" to a point of full inclusion of women in all ministries. France explains:

> The gospels do not, perhaps, record a total reversal of Jewish prejudice against women and of their total exclusion from roles of leadership. But *they do contain the seeds from which such a reversal was bound to grow.* Effective revolutions are seldom completed in a year or two. In this, as in other matters, the disciples were slow learners. But the fuse, long as it might prove to be, had been ignited.[1]

---

1. R. T. France, *Women in the Church's Ministry: A Test Case for Biblical Interpretation*, 78 (italics added). I. Howard Marshall also seems to adopt a similar "trajectory" argument when he speaks of Paul not taking the final step along the direction to which his own teaching was leading when he commanded husbands to love their wives ("Mutual Love and Submission in Marriage," in DBE, especially 194–95).

France later comments on "there is no longer male and female" in Galatians 3:28:

> Paul here expresses *the end-point of the historical trajectory* which we have been tracing…from the male-dominated society of the Old Testament and of later Judaism, through the revolutionary implications and yet still limited actual outworking of Jesus' attitude to women, and on to the increasing prominence of women in the apostolic church and in its active ministry. At all points within the period of biblical history *the working out of the fundamental equality* expressed in Galatians 3:28 *remained constrained by the realities of the time*, and yet there was the basis, indeed the imperative, for the dismantling of the sexual discrimination which has prevailed since the fall. *How far along that trajectory it is appropriate and possible for the church to move* at any subsequent stage in history must remain a matter for debate, as it is today.[2]

And he says that he has found his "basic position" regarding women in ministry

> not in these few texts [1 Corinthians 14:34–36 and 1 Timothy 2:11–15] but *in a trajectory of thought and practice developing through Scripture, and arguably pointing beyond itself* to the fuller outworking of God's ultimate purpose in Christ in ways which the first-century situation did not yet allow.[3]

A similar position is argued by Asbury Seminary professor David L. Thompson in a 1996 article in *Christian Scholar's Review*:[4]

[1. *continued*] William Webb also adopts a "trajectory" hermeneutic in *Slaves, Women and Homosexuals* and in his chapter "A Redemptive-Movement Hermeneutic: The Slavery Analogy," in DBE, 382–400. I have responded to Webb in an extensive analysis elsewhere: see Grudem, EFBT, 350–57, 397–402, and 600–45.

2. Ibid., 91, italics added.

3. Ibid., 94–95.

4. David Thompson, "Women, Men, Slaves and the Bible," *Christian Scholars' Review* 25:3 (March, 1996), 326–49. For a more detailed response to Thompson's article, especially his hermeneutical principles and his approach to the authority of Scripture, see Grudem, "Asbury Professor," *CBMW News* 2:1 (Dec. 1996): 8–12 (also available at www.cmbw.org).

Sensing the direction of the canonical dialogue and prayerfully struggling with it, God's people conclude that they will most faithfully honor his Word by *accepting the target already anticipated in Scripture and toward which the Scriptural trajectory was heading* rather than the last entry in the Biblical conversation.... The canonical conversation at this point closed without final resolution. But *the trajectory was clearly set toward egalitarian relationships.*[5]

— Answer #1: This trajectory argument invalidates the Bible as our final authority.

Both France and Thompson admit that the New Testament authors did not teach the full inclusion of women in all forms of church leadership. As France says, the first-century situation "did not yet allow" this "fuller outworking of God's ultimate purpose," which they say should be our standard today.

But this means that the teachings of the New Testament are no longer our final authority. Our authority now becomes *our own ideas of the direction the New Testament was heading* but never quite reached.

— Answer #2: This trajectory argument denies the doctrine of Scripture and the principle of sola Scriptura as they have been believed in the major confessions of faith.

In order to guard against making our authority something other than the Bible, major confessions of faith have insisted that the words of God *in Scripture* are our authority, not some position arrived at after the Bible was finished. This is the Reformation doctrine of *sola Scriptura*, or "the Bible alone," as our ultimate authority for doctrine and life. The Westminster Confession of Faith says:

> The *whole counsel of God* concerning all things necessary for his own glory, man's salvation, faith and life, is either expressly set down in Scripture, or by good and necessary consequence may be deduced from Scripture: unto which nothing at any time is to be added, whether by new revelations of the Spirit, or traditions of men.[6]

---

5. Thompson, "Women, Men, Slaves and the Bible," 338–39.
6. Chapter 3, paragraph 6 (italics added).

More recently, the widely acknowledged "Chicago Statement on Biblical Inerrancy" said:

> We affirm that God's revelation in the Holy Scriptures was progressive. We deny that later revelation, which may fulfill earlier revelation, ever corrects or contradicts it. We further deny that any normative revelation has been given since the completion of the New Testament writings.[7]

But this trajectory position would have the later standard (the supposed "goal" to which the New Testament was headed) contradict earlier revelation (which limited certain roles in the church to men). It would have the "normative revelation" be, in effect, the developments in thought that occurred after the New Testament was completed. Thus this position is contrary to both the Westminster Confession of Faith and the "Chicago Statement on Biblical Inerrancy."

— Answer #3: This trajectory argument fails to understand the uniqueness of the New Testament in distinction from the Old Testament.

France argues that we already see change from the Old Testament to the New Testament, and within the New Testament we see the apostles gradually growing in their understanding of the way Gentiles can be fully included in the church (as in the Jerusalem Council in Acts 15).[8] So why should we not allow change beyond what is in the New Testament?

This view fails to recognize the uniqueness of the New Testament. Yes, the New Testament explicitly tells us that we are no longer under the regulations of the Old Covenant (Hebrews 8:6–13), so we have clear warrant for saying that the sacrificial laws and dietary laws are no longer binding on us. And we do see the apostles in a process of coming to understand the inclusion of the Gentiles in the church (Acts 15; Galatians 2:1–14; 3:28). But *that process was completed within the New Testament*, and the commands given to Christians in the New Testament say nothing about excluding Gentiles from the church. We do not have to progress on a "trajectory" beyond the New Testament to discover that.

Christians living in the time of Paul's epistles were living under the New

---

7. Article V, *Journal of the Evangelical Theological Society* 21:4 (Dec. 1978), 290–91. Italics added.
8. France, *Women in the Church's Ministry*, 17–19.

Covenant. And we Christians living today are also living under the New Covenant. This is "the new covenant in my blood" (1 Corinthians 11:25), which Jesus established and which we affirm every time we take the Lord's Supper. That means we are living in the same period in God's plan for "the history of redemption" as the first-century Christians. And that is why we can read and apply the New Testament directly to ourselves today.

To attempt to go beyond the New Testament documents and derive our authority from "where the New Testament was heading" is to reject the very documents God gave us to govern our life under the New Covenant until Christ returns.

— Answer #4: This trajectory argument is far different from later doctrinal formulations that were based on Scripture alone.

I agree that the church later formulated doctrines, such as the Trinity, that are not spelled out explicitly in the New Testament. But that is far different from what France and Thompson advocate, because Trinitarian doctrine was always *based on the actual teachings of the New Testament*, and its defenders always took the New Testament writings as their final authority. By contrast, France and Thompson do not take the New Testament statements as their final authority, but "go beyond" the New Testament to a "target" that *contradicts or nullifies* the restrictions on women's ministry given by Paul. No Trinitarian doctrine was ever built by saying we need a view that contradicts and denies what Paul wrote.[9]

— Answer #5: This trajectory argument is similar to the view of the Roman Catholic church, which bases doctrine not only on the Bible but also on the authoritative teachings of the church that have come after the Bible was written.

One of the distinctive differences between historic, orthodox Protestants and the Roman Catholic church has been that Protestants base doctrine on "Scripture

---

9. I. Howard Marshall, "Mutual Love and Submission in Marriage," in DBE, 186–204, takes a similar approach: "The raw materials for this deeper understanding [that is, mutual submission in marriage] are there in Scripture, but their full significance was not yet realized, just as we recognize that the doctrines of the Trinity and Christology were formulated only at a later point" (203). But he does not address the objection that these later doctrinal formulations did not nullify or contradict any statements or commands in the New Testament, as the mutual submission view would have us do with respect to the commands for wives to be subject to their husbands.

alone" (in Latin, *sola Scriptura*), while Catholics base doctrine on Scripture *plus* the authoritative teaching of the church through history. This trajectory argument of France and Thompson is disturbingly similar to Roman Catholicism in this regard, because Roman Catholics place final authority not in the New Testament writings, but in their ideas of where that teaching was leading. Yet a Roman Catholic could argue that more reliable than their *speculation* on where the teaching was leading are the *historical facts* of where the teaching did lead. So the trajectory (which actually was fulfilled in church history) would look like this:

FROM JESUS' TEACHINGS	TO PAUL'S TEACHINGS	TO THE FINAL TARGET FOR THIS TRAJECTORY	APPLICATION TODAY
No local church officers or governing structure mentioned	Increased authority given to elders and deacons	Worldwide authority given to the Pope, cardinals, and bishops	We should submit to the authority of the Pope and the Roman Catholic Church

The Reformation principle sola Scriptura was formulated to guard against the kind of procedure France and Thompson advocate, because the Reformers knew that once our authority becomes "Scripture plus some later developments" rather than "Scripture alone," the unique governing authority of Scripture in our lives is lost.

On several grounds, then, this trajectory argument must be rejected as inconsistent with the view that "all Scripture is breathed out by God" (2 Timothy 3:16), and

Every word of God proves true.…
Do not add to his words,
lest he rebuke you and you be found a liar. (Proverbs 30:5–6)

35

STOP FIGHTING ABOUT A MINOR ISSUE

⌐· EGALITARIAN CLAIM: This Is Not a Core Issue, and It Is Not a Major Doctrine. We Should Stop Fighting About This, Allow Different Views and Practices to Exist in the Church, and Get on with More Important Ministries to a Needy, Hurting, Lost World.

This objection is often heard when churches or organizations try to decide what their policy should be on men and women in the home and the church. This claim finds implicit voice in Ann Brown's statement:

Why are there so many interpretations of Paul's letters? Is the apostle's teaching so confused and contradictory? I do not believe that it is, though *we* may be confused in expecting to discover dogmatic answers to questions which were not asked in the New Testament. Paul did not share the same ideological concerns as his twentieth century readers.[1]

---

1. Ann Brown, *Apology to Women: Christian Images of the Female Sex*, 157. The need to stop fighting about a relatively unclear and unimportant issue is a major theme in Brown's book, as indicated by her quotation from Milton which appears on the inside cover of her book (with archaic spelling preserved). It reads:

    "Thus, they in mutual accusation spent / The fruitless hours, but neither self-condemning, / And of thir vain contest appeerd no end."

    Similarly, Sarah Sumner, *Men and Women in the Church*, tells complementarians and egalitarians to "stop playing tug-of-war with each other" and to cooperate, not compete against each other (321).

Regarding 1 Corinthians 14 and 1 Timothy 2, in answer to the question, "Why didn't Paul make it clearer?" Brown responds:

> I suspect that it is not clearer because it was not that important in the early church. Part of the problem is that we look at the New Testament through twentieth-century spectacles. I am not sure that the first-century church shared our preoccupation with ecclesiastical structures and status. Maybe they were too busy spreading the gospel to be concerned about precise job descriptions for women in their churches.[2]

— Answer #1: The basic question underlying this controversy is obedience to the Bible. That is a major doctrine and it is a core issue.

Throughout this book and throughout *Evangelical Feminism and Biblical Truth*, I have pointed out various ways in which egalitarian claims result in a rejection of the authority of the Bible over our lives.[3] This happens through saying that certain passages no longer apply to us today, or saying that certain verses are not really part of the Bible, or saying Paul's reasoning from the Old Testament was wrong, or saying that the reason for Paul's command was something other than what he gave as the reason, or saying that the New Testament epistles are descriptive rather than prescriptive (and show us what was happening in the first century, not what we should do today), or saying that people can disobey what the Bible says if the elders or pastor give them permission, or saying that what we should obey is not what the New Testament says but our best guess as to where its "trajectory" was leading, and so forth.

But this repeated theme in the egalitarian position shows that *what is really at stake in this controversy is the authority of the Bible.* I am convinced that if the egalitarian position prevails, the principles it has used to interpret and apply Scripture will soon be broadened to many other areas of life, and no moral command of Scripture will be safe from its destructive procedures. Then the church will simply mimic the popular views of its culture in one issue after another, and Christians

---

2. Ibid., 159.
3. For a more detailed discussion, see also Wayne Grudem, *Evangelical Feminism: A New Path to Liberalism?* (Wheaton: Crossway, 2006).

will no longer be subject to the authority of God speaking through His Word. I believe this is the direction egalitarianism is pushing the church. Therefore I believe this is an issue of major importance.

— Answer #2: The teaching of Scripture on men and women is not a minor or trivial issue, but has a massive effect on how we live our lives.

Is the teaching of the Bible on how men and women relate to each other in marriage a trivial issue? Is the teaching of the Bible about who should have authoritative leadership in the church a trivial issue? I do not believe so. The teaching of the Bible on men and women has a massive impact on marriages, families, and on children as they develop a sense of gender identity. And outside the realm of individual family life, feminism in our society, with its systematic denial of biblical roles for men and women, has had a massive impact in our educational system, our laws, our movies and TV and literature, our language, our military forces, our laws and expectations concerning sexual morality, and how we think of ourselves and relate to one another as men and women. Certainly some of these influences have been very good and have brought about needed change, but many other changes have not been good and have not been consistent with biblical teachings. Whether we agree or disagree about specific changes, this matter is anything but a minor issue or one without consequence. The issue has massive consequences.

In addition, the influence of evangelical feminist teaching in our churches has been very significant, because in many churches the eldership and the ordained pastorate have been opened to thousands of women. Whether someone agrees with this change or not, the change is anything but minor or trivial. And I believe we will see increasingly significant consequences from this change. Over the next decade or two, I believe that including women as pastors and elders in evangelical churches will bring harmful effects as churches become more and more "feminized," resulting in a massive loss in male membership and male participation.[4]

This has already happened in liberal Protestant denominations that adopted egalitarian views in the 1960s and 1970s. Leon Podles quotes several studies showing this trend:

---

4. For extensive documentation for how this has happened in liberal Protestant churches and Roman Catholic churches, see Leon J. Podles, *The Church Impotent: The Feminization of Christianity* (Dallas: Spence Publishing, 1999).

Lyle E. Schaller, an authority on church growth, observes that "In 1952 the adult attenders on Sunday morning in the typical Methodist, Presbyterian, Episcopal, Lutheran, Disciples, or Congregational worship service were approximately 53 percent female and 47 percent male, almost exactly the same as the distribution of the adult population. By 1986...these ratios were closer to 60 percent female and 40 percent male with many congregations reporting a 67–37 or 65–35 ratio." In 1992, 43 percent of men attended church, in 1996 only 28 percent. Patrick Arnold...notes, "some liberal Presbyterian or Methodist congregations are practically bereft of men." Kenneth Woodward reports that Protestant pastors "say that women usually outnumber the men three to one."[5]

— Answer #3: If we allow different views and practices on this issue to exist in the church, we are essentially admitting that both views are right. But that is all egalitarians want–at least until they attain majority control, and then the complementarian view is not allowed.

The plea that we should allow different views and practices to exist in the church is essentially a plea to stop saying that the egalitarian view is wrong and contrary to Scripture. But if we are convinced that it *is wrong*, and that it *is contrary to Scripture*, then we cannot support any policy that says we should allow both views and practices to exist in church and just get along with our differences.

There are some doctrines on which Christians can "agree to disagree," such as details about the end times, and go on ministering together in the same church. Christians can differ on issues such as these *because they do not involve a rejection of the authority of Scripture on either side* and also *because differences do not have any significant effect on how we live or on how our church functions.*

But neither of those things is true with the question of women's roles in the church. As I mentioned in the previous section, it seems to me that the authority of Scripture *is* at stake in this controversy. And either a church has women elders or it does not. Either it allows women to be ordained as pastors or it does not. You cannot have it both ways. For example, if a church were to ordain "a few" women as elders, the egalitarian position would have won, because this action would establish the validity of having women as elders.

5. Ibid., 11–12.

I have also observed a regular pattern in which egalitarians first gain acceptance for their view, and then promote it more and more, and then force out the complementarians who still differ with them. I have seen this pattern, for example, in the United Presbyterian Church—USA, in which the ordination of women was approved in 1956 (in the North) and 1964 (in the South), but then in 1974 the denomination decided that it would require all candidates for ordination *to agree that they would participate in the ordination of women.*[6]

In a similar way, Willow Creek Community Church in South Barrington, Illinois, from at least 1997 has required that all members be willing to "joyfully sit under the teaching of women teachers at Willow Creek" and "joyfully submit to the leadership of women in various leadership positions at Willow Creek."[7]

So I am not persuaded that "allowing different views and practices to exist in the church" is where the egalitarian position will ultimately lead. In practice, it often leads to the exclusion of the other view.[8]

— Answer #4: When people say we should "stop fighting," it implies that complementarians are doing something wrong when we criticize egalitarians. But people who promote false doctrine will always say, "Let's stop fighting about this topic," because they want to stop the criticism.

It is not surprising that egalitarians say that Christians should "stop fighting" about this question, because to stop fighting means that any criticism of their view will be silenced, and their view will gain acceptance in the church. By calling the criticism of their view "fighting," they imply that the critics are doing wrong (for who wants to support fighting?). But using the term "fighting" is just giving a negative spin to what may well be very healthy and godly criticism of an incorrect position.

---

6. See more information in Grudem, EFBT, 379–80. See also Lois A. Boyd and R. Douglas Brackenridge, *Presbyterian Women in America* (Westport, Conn.: Greenwood Press, 1996), 138–39.

7. These quotations are from p. 3 of "The Elders' Response to the Most Frequently Asked Questions About Membership at Willow Creek," a paper distributed by the church and quoted in Wayne Grudem, "Willow Creek Enforces Egalitarianism," in *CBMW News* 2:5 (December 1997): 1.

8. Someone could object that complementarians likewise eventually exclude egalitarians from influence in their churches. This does happen eventually, but often after a long period of allowing different views to be studied and taught. This is probably inevitable because the two views are mutually exclusive and only one side's position can be implemented (either a church has women elders or it does not). My own position is that the complementarian position is the right one and should be incorporated into governing documents of churches. At that point it takes on a status like other doctrines a church affirms, such as believer's baptism, for example. It is not that people can't read books and hear speakers who hold another view, but people who hold another view will not be given leadership roles in the church.

OKAY IF UNDER THE AUTHORITY OF PASTOR AND ELDERS

⌐· EGALITARIAN CLAIM: If a Woman Is Teaching "Under The Authority of the Pastor or Elders," She May Teach the Scriptures to the Assembled Congregation.

This position is found frequently in evangelical churches. Many people who hold this position say they genuinely want to uphold male leadership in the church, and they say they are doing so when the woman teaches "under the authority of the elders," who are men (or of the pastor, who is a man).

This is not a commonly held view among egalitarian authors, for they do not think that only men should be elders, or that women need any approval from men to teach the Bible. But this view is often stated in phone calls or e-mails to the Council on Biblical Manhood and Womanhood office (www.cbmw.org), and I often hear it in personal conversations and discussions of church policies.

Is it true that a woman is obeying the Bible if she preaches a sermon "under the authority of the pastor and elders"?

— Answer #1: Pastors and elders cannot give someone permission to disobey the Bible.

The question here is, what does the Bible say? It does not merely say, "Preserve some kind of male authority in the congregation." It does not say, "A woman may

226

not teach men *unless she is under the authority of the elders.*" Rather, it says, "I do not permit a woman to teach or to exercise authority over a man" (1 Timothy 2:12).

Can a pastor or the elders of a church rightfully give a woman permission to disobey this statement of Scripture? Certainly not! Should a woman do what the Bible says *not* to do and excuse it by saying "I'm under the authority of the elders"? No.

Would we say that the elders of a church could tell people "under their authority" that they have permission to disobey *other* passages of Scripture? What would we think of someone who said, "I'm going to rob a bank today because I need money, and my pastor has given me permission, and I'm under his authority"? We would dismiss that statement as ridiculous, but it highlights the general principle that *no pastor or church elder or bishop or any other church officer has the authority to give people permission to disobey God's Word.*

Someone may answer, "But we are respecting the Bible's *general principle* of male headship in the church." But Paul did not say, "*Respect the general principle of male headship* in your church." He said, "*I do not permit a woman to teach or to exercise authority over a man*" (1 Timothy 2:12). We do not have the right to change what the Bible says and then obey some new "general principle of the Bible" we have made up.

Nor do we have the right to take a specific teaching of Scripture and abstract some general principle from it (such as a principle of "male headship") and then say that principle gives us the right *to disobey the specific commands of Scripture* that fall under that principle. We are not free to abstract general principles from the Bible however we wish and then invent opinions about how those principles will apply in our situations. Such a procedure would allow people to evade any command of Scripture they were uncomfortable with. We would become a law unto ourselves, no longer subject to the authority of God's Word.

— Answer #2: To add "unless you are under the authority of your elders" to any of Paul's directions to churches would empty Paul's commands of their divine authority and reduce them to the level of advice that Paul hoped people would follow most of the time.

We could try this same procedure with some other passages. Would we think it right to say that the Bible teaches that men should pray "without anger or quarreling, *unless they quarrel under the authority of the elders*"? Or that women should adorn themselves "with modesty and self-control, *unless the elders give them permission to dress immodestly*"? Or would we say that those who are "rich in this present age" should "be generous and ready to share, *unless the elders give them permission to be stingy and miserly*"? (See 1 Timothy 6:17–19.)

But if we would not add "unless the elders give permission to do otherwise under their authority" to any of the other commands in Scripture, neither should we add that evasion to 1 Timothy 2:12.

— Answer #3: This answer actually results in no differences between men and women regarding teaching the Bible to men.

If a woman says, "I will teach the Bible to men only when I am under the authority of the elders," she has become no different from men who teach the Bible. No man in any church should teach the Bible publicly unless he also is under the authority of the elders (or pastor, or other church officers) in that church. The general principle is that anyone who does Bible teaching in a church should be subject to the established governing authority in that church, whether it is a board of elders, a board of deacons, a church governing council, or the church board. Both men and women alike are subject to that requirement. Therefore this "under the authority of the elders" position essentially says there is no difference between what men can do and what women can do in teaching the Bible to men.

Do we really think that is what Paul meant? Do we really think that Paul did not mean to say anything *that applied only to women* when he said, "I do not permit a woman to teach or to exercise authority over a man" (1 Timothy 2:12)?[1]

---

1. For a response to another egalitarian objection, "We are not a church but a parachurch organization, so we don't have to follow Paul's instructions in 1 Timothy 2," see Grudem, EFBT, pp. 384–92, and Grudem, *Evangelical Feminism: A New Path to Liberalism?*, pp. 107–13. All of the NT epistles were written to churches or to people in churches, so if we don't have to obey commands written to churches in the NT, we would not have to obey anything written in the epistles! Surely this argument is not correct.

PART NINE

EVANGELICAL FEMINIST CLAIMS FROM THEOLOGY AND FROM IDEAS OF FAIRNESS AND JUSTICE

We have considered many egalitarian claims concerning marriage and the church in part 8, but in the end none of them are persuasive in their attempts to overturn the vision we saw in chapters 1 and 2 of our equality and differences as men and women created in the image of God.

Some egalitarian claims are based on theological doctrines or on the general ideas of fairness and justice. For instance, is the complementarian claim about parallels of subordination within the Trinity really valid? Might there not be a kind of "mutual submission" among the members of the Trinity? And wasn't Jesus' submission to His Father only for His time on the earth in any case? With regard to questions of fairness, is it really fair to allow women to assume leadership roles on the mission field but prohibit them from taking these same roles here in the United States?

It is questions such as these that we consider next.

37

NO ETERNAL SUBMISSION OF THE SON

⌐· EGALITARIAN CLAIM: Complementarians Mistakenly Appeal to the Son Being Subject to the Father Within the Trinity. This Subjection Existed Only During Jesus' Life on Earth and Did Not Exist Eternally Within the Trinity.

This objection to a parallel (discussed above, pp. 27–28) between the Father-Son relationship and the husband-wife relationship occurs several times in egalitarian writings. Gilbert Bilezikian claims:

It is much more appropriate, and theologically accurate, to speak of Christ's self-humiliation rather than of his subordination. Nobody subordinated him, and he was originally subordinated to no one....

The frame of reference for every term that is found in Scripture to describe Christ's humiliation pertains to his ministry and not to his eternal state....

Because there was no order of subordination within the Trinity prior to the Second Person's incarnation, there will remain no such thing after its completion. If we must talk of subordination it is only a functional or economic subordination that pertains exclusively to Christ's role in relation to human history.[1]

---

1. Gilbert Bilezikian, *Community 101*, 190–91.

Rebecca Groothuis writes:

> It is by no means clear from Scripture that the members of the Godhead are related to one another in terms of an eternal structure of rule and submission. This is a debatable point of theology on which conservative scholars disagree.[2]

— Answer #1: There is substantial testimony in Scripture that the Son was subject to the Father before He came to live on earth.

Scripture frequently speaks of the Father-Son relationship within the Trinity, a relationship in which the Father "gave" His only Son (John 3:16) and "sent" the Son into the world (John 3:17, 34; 4:34; 8:42; Galatians 4:4). But if the Father shows His great love by the fact that He gave His Son, then He had to *be* Father *before* He could give His Son. The Son did not suddenly decide to become Son on the day He came to earth. The Trinity was not just Person A and Person B and Person C before Christ came to earth, for then there would have been no Father who could give and send His Son. The idea of giving His Son implies a headship, a unique authority for the Father *before* the Son came to earth. So even on the basis of John 3:16, the egalitarian claim that Jesus' submission to His Father was only during His time on earth is incorrect.

But the Father-Son relationship also existed *before* creation.[3] The Father created through the Son, for "all things were made *through* him" (John 1:3), and "there is one God, the Father, *from* whom are all things…and one Lord, Jesus Christ, *through* whom are all things" (1 Corinthians 8:6). The Bible tells us that in these last days God "has spoken to us by his Son, whom he appointed the heir of all things, *through whom* also he created the world" (Hebrews 1:2). When the Bible discusses distinct actions of the members of the Trinity in creation, this is the pattern: Things were made "by" or "from" the Father and "through" the Son. But this also means that *before* creation, the Father was Father and the Son was Son.

---

2. Rebecca Groothuis, *Good News for Women*, 57.
3. Kevin Giles, *The Trinity and Subordinationism: The Doctrine of God and the Contemporary Gender Debate*, incorrectly says that complementarians only argue from revelation concerning the Incarnation when they argue for the eternal subordination of the Son (17).

The Father had to *have* a Son before He could create a world *through* His Son. This means that they related as Father and Son before creation. Again, the egalitarian claim that limits the Son's submission to the Incarnation[4] is incorrect.

In some places the Bible speaks of different roles for Father and Son *before* creation. It was the Father who "predestined" us to be conformed to the image of His Son (Romans 8:29; compare 1 Peter 1:2). But if He "predestined" us to be like His Son, then in the counsels of eternity in which predestination occurred, there had to be a Father who was predestining and a Son whom He decided we would be like. Paul also says that God the Father "chose us" in the Son *"before the foundation of the world"* (Ephesians 1:4). This means that before there was any creation, before anything existed except God Himself, the Father was the one who chose, who initiated and planned, and, before creation, it was already decided that the Son would be the one to come to earth in obedience to the Father and die for our sins. Here is Paul's statement:

> Blessed be the God and Father of our Lord Jesus Christ, who has blessed us in Christ with every spiritual blessing in the heavenly places, even as he chose us in him *before the foundation of the world,* that we should be holy and blameless before him. In love he *predestined* us for adoption through Jesus Christ, according to the purpose of his will. (Ephesians 1:3–5)

Once again, the egalitarian claim that the Son's subordination to the Father was only for His time on earth is surely incorrect.

Bruce Ware adds a similar consideration from Revelation 13:8, which says, "And all who dwell on earth will worship [the beast], everyone whose name has not been written before the foundation of the world in the book of life of the Lamb that was slain." Ware writes:

> Revelation 13:8 likewise indicates that "the book of life" in which believers' names have been recorded is (1) "from the *foundation of the world,*" and (2) is "of the *Lamb who has been slain.*" Again we see clear evidence that the Father's purpose from eternity past was to send His Son, the Lamb of God,

---

4. The word "Incarnation" refers to Christ's taking to Himself a human nature, like ours but free from sin.

by which His own would be saved. The authority-obedience relation of Father and Son in the immanent Trinity is mandatory if we are to account for God the Father's eternal purpose to elect and save His people through His beloved Son.[5]

How do egalitarians answer these verses that show an eternal difference in role between the Father and Son before the world began? They ignore them. Most egalitarians who deny an eternal subordination of the Son to the Father do not treat these verses at all.

— **Answer #2: Christ was also subject to the authority of the Father while He was on earth as a man.**

While Jesus was on earth, He was obedient to the commands of the Father, as many passages indicate.[6] In several of these verses there are also indications of a prior authority of the Father, an authority that reaches back before the Incarnation and indicates an eternal Father-Son relationship. Jesus says, "The Father is greater than I" (John 14:28). He says, "My food is to do the will of him who sent me and to accomplish his work" (John 4:34). He says, "I have come down from heaven, not to do my own will but the will of him who sent me" (John 6:38). But this means that prior to the Incarnation, there was a will of the Father that directed and guided what the Son would do when He came to earth.

Jesus also says, "The Father judges no one, but has given all judgment to the Son" (John 5:22). But if the Father *gave* the Son this authority to judge, then it had to be the Father's to give. There had to be a prior authority on the part of the Father, greater than the authority of the Son, by which the Father could have the ability and right to give judgment to the Son. One has to *have* authority before one can *delegate* authority. Similarly, Jesus says, "Truly, truly, I say to you, the Son can do nothing of his own accord, but only what he sees the Father doing. For whatever the Father does, that the Son does likewise" (John 5:19). Even when the Son prays to the Father and the Father grants what the Son asks (as in John

---

5. Ware, "Tampering with the Trinity: Does the Son Submit to His Father?" in *Biblical Foundations for Manhood and Womanhood,* ed. Wayne Grudem (Wheaton, IL: Crossway Books, 2002), 250.

6. Bruce Ware, for example, notes the following passages that indicate that Christ was sent to do the will of His Father: John 4:34; 5:23, 30, 37; 6:37–38, 57; 12:49 (Ware, "Tampering with the Trinity," 245).

14:16), the relationship is the same, for the Son asks, and it is the Father's decision to grant or not to grant what is asked.

— Answer #3: After Christ returned to heaven, He was still subject to the authority of the Father, and will be so forever.

In the future, the Son will be subject to the Father for all eternity. This is contrary to Gilbert Bilezikian's claim, "Because there was no order of subordination within the Trinity prior to the Second Person's incarnation, there will remain no such thing after its completion."[7] This is a baffling statement. It is baffling, first, because it talks about "no order of subordination within the Trinity prior to the Second Person's incarnation," but Bilezikian does not deal with any of those texts that speak of the Father predestining us in the Son or choosing us in the Son even "before the foundation of the world" (see above). How he can say "there was no order of subordination within the Trinity prior to the Second Person's incarnation" without dealing with those verses is unclear to me.

Bilezikian's statement is also baffling because it says "there will remain no such thing after its completion." But what could Bilezikian mean by speaking of a time "after its completion" (that is, after the completion of the Incarnation)? If he means after Jesus returned to heaven in Acts 1, then many verses contradict him, for they say that Jesus ascended into heaven and assumed a place at the Father's right hand, which implies being subject to the Father's authority (for example, "Being therefore exalted *at the right hand of God*, and having received from the Father the promise of the Holy Spirit, he has poured out this that you yourselves are seeing and hearing," Acts 2:33; see more verses below). But if by the phrase "after its completion" Bilezikian means a time after Jesus ceases to be both fully man and fully God, then he has a strange view indeed of the Incarnation, for Scripture gives no indication that Jesus will ever cease to be both God and man: "Jesus Christ is the same yesterday and today and forever" (Hebrews 13:8). Jesus will remain both truly God and truly man forever, and it is troubling to see Bilezikian suggest otherwise, as if he thinks Christ's Incarnation will sometime come to an end.

There is much evidence in Scripture that after Christ returned to heaven, He was still subject to the authority of the Father. For example, the author of

---

7. Bilezikian, *Community 101*, 191.

Hebrews says, "After making purification for sins, he sat down at the *right hand* of the Majesty on high" (Hebrews 1:3). To sit at the king's right hand in the ancient world indicated that one was second only to the king in authority, but it did not indicate authority equal to the king. For example, when the mother of James and John came to Jesus and asked, "Say that these two sons of mine are to sit, one at your right hand and one at your left, in your kingdom" (Matthew 20:21), she was not asking that they have authority equal to Jesus, but only that they be second to Him in authority. Jesus told James and John that that decision belonged to God the Father:

> He said to them, "You will drink my cup, but to sit at my right hand and at my left is not mine to grant, but it is for those for whom it has been prepared by my Father." (Matthew 20:23)[8]

Why is this important? Because it shows that someone can be subordinate in authority to someone else but still be equal in being, equal in importance, equal in personhood. And if the Father and Son can be both equal and different in this way, then husband and wife in the image of God can be equal and different too. And thus the fundamental egalitarian objection, "If different, then not equal, and if equal, then not different," falls apart. This is why the debate about the Trinity is so important to this whole controversy.[9]

The promise that Jesus would sit at the Father's right hand is fulfilled after Jesus completes His work dying for us and rising from the dead. It is interesting to see how many times the Bible affirms that after Jesus' return to heaven He is still at the right hand of the Father, and therefore subordinate to the authority of the Father:

> Being therefore exalted *at the right hand of God*, and having *received from the Father* the promise of the Holy Spirit, he has poured out this that you yourselves are seeing and hearing. (Acts 2:33)

---

8. See also Psalm 45:9: The queen is at the "right hand" of the king.
9. Over twenty-five years ago I wrote, "A proper understanding of the doctrine of the Trinity may well turn out to be the most decisive factor in finally deciding this current debate" (Grudem, review of George Knight, *The New Testament Teaching on the Role Relationship of Men and Women*, for the *Journal of the Evangelical Theological Society* 22:4 [December 1979]: 375–76).

God exalted him *at his right hand* as Leader and Savior, to give repentance to Israel and forgiveness of sins. (Acts 5:31)

Who is to condemn? Christ Jesus is the one who died—more than that, who was raised—who is *at the right hand of God*, who indeed is interceding for us. (Romans 8:34)

If then you have been raised with Christ, seek the things that are above, where Christ is, seated *at the right hand of God.* (Colossians 3:1)

He is the radiance of the glory of God and the exact imprint of his nature, and he upholds the universe by the word of his power. After making purification for sins, he sat down *at the right hand of the Majesty on high.* (Hebrews 1:3)

Looking to Jesus, the founder and perfecter of our faith, who for the joy that was set before him endured the cross, despising the shame, and is seated *at the right hand of the throne of God.* (Hebrews 12:2)

Who has gone into heaven and is *at the right hand of God*, with angels, authorities, and powers having been subjected to him. (1 Peter 3:22)

Nowhere is this pattern reversed. Nowhere is it said that the Father sits at the Son's right hand. Nowhere does the Son give the Father the authority to sit with Him on His throne. The supreme authority always belongs to the Father. The egalitarian claim that Jesus was subject to the Father only during His life on earth is simply wrong.

Gilbert Bilezikian objects that other verses show the Son sitting *with* the Father on His throne.[10] This is true, as we see stated in various ways in the following verses:

"The one who conquers, I will grant him to sit with me on my throne, as I also conquered and sat down with my Father on his throne." (Revelation 3:21)

---

10. A similar objection is made by Sarah Sumner, *Men and Women in the Church*, 175.

"For the Lamb in the midst of the throne will be their shepherd, and he will guide them to springs of living water, and God will wipe away every tear from their eyes." (Revelation 7:17)

But these verses do not contradict the other verses that show Jesus at the right hand of God. Revelation 3:21 gives the answer: Just as we will sit *with* Christ on His throne, but He will still have the supreme authority, so Christ sits with the Father on His throne, but the Father still has supreme authority. (Bilezikian does not quote the first half of Revelation 3:21, which disproves his argument.) Both facts are true: Jesus sits with the Father on His throne, and Jesus is still at the right hand of the Father and the throne can still be called "his [that is, the Father's] throne." Similarly, Revelation 7, which refers to "the Lamb in the midst of the throne" (v. 17), also can say, "Salvation belongs to our God who sits on the throne, and to the Lamb!" (v. 10).

In addition to these there are passages that say that Christ in heaven "intercedes" for us—that is, He brings requests on our behalf to the Father:

Who is to condemn? Christ Jesus is the one who died—more than that, who was raised—who is at the right hand of God, who indeed *is interceding for us.* (Romans 8:34)

Consequently, he is able to save to the uttermost those who draw near to God through him, since *he always lives to make intercession for them.* (Hebrews 7:25)

These passages also indicate that the Father has greater authority than the Son, for the Son does not command the Father; rather, He brings requests, and these actions are appropriate to a relationship in which the Father is the one in authority over the Son.

The very names "Father" and "Son" also attest to this, and those names have belonged to the Father and the Son forever. From eternity past to infinite eternity future the Son is subject to the Father's authority yet equal to Him in being, in value, in personhood, and in honor. Similarly in marriage as God created it, husbands and wives are equal in value and personhood, and should be equally honored as bearers of the image of God, but wives are also to be subject to the authority of their husbands. Equal *and* different. (See answer #7 below, pp. 246–50, on the failure of egalitarians to deal with these verses.)

— Answer #4: The Son will forever be subject to the authority of the Father.

The authority of the Father over the Son (and the Holy Spirit), an authority that never began but was always part of the eternal relationship among the members of the Trinity, will also never end. Paul tells us that after the last enemy, death, is destroyed, "the Son himself will also be subjected to him who put all things in subjection under him, that God may be all in all" (1 Corinthians 15:28).

Does this mean that the Son is eternally inferior to the Father? No, He is equal to the Father in His being or essence, for He is fully God. It simply means that along with equality in attributes and deity and value and honor, there is also a subordination in role, and the Son is subject to the Father's authority.

This relationship between Father and Son that is seen in so many passages is never reversed, not in predestination before the foundation of the world, not in creation, not in sending the Son, not in directing what the Son would do, not in granting authority to the Son, not in the Son's work of redemption, not in the Son's return to sit at the Father's right hand, not in the Son's handing over the kingdom to God the Father, never. Never does Scripture say that the Son sends the Father into the world, or that the Holy Spirit sends the Father or the Son into the world, or that the Father obeys the commands of the Son or the Holy Spirit. Never does Scripture say that the Son predestined us to be conformed to the image of the Father. The role of planning, directing, sending, and commanding the Son belongs to the Father only.

And just as Father and Son are equal and different, so God has made husband and wife to be equal and different.

— Answer #5: The Christian church throughout history has affirmed both the subordination of the Son to the Father with respect to their roles, and the equality of the Son with the Father with respect to their being.

It is not responsible scholarship, nor is it fair to readers who may have little knowledge of church history, for Gilbert Bilezikian to claim that the position he holds is the historical doctrine of the Trinity, for it is not. Bilezikian first denies any subordination of the Son to the Father prior to the Incarnation:

Because there was no order of subordination within the Trinity prior to the Second Person's incarnation, there will remain no such thing after its completion. If we must talk of subordination it is only a functional or economic subordination that pertains exclusively to Christ's role in relation to human history.

Then he says:

Except for occasional and predictable deviations, *this is the historical Biblical trinitarian doctrine* that has been defined in the creeds and generally defended by the Church, at least the western Church, throughout the centuries.[11]

But when Bilezikian denies the eternal subordination of the Son to the Father (which exists along with equality in essence or being), he is denying the teaching of the church throughout history, and it is significant that he gives no quotations, no evidence, to support his claim that his view "is the historical Biblical trinitarian doctrine." This statement is simply not true. The vast majority of the church has affirmed equality in being *and* subordination in role among the persons in the Trinity, not simply during the time of Incarnation, but in the eternal relationships between the Father and the Son. The great, historic creeds affirm that there is an eternal difference between the Father and Son, not in their being (for they are equal in all attributes, and the three persons are just one "being" or "substance"), but in the way they relate to one another.

There is an ordering of their relationships such that the Father eternally is first, the Son second, and the Holy Spirit third.

The doctrine of the "eternal generation of the Son" or the "eternal begetting of the Son" found expression in the Nicene Creed (AD 325) in the phrase "begotten of the Father before all worlds," and in the Chalcedonian Creed (AD 451) in the phrase "begotten before all ages of the Father according to the Godhead." In the Athanasian Creed (4th–5th century AD) we read the expressions "The Son is of the Father alone: not made, nor created: but begotten" and "the Son of God

---

11. Bilezikian, *Community 101*, 191–92. For a discussion of the claims of Kevin Giles in his book *The Trinity and Subordinationism*, see answer #7 below, pp. 246–50.

is…God, of the Substance of the Father; begotten before the worlds." It is open to discussion whether these were the most helpful expressions,[12] but it is not open to discussion whether the entire church throughout history has in these creeds affirmed that there was an *eternal* difference between the way the Son related to the Father and the way the Father related to the Son; that in their relationships the Father's role was primary and had priority, and the Son's role was secondary and was responsive to the Father; and that the Father was eternally Father and the Son was eternally Son.

We may describe this difference in relationship in other terms, as later theologians did (such as speaking of the eternal subordination of the Son with respect to role or relationship, not with respect to substance), and still say we are holding to the historic Trinitarian doctrine of the church. Yet we may not deny that there is *any* eternal difference in relationship between the Father and the Son, as Bilezikian and others do, and still claim to hold to the historic Trinitarian doctrine of the church.

Bilezikian gives no explanation of how he understands "begotten of the Father before all worlds" or "eternal generation" or "eternal begetting." It is remarkable that Bilezikian, in denying *any* eternal difference in relationship between the Father and the Son, gives no explanation for why he thinks he has not placed himself outside the bounds of the great Trinitarian confessions through history. And it is simply irresponsible scholarship to accuse all those who hold to the historic doctrine of the eternal subordination of the Son to the Father (in role, not in being) of "tampering with the doctrine of the Trinity" and coming close to Arianism and engaging in "hermeneutical bungee jumping."[13] It is Bilezikian, not complementarians, who is tampering with the doctrine of the Trinity. Bilezikian is certainly free to deny any eternal differences in the Father-Son relationship if he wishes, but he may not truthfully say that a denial of these eternal differences has been the historic doctrine of the church.

Here is a sampling of these creeds and the relevant expressions from them:

---

12. For further discussion of the phrase "only begotten" and the Greek term *monogenēs* on which it is based, see Grudem, "The *Monogenēs* Controversy: 'Only' or 'Only Begotten'?" Appendix 6 in *Systematic Theology*, 1233–34. (This appendix is in the revised printing only, from 2000 onward.)

13. For these accusations see Bilezikian, "Hermeneutical Bungee-Jumping," JETS 40/1 (March, 1997), 57–68. The same article is found in Bilezikian, *Community 101*, 187–202.

NICENE CREED (AD 325/381):

And in one Lord Jesus Christ, the only-begotten Son of God, *begotten of the Father before all worlds*, Light of Light, very God of very God, begotten, not made, being of one substance with the Father...and ascended into heaven, and sitteth on the right hand of the Father

CHALCEDONIAN CREED (AD 451):

begotten before all ages of the Father according to the Godhead

ATHANASIAN CREED (4TH–5TH CENTURY AD):

The Son is of the Father alone: not made, nor created: but begotten.... Our Lord Jesus Christ, the Son of God, is God and Man; God, of the Substance of the Father; *begotten before the worlds*: and Man, of the Substance of his Mother, born in the world.... He sitteth on the right hand of the Father God Almighty

THIRTY-NINE ARTICLES (CHURCH OF ENGLAND, 1571):

The Son, which is the Word of the Father, *begotten from everlasting of the Father*, the very and eternal God, and of one substance with the Father

WESTMINSTER CONFESSION OF FAITH (1643–46):

The Father is of none, neither begotten, nor proceeding; *the Son is eternally begotten of the Father* (chapter 2, paragraph 3)

Bilezikian quotes no church historians, no creeds, no other recognized theologians when he affirms that his view is the historic doctrine of the church. But it is not difficult to find many theologians and historians of doctrine who differ with Bilezikian's unsubstantiated affirmation. For example, concerning this inter-Trinitarian relationship between the Father and the Son, Charles Hodge (1797–1878), the great Princeton theologian whose monumental *Systematic Theology* has now been in print for 140 years, wrote about the Nicene Creed:

The Nicene doctrine includes…the principle of the subordination of the Son to the Father, and of the Spirit to the Father and the Son. But this subordination does not imply inferiority…. The subordination intended is only that which concerns the mode of subsistence and operation…. The creeds are nothing more than a well-ordered arrangement of the facts of Scripture which concern the doctrine of the Trinity. They assert the distinct personality of the Father, Son, and Spirit…*and their consequent perfect equality*; and *the subordination of the Son to the Father, and of the Spirit to the Father and the Son, as to the mode of subsistence and operation.* These are scriptural facts, to which the creeds in question add nothing; and it is *in this sense they have been accepted by the Church universal.*[14]

The section in the Nicene Creed to which Hodge refers is this:

And in one Lord Jesus Christ, the *only-begotten Son of God, begotten of the Father before all worlds,* Light of Light, very God *of very God, begotten, not made,* being of one substance with the Father.

Hodge is saying that in the phrases "only-begotten Son of God," and "begotten of the Father before all worlds," and "of very God," and "begotten, not made," the Nicene Creed is referring to an *eternal* distinction in relationship between the Father and the Son such that the Son was seen to be eternally "of " or "from" the Father (the Father was not "of" or "from" the Son). The Father has eternally been Father and the Son has eternally been Son. The expressions "only-begotten" and "begotten, not made," indicated to the authors of the Nicene Creed that there was a difference in the relationship between Father and Son such that the Son was the one "begotten" by the Father. But this difference in their relationship *never began* ("begotten of the Father before all worlds"), and it did not mean that the Son was created or derived His being from the Father ("begotten, not made"), because the

---

14. Charles Hodge, *Systematic Theology* (3 vol. reprint edn.; Grand Rapids: Eerdmans, 1970; first published 1871–73), 1:460–62 (italics added). A survey of historical evidence showing affirmation of the eternal subordination of the Son to the authority of the Father is found in Stephen Kovach and Peter Schemm, "A Defense of the Doctrine of the Eternal Subordination of the Son," in *Journal of the Evangelical Theological Society* 42/3 (Sept., 1999), 461–76. See also Grudem, *Systematic Theology*, 248–52.

Father and Son are of the same substance or essence ("of one substance with the Father"). It simply meant that the Father and Son *related* as Father and Son for all eternity. But that means there was an eternal difference in their roles, and it implies that the Father eternally was the one who initiated, planned, and directed, and the Son was the one who eternally responded to the Father and agreed to carry out the will of the Father, as He subsequently did in creation and in redemption.

Other theologians in the history of the church have made similar affirmations, confirming Charles Hodge's statement that these concepts "have been accepted by the church universal."[15]

The eminent church historian Philip Schaff (1819–1893) wrote:

The Nicene fathers still teach, like their predecessors, a certain *subordinationism*,[16] which seems to conflict with the doctrine of consubstantiality. But we must distinguish between a subordinationism of essence (*ousia*) and a *subordinationism of hypostasis, of order and dignity.* The former was denied, the latter affirmed.[17]

Similarly, church historian Geoffrey Bromiley writes:

Eternal generation...is the phrase used to denote the inter-Trinitarian relationship between the Father and the Son as is taught by the Bible. "Generation" makes it plain that there is a divine sonship prior to the incarnation (cf. John 1:18; 1 John 4:9), that there is thus a distinction of persons within the one Godhead (John 5:26), and that between these persons *there is a superiority and subordination of order* (cf. John 5:19; 8:28). "Eternal" reinforces the fact that the generation is not merely economic (i.e. for the purpose of human salvation as in the incarnation, cf. Luke 1:35), but essential, and that as such it cannot be construed in the

---

15. Hodge, *Systematic Theology,* 1:462. For several other lengthy quotations by prominent theologians throughout history supporting this view, see Grudem, EFBT, 418–22.

16. Schaff uses *subordinationism* to refer not to the heresy by which the Son is thought to have an *inferior* being to the Father, but to the orthodox teaching that the Son has a subordinate *role* to the Father.

17. Philip Schaff, *History of the Christian Church* (reprint edn.; Grand Rapids: Eerdmans, 1971; originally published 1910), 3:681.

categories of natural or human generation. Thus it does not imply a time when the Son was not, as Arianism argued.... Nor does his subordination imply inferiority.... The phrase...corresponds to what God has shown us of himself in his own eternal being.... It finds creedal expression in the phrases "begotten of his Father before all worlds" (Nicene) and "begotten before the worlds" (Athanasian).[18]

This then has been the historic doctrine of the church. Egalitarians may differ with this doctrine today if they wish, and they may attempt to persuade us that they are right if they wish, but they must do this on the basis of arguments from Scripture, and they should also have the honesty and courtesy to explain to readers why they now feel it necessary to differ with the historic doctrine of the church as expressed in its major creeds.

— Answer #6: But the Son was also fully God. Therefore the very nature of the Trinitarian God shows that equality in personhood and value and abilities can exist along with being subject to the authority of another.

The subjection of the Son to the Father for all eternity, a subjection that never began but always existed, and a subjection that will continue eternally in the future, does not nullify the full deity of the Son. The Bible is very clear that the Son is fully God (see John 1:1–3; John 10:30; Romans 9:5; Titus 2:13; Hebrews 1:3, 8–10). Therefore the Son is both subject to the authority of the Father and at the same time equal to the Father in every attribute and in value and personhood forever. Equality in being and eternal differences in role exist together in the Trinity. Therefore equality in being and in value and in honor can exist together with differences in roles between husband and wife as well.

Sarah Sumner at first seems to affirm the orthodox doctrine of the subordination of the Son to the Father,[19] but then she modifies it with a novel proposal:

So then, to whom is Christ finally subjected? God. Christ the Son is subject to the triune God of three persons. The Son is subjected to "the God

---

18. Geoffrey W. Bromiley, "Eternal Generation," in *EDT*, ed. Walter Elwell, 368; see also J. N. D. Kelly, *Early Christian Doctrines*, 2nd edn. (New York: Harper and Row, 1960), 263.
19. Sarah Sumner, *Men and Women in the Church*, 177.

and Father." And in that sense, the Son is subjected to himself. This is the doctrine of the Trinity.[20]

But this is not the doctrine of the Trinity. It sounds more like ancient modalism (the view that there is only one person in God) than Trinitarianism.[21] We should not understand the doctrine of the Trinity in a way that denies the distinctions between the Persons or that prevents us from saying that one Person in the Trinity does something the others do not do.

The Bible simply does not speak the way Sumner does. The Father did not send *Himself* into the world to become man and die for our sins; He sent the Son. The Father did not *Himself* bear the penalty for our sins (which is the ancient heresy of *patripassianism*, one form of modalism), nor did the Holy Spirit, but the Son did. The Son did not pray to *Himself*; He prayed to the Father. The Son does not sit at the right hand of *Himself* but at the right hand of the Father.

And (contrary to Sumner) the Son is not subjected to *Himself*; He is subjected to the Father. To deny these distinctions is to deny that there are different persons in the Trinity, and thus it is to deny the Trinity.

This misunderstanding carries over into Sumner's statement about wives submitting to their husbands: She says, "the paradox of their oneness means that in submitting to her husband (with whom she is one), the wife ends up submitting to herself." She claims this is parallel to "Christ's submission to himself."[22] But Paul says husbands should love their wives "*as* their own bodies" (that is, in the same way as they love their own bodies),[23] and this is not because a husband's wife is

---

20. Ibid., 178. She returns to a similar theme later when she appeals to the doctrine of *perichoresis* or *circumincession* and says, "Circumincession also affirms that the action of one of the persons of the Trinity is also fully the action of the other two persons" (289n10). But Sumner misunderstands this doctrine. The term refers to the mutual indwelling of the persons of the Trinity in one another, and it may be used to affirm that the action of one person is the action of the being of God, but it should never be understood to deny that there are some things that one person of the Trinity does that the other persons do not do.

21. Modalism is also called modalistic monarchianism. See Craig Blaising, "Monarchianism," *EDT*, 727; also Grudem, *Systematic Theology*, 242.

22. Sumner, *Men and Women in the Church*, 198.

23. Ephesians 5:28. Greek *hōs* here is best understood to tell the manner in which husbands should love their wives. When Paul says later in that same verse, "He who loves his wife loves himself," he does not mean, "He who loves himself loves himself." He means that he who loves his wife will *also* bring good to himself as a result.

identical with his own physical body, which would be nonsense.[24] If in submitting to her husband a wife is really just submitting to herself and not to a different person, then her husband has no distinct existence as a person. This also is nonsense.

Would Sumner say that when a wife disagrees with her husband, she should simply give in to him, since this is just giving in to herself? This too is nonsense.

Answer #7: Scholars who deny that the Son is eternally submissive to the Father do not prove their position from Scripture.

Regarding the eternal submission of the Son to the Father, Rebecca Groothuis says, "This is a debatable point of theology on which conservative scholars disagree." But egalitarian scholars who say that the Son was not eternally submissive to the authority of the Father *have not proven their position from Scripture*. Their general approach is to quote other theologians rather than dealing with the passages of Scripture that indicate such eternal differences in relationship within the Trinity. Usually they overlook or fail to deal with passages such as Ephesians 1:4, Romans 8:29, and 1 Peter 1:2, or passages such as John 1:3, 1 Corinthians 8:6, and Hebrews 1:2, which indicate that the Son was subject to the Father before the work of creation began.

Nor do they deal with 1 Corinthians 15:28 or the many passages in the epistles that indicate that the Son intercedes before the Father, that the Son is seated at the right hand of the Father, and that it is the Father's throne—passages that indicate that the Son will be subject to the authority of the Father for all eternity (see discussion of these passages on pp. 231–38, above).

The primary example of failure to argue from Scripture on this topic is Kevin Giles in *The Trinity and Subordinationism*. He tells readers that he will not argue from Scripture:

---

24. Sumner several times wrongly says that the wife *is* the husband's body (161, 167, 184). She derives this idea by drawing unjustified deductions from the metaphor of the husband being the "head" of the wife, but Scripture never says "the wife is the body of the husband." If the wife *is* the husband's body, then either he himself has two bodies, or he has no body and his wife is his body, and neither of these ideas can be true. Someone could draw all sorts of weird deductions from the metaphor of the husband as the head of the wife (she has no eyes, she can't see; she can't eat because she has no mouth; he can't walk, she is his feet and must walk for him; and so forth), but none of these are intended by the metaphor, which conveys the idea of authority and leadership but none of these other ideas.

In seeking to make a response to my fellow evangelicals who subordinate the Son to the Father, I do not appeal directly to particular scriptural passages to establish who is right or wrong.... I seek rather to prove that orthodoxy rejects this way of reading the Scriptures.[25]

Giles *does not think that citing verses from the Bible can resolve theological questions in general.* He thinks that the Bible can be read in different ways, and even though "given texts cannot mean just anything," he says that "more than one interpretation is possible."[26]

Giles even admits that it is possible to find evidence for the eternal subordination of the Son in Scripture: "I concede immediately that the New Testament *can* be read to teach that the Son is *eternally* subordinated to the Father."[27] But for him that is not decisive, because, as he tells us at the outset, "This book is predicated on the view that the Bible can often be read in more than one way, even on important matters."[28] Giles's fundamental approach should disturb evangelicals, for it means that appeals to Scripture can have no effect in his system. He can just reply, "Yes, the Bible can be read that way, but other readings are possible." And thus the voice of God's Word is effectively silenced.

How then does Giles think we should find out which view is right? His answer is found in church history, but his reading of the historical data is deeply flawed.[29] He continually blurs the distinction between the heresy of subordinationism (the view that the Son had a lesser being than the Father) and the orthodox view that the Son had a subordinate role but was equal in His being (this he also calls subordinationism, making the book simply a contribution to confusion on this topic).[30]

---

25. Kevin Giles, *The Trinity and Subordinationism*, 25. The back cover identifies Giles as "vicar of St. Michael's Church (Anglican) in North Carlton, Australia." Giles repeats his arguments in DBE, 334–52, and he has been answered in detail by Peter Schemm in his review article in JBMW 10:1 (Spring 2005): 81–87. Schemm says of Giles's chapter in DBE, "Most of the theologians cited in this chapter have been unfairly represented, if not misrepresented" (84). (See also note 32 below.)
26. Ibid., 10.
27. Ibid., 25.
28. Ibid., 9.
29. See the discussion in Grudem, EFBT, 426–27.
30. Ibid., 16–17, 60–69. He even equates modern complementarians with ancient Arians who denied the deity of the Son (66), which is preposterous.

If we are to accept Giles's thesis, we will have to believe that he is right and that world-renowned theologians and church historians such as Charles Hodge, Augustus Strong, Louis Berkhof, Philip Schaff, J. N. D. Kelly, and Geoffrey Bromiley have all misunderstood the history of the doctrine of the Trinity.[31] It seems more likely that Giles has misunderstood the historic view of the Trinity and has wrongly decided to believe that the teaching of the Bible cannot be used to settle doctrinal disputes.[32]

Another example of a failure to deal adequately with Scripture on this issue is Millard Erickson, in *God in Three Persons*,[33] where he argues against the eternal subordination of the Son. In dealing with the eternal relationships among the members of the Trinity, Erickson depends primarily not on Scripture but on several quotations from B. B. Warfield (some that are merely speculative statements in the original Warfield article and several that simply show Warfield attempting to protect the doctrines of the Son and the Spirit from any thought of inferiority or derivation of being).[34] Erickson questions the idea of the eternal subordination of the Son to the Father,[35] but he fails to treat any of the passages just mentioned that indicate the Father's authority and primacy in the Father-Son relationship before the world was created (such as Ephesians 1:4; Romans 8:29; 1 Peter 1:2; John 1:3; 1 Corinthians 8:6; Hebrews 1:2). It is surprising that Erickson can sug-

---

31. See Grudem, EFBT, 417–22 for quotations from these authors. Every one of these scholars has produced monumental works that have lasted or will last long beyond their lifetimes. Their names represent some of the highest scholarly achievements of evangelical scholarship in theology and in the history of doctrine in the nineteenth and twentieth centuries. This is significant because Giles differs with them not in the first instance over what people should believe today, but over a far simpler historical fact: What has the church believed throughout history? To claim that they have all been wrong about the history of a doctrine as central as the doctrine of the Trinity is a bold claim, to say the least.

32. An extensive and insightful review of Giles's book is Peter Schemm, "Kevin Giles's *The Trinity and Subordinationism*: A Review Article," *JBMW* 7/2 (Fall 2002): 67–78 (also available online at www. cbmw.org). Schemm points out several significant inaccuracies in Giles's reporting of the views of others (74), so his book should be read with caution. In addition, Mark Baddeley, "The Trinity and Subordinationism: A Response to Kevin Giles," *Reformed Theological Review* 63:1 (April 2004): 1–14, shows that Giles has quoted Karl Barth and Karl Rahner as saying exactly the opposite of what they actually say and has seriously misrepresented the findings of the 1999 Sydney Anglican Diocese Doctrine Commission Report on the Trinity.

33. Millard Erickson, *God in Three Persons*, 291–310.

34. See B. B. Warfield, "The Biblical Doctrine of the Trinity," in Warfield, *Biblical Doctrines*, 164–67, as well as the discussion of Warfield in note 27, above.

35. Erickson, *God in Three Persons*, 309–10.

gest that Christ's subordination to the Father while on earth is not representative of their relationship "before, or for that matter, after the earthly presence of the second person"[36] without dealing with any of these passages that talk about their relationship before Christ came to earth, or without dealing with 1 Corinthians 15:28, or the passages that talk about Christ being at the Father's right hand after His return to heaven.

Erickson writes, regarding Geoffrey Bromiley's summary of the doctrine of eternal generation as it has been held through the history of the church:

> Bromiley has correctly seen that generation, thought of as an eternal occurrence, involves subordination of the Son to the Father. His attempt to separate eternal subordination and superiority from inferiority seems to be a verbal distinction to which no real distinction corresponds. A temporal, functional subordination without inferiority of essence seems possible, but not an eternal subordination. And to speak of the superiority of the Father to the Son while denying the inferiority of the Son to the Father must be contradictory, unless indication is given of different senses in which these are being used.[37]

But this paragraph by Erickson is just stating the historic position of the church (which Bromiley correctly summarizes)[38] in apparently contradictory terms by leaving off the senses in which "superiority" and "inferiority" are intended. Bromiley specifies that it is a "superiority and subordination of order,"[39] similar to what I have here called "relationship." And yet there is no inferiority (or superiority) of being or essence: Father, Son, and Holy Spirit are each fully God and equal in all attributes.

Erickson's statement (that this is a "verbal distinction" but no "real distinction") is just another way of affirming the fundamental egalitarian claim that if there is equality, there cannot be difference in role, and if there is difference in role, there cannot be equality. Erickson himself admits that such a distinction is possible for a time ("a temporal, functional subordination without inferiority of essence seems possible"), but if it is possible for a time without denying the equality of the

---

36. Ibid., 307.
37. Ibid., 309.
38. See Bromiley's statement above, p. 243–44.
39. Bromiley, "Eternal Generation," in EDT, 368.

Son with the Father in essence, then why is it not possible for eternity? That is what many texts of Scripture (not treated by Erickson) lead us to believe.

As for Erickson's suggestion that the roles of the Father, Son, and Holy Spirit may have been voluntarily assumed by each person,[40] the fact that this would have been an *eternal* decision (with which I think Erickson agrees[41]) implies that in all their interaction with the entire creation for all eternity, the Father, Son, and Holy Spirit have related to one another in ways that reflect the headship and authority of the Father, whom the Son and Spirit obey. So for all eternity we would still have this voluntary decision and thus a relationship that indicates both *equality of being* and *subordination in role* with respect to actions in the creation. This still provides a clear parallel to the headship of a husband over his wife (both equality and differences). Therefore, for the sake of the current argument there does not seem to be much difference between Erickson's view and one that holds to an eternal subordination of the Son to the Father in terms of relationship, together with equality in being. (However, I would affirm that the eternal relationships could not have been otherwise because the persons have eternally been Father, Son, and Holy Spirit, and those identities are appropriate to the differing eternal relationships that exist among them.)

— Answer #8: The idea of authority and submission never began; it existed forever in the very being of God.

The idea of authority and submission in an interpersonal relationship did not begin with the Council on Biblical Manhood and Womanhood in 1987. Nor did it begin with a few patriarchal men in the Old Testament. Nor did it begin with the Fall of Adam and Eve in Genesis 3. Nor did the idea of authority and submission to authority begin with the creation of Adam and Eve in the Garden in Genesis 1 and 2. No, the idea of authority and submission has always existed in the eternal relationship between the Father and Son in the Trinity. And this means that the idea of authority and submission in interpersonal relationships *never began*—it has always existed in the eternal relationship between the Father and Son.

The doctrine of the Trinity thus indicates that equality of being together with authority and submission to authority are perhaps the most fundamental aspects of interpersonal relationship in the entire universe.

---

40. Erickson, *God in Three Persons*, 303.
41. Ibid., 310.

38

MUTUAL SUBMISSION
IN THE TRINITY

↩· EGALITARIAN CLAIM: Within the Trinity, the Father Also Submits to the Son, So There Is No Unique Authority for the Father in Relation to the Son.

E galitarians such as Stanley Grenz now argue that there is mutual submission among the members of the Trinity:

The argument from Christ's example often overlooks the deeper dynamic of mutual dependence within the Trinity.... The Father is dependent on the Son for his deity. In sending his Son into the world, the Father entrusted his own reign—indeed his own deity—to the Son (for example, Lk. 10:22). Likewise, the Father is dependent on the Son for his title as the Father. As Irenaeus pointed out in the second century, without the Son the Father is not the Father of the Son. Hence the subordination of the Son to the Father must be balanced by *the subordination of the Father to the Son.*[1]

---

1. Stanley Grenz, *Women in the Church*, 153–54. For a fuller discussion of this novel kind of egalitarian tampering with the doctrine of the Trinity see Ware, "Tampering with the Trinity: Does the Son Submit to His Father?" in *Biblical Foundations for Manhood and Womanhood*, ed. Wayne Grudem (Wheaton, IL: Crossway Books, 2002), 233–53. Statements by Bilezikian affirming "mutual submission" in the Trinity are found in Gilbert Bilezikian, "Hermeneutical Bungee-Jumping," JETS 40/1 (March, 1997), 57–68. See also Stanley Grenz, "Theological Foundations for Male-Female Relationships," JETS 41/4 (December 1998), 618; Royce Gruenler, *The Trinity in the Gospel of John* (Grand Rapids: Baker, 1986), xvi.

— Answer #1: Grenz has confused the categories under discussion.

The question under discussion is the submission of the Son to the authority of the Father. All of the passages that I quoted above show the Father planning, initiating, directing, sending, and commanding, and they show the Son responding, obeying the Father, and carrying out the Father's plans. In order to show "mutual submission" in the Trinity or "the subordination of the Father to the Son" in a way that is parallel, Grenz would have to find some passages that show the Son commanding the Father, or the Son sending the Father, or the Son directing the activities of the Father, or the Father saying that He is obedient to the Son. But no verses like that are found.

So how does Grenz argue for the "subordination of the Father to the Son"? He changes the topic under discussion and confuses the categories. He says nothing about any submission of the Father to the Son's authority. He rather says, "Without the Son the Father is not the Father of the Son." But this does not address the topic at hand. It is a linguistic sleight of hand argument that shifts the discussion to whether the Father would be Father without the Son (the answer is, of course not, but all that tells us is that if God were not a Trinity, He would not be a Trinity, or if God were different, He would be different). This statement tells us nothing about who the true God is or about the relationships that *actually* exist among the persons of the Trinity. And it says nothing to show that the Father submits to the authority of the Son—which He never does. Grenz has just confused the categories under discussion.

— Answer #2: No recognized writer throughout the history of the church supports the idea of "mutual submission" in the Trinity. It is an egalitarian invention created to justify the egalitarian idea of mutual submission in marriage.

As far as I know, no recognized writer or teacher in the entire history of the church ever taught that there is "mutual submission" in the Trinity whereby the Father submits to the Son. In spite of this, so deep is the egalitarian commitment to "mutual submission" in marriage that they have invented a new doctrine of "mutual submission" in the Trinity to support it.

— Answer #3: If the Father also submitted to the authority of the Son, it would destroy the Trinity, because there would be no Father, Son, and Holy Spirit, but only Person A, Person A, and Person A.

The differences in authority among Father, Son, and Holy Spirit are the only interpersonal differences that the Bible indicates exist eternally among the members of the Godhead. They are equal in all their attributes and perfections, but for all eternity there has been a difference in authority, whereby the Father has authority over the Son that the Son does not have over the Father, and the Father and Son both have authority over the Holy Spirit that the Holy Spirit does not have over the Father and the Son. These differences, in which there is authority and submission to authority, seem to be the means by which Father, Son, and Holy Spirit differ from one another and can be differentiated from one another.

If we did not have such differences in authority in the relationships among the members of the Trinity, then we would not know of any differences at all, and it would be unclear whether there *are* any differences among the persons of the Trinity. But if there are no differences among them eternally, *then how does one person differ from the other?* They would no longer be Father, Son, and Holy Spirit, but rather Person A, Person A, and Person A, each identical to the other not only in being but also in role and in the way they relate to one another. This would be very troubling, for once we lose personal distinctions among the members of the Trinity, we sacrifice the very idea that personal differences are eternally and fundamentally good, and we no longer have in the being of God a guarantee that God will eternally preserve our own individual, personal distinctiveness either. (Probably egalitarians will not go that far in this generation, but that is the direction such ideas are heading.)

39

SUBORDINATION
IN ESSENCE

↶ EGALITARIAN CLAIM: If Female Subordination Is Based on Who a Woman Is (As Female) Rather than Her Ability or Choice, Then It Is a Subordination in Essence. Therefore the Complementarian Position Leads to the Conclusion That Women Are Lesser Beings.

This objection is stated by Rebecca Groothuis:

> Regardless of how hierarchalists try to explain the situation, the idea that women are equal *in* their being, yet unequal *by virtue of* their being, is contradictory and ultimately nonsensical. If you cannot help but be what you are, and if inferiority in function follows inexorably from what you are, then you are inferior in your essential being.... A permanent and comprehensive subordination based on a person's essence is an essential (not merely a functional) subordination.[1]

---

1. Rebecca Groothuis, *Good News for Women*, 55 (italics in original). Groothuis repeats this argument in her chapter, "Equal in Being, Unequal in Role" in DBE, 301–33, and Dorothy Patterson responded to her in JBMW 10:1 (Spring 2005): 72–80. See also Judy Brown, *Women Ministers*, 8. (For a response to Groothuis's claim that analogies with other, temporary kinds of human subordination are not valid comparisons for marriage, see Grudem, EFBT, 437–41.)

— Answer #1: No, it is a subordination in function.

To state it again, the complementarian position is equality in being (in the sense of equal value, honor, personhood, and importance) with differences in authority. The complementarian position holds to subordination in function, not subordination in being.

Groothuis states our position in a misleading way, because her phrase "inferiority in function" carries connotations of lesser value. The complementarian position is that greater or lesser *authority* does not imply "*inferior* function" or "*superior* function," just *different* function. Groothuis also states the position in a misleading way when she says, "The idea that women are equal *in* their being, yet unequal *by virtue of* their being, is contradictory and ultimately nonsensical."

The problem is that she uses "equal" and "unequal" with different meanings. If we reword her sentence so the meanings are explicit and the complementarian view is represented fairly, it would say: "The idea that women are *equal in value and honor and personhood* but *unequal in authority* by virtue of their being *women* is contradictory and ultimately nonsensical." But this idea is not at all contradictory and nonsensical. A contradiction would be to say, for example, "women are equal in value and women are not equal in value." That sentence takes the form, "A and not A," which is a contradiction. But to say, "women are equal in value and different in authority" is not at all a contradiction or nonsensical. Groothuis may disagree with that statement, but for her to use "equal" in two different ways and then call it a contradiction is simply a word trick.

— Answer #2: Women's submission to male headship is based on their having a different being, not an inferior being.

What Groothuis is really objecting to is women having different roles that are not based on ability or choice, but just on the fact that a person is a woman.

In fact, Groothuis herself does not object to the idea that people can be equal but different in some ways. She agrees, for example, that people can have different skills or social position and still be of equal value to God.[2] So she agrees that *some* kinds of differences are compatible with *some* kinds of equality.

---

2. Ibid., 46.

But the only kinds of differences she allows are those based on ability or voluntary choice. This is evident when she assumes over and over again that, apart from voluntary choice, the only rightful submission to authority has to be based on inferior ability. She says, for example:

> Subordinating a woman solely by reason of her femaleness can be deemed fair and appropriate only if all females are, without exception, inferior to all males in their *ability* to perform the particular function for which they have been subordinated.[3]

That is just saying that *greater ability* is the *only* "fair and appropriate" basis for a husband to have leadership in the family. By contrast to Groothuis's idea of what is "fair and appropriate," the Bible never bases a husband's leadership on ability, but simply on the fact that he is a man. Are we to say that the Bible is not "fair and appropriate"? Are we to say that God's choice of the Levites to be priests, or of the Jews to be His people, was not "fair and appropriate"?

Are we to say that the eternal authority of God the Father over the Son and the Holy Spirit, based not on greater ability but just on being Father, is not "fair and appropriate"? Surely Groothuis is wrong here.

In the case of different roles for men and women in marriage, God can (and does) assign roles based on something other than abilities. He bases roles on the fact that one is a man and one is a woman ("The husband is the head of the wife even as Christ is the head of the church," Ephesians 5:23). God looks at these equal but different beings and assigns headship to the husband. And He bases it on the fact that they are different, not on any inferiority or superiority. Egalitarians may say, "That's not fair," or "I can't understand why God does this," but it still remains the decision God has made. Any egalitarian opinions of whether God's actions are fair or reasonable need adjustment in light of the testimony of Scripture.

---

3. Ibid., 53 (italics added).

40

MISSION FIELD

⌐· EGALITARIAN CLAIM: It Is Inconsistent to Restrict Women from Church Leadership Positions in the Western World and at the Same Time Approve of Women Having Such Positions on the Mission Field.

I have heard this objection a number of times in personal conversation. Why should we allow women to plant churches, teach the Bible, and serve as pastors on the mission field while at the same time prohibiting them from such work here at home?

Rich Nathan writes, "How can churches justify women preaching the gospel and instructing men in other nations, while not allowing them to do the same here?"[1]

— Answer #1: It is not right to say that the Bible is authoritative in one country and not in another.

We should never say that the Bible has authority in one country of the world and not in another! If anyone does this, he or she is being inconsistent and not respecting the authority of the Bible as the very Word of God. I would never want to support such a procedure.

Therefore whatever we decide the Bible teaches about women's roles in ministry, we should apply those principles consistently in every part of the world.

---

1. Rich Nathan, *Who Is My Enemy?* 148.

— Answer #2: Many kinds of women's ministries are approved by Scripture because they do not include teaching or governing over an assembled church or some equivalent activity.

As I pointed out in chapter 2, many ministries are entirely valid for women and are not prohibited by Scripture. For example, evangelistic ministry of various kinds is valid and should be encouraged for both men and women anywhere in the world.

More specifically, while people may have legitimate differences on whether it is wise for a mission board to send a single woman to evangelize an unreached group of people, I personally see no compelling objection to a woman doing evangelism in this way. Indeed, the history of missions is filled with the stories of courageous women who have carried out this kind of evangelism.

But what happens, time after time, is that as people become Christians, at first the woman missionary teaches the new converts in an informal way, analogous to the situation of Priscilla and Aquila teaching Apollos in Acts 18:26. Eventually, indigenous male leaders develop and a church is formed, and men in the village or tribe assume the leadership roles in the new church.

This is a natural transition from an informal Bible study with a group of new Christians to an established church with men in leadership.[2]

---

2. See a specific example of this in chapter 2, p. 48, above.

PART TEN

EVANGELICAL FEMINIST CLAIMS FROM HISTORY AND EXPERIENCE

In this part we move beyond egalitarian claims based on theology and on the ideas of fairness and justice to consider egalitarian objections based purely on their observations of church history and contemporary experience. Haven't there been many women pastors and elders in the history of the church, giving us a precedent for women to be leaders in the church today? Haven't many denominations already approved women's ordination?

And who are we to oppose the evident blessing of God on numerous women who currently serve as pastors and Bible teachers to men? Moreover, if a woman has a genuine call from God for pastoral ministry, how can we rightfully oppose that call?

It is questions such as these that we consider in this part.

41

MANY HISTORICAL
PRECEDENTS

✑· EGALITARIAN CLAIM: There Are Many Examples
of Women Pastors and Women Preachers in Church History,
So the Egalitarian Position Is Not As Novel As Some People Think.

This is the main argument of Janette Hassey's book *No Time for Silence*. She writes:

In 1927, the Moody Bible Institute *Alumni News* proudly published a letter containing an astounding personal account of the ministry of Mabel C. Thomas, a 1913 MBI graduate. Thomas, called to the pastorate in a Kansas church, has preached, taught weekly Bible classes, and baptized dozens of converts. She concluded her letter with praise, since she "could not have met the many and varied opportunities for service without the training of MBI" [Hassey's footnote indicates this is from *Moody Alumni News* (June 1927), 12].

Today, because of gender, female students at MBI and other Evangelical institutions are barred from pastoral training courses. Why has such an enormous shift occurred since the turn of the century? Why do many Evangelical groups who used women as pastors and preachers *then* now prohibit or discourage such ministry?…

How could Evangelicals a century ago hold high their inerrant, verbally inspired Bible in one hand while blessing the ministry of women preachers, pastors, Bible teachers, and evangelists with the other?... Those who endorsed women's public ministry were convinced that a literal approach to the Bible, and especially to prophecy, demanded such leadership by women.[1]

Hassey then details the history of women's involvement in public ministry in the United States. In addition, she notes the following:

1. In the early 1900s, many Bible institutes had both men and women students. Some women became pastors, usually in smaller, rural churches where no trained men were available. The alumni publications of these Bible institutes (such as Moody Bible Institute in Chicago and Northwestern in Minneapolis) published the ministry reports of these women.[2]

2. Some early evangelical leaders in the United States supported the idea of women preachers, even if they were ambivalent on the idea of women's ordination as pastors. However, these leaders generally did not support an egalitarian view of marriage. Leaders who supported the right of women to preach included A. B. Simpson (founder of the Christian and Missionary Alliance), A. J. Gordon (prominent Baptist pastor, 1836–1895), and both Fredrik Franson and John Gustaf Princell (both influential in founding what became the Evangelical Free Church of America).[3]

What shall we make of Hassey's arguments? Do these historical facts indicate clear precedents that should lead us to think that the ordination of women is consistent with evangelical beliefs and especially with the conviction that the Bible is the inerrant Word of God? That is the intent of Hassey's book, and some have found the argument persuasive. But several other factors need to be considered before we reach such a conclusion.

---

1. Janette Hassey, *No Time for Silence*, xi–xii.
2. Hassey, *No Time for Silence*, quotes several of these reports on 11–46.
3. Hassey discusses Simpson's views on 15–16 and 19. A. J. Gordon's position is explained on 20 and 105–8. Franson is discussed on 84–86 and 108–10. Princell's views are reported on 89–90. Hassey summarizes her same argument from historical precedent in "Evangelical Women in Ministry a Century Ago," in DBE, 39–75.

— Answer #1: While Hassey has emphasized isolated examples, the entire history of the church, and the entire history of evangelicalism in America, looks far different: The vast majority of churches, and of evangelicals in particular, clearly rejected the idea of women as pastors throughout church history.

Several egalitarian books, in addition to Janette Hassey's book, provide helpful surveys of women who have played influential roles at various times in the history of the church.[4] The conclusion from these studies is not in dispute: For the first eighteen hundred years of the history of the church, women played influential roles in evangelism, prayer, ministries of mercy, writing, financial support, political influence, private exhortation and encouragement and counsel, and teaching of women and children. But they never became pastors of churches, and rarely did they speak or teach publicly in mixed assemblies of men and women. When women did preach or teach the Bible to men, it was generally in "sectarian" movements such as the Quakers.[5] Tucker and Liefeld say: "Women were very prominent in church history…even though they were systematically denied positions of authority."[6]

After detailing other examples of women who spoke publicly in Baptist groups or among women who claimed extraordinary visions or revelations from the Holy Spirit,[7] Tucker and Liefeld conclude:

> The seventeenth and eighteenth centuries provided women with more opportunities for ministry than they had previously enjoyed, but only if they were willing to defy male leadership in the institutionalized churches or be

---

4. Probably the most comprehensive study is *Daughters of the Church: Women and Ministry from New Testament Times to the Present* by Ruth Tucker and Walter Liefeld, 141–90. From a complementarian perspective, a helpful historical survey is the article by William Weinrich, "Women in the History of the Church: Learned and Holy, but Not Pastors," in Piper and Grudem, *Recovering Biblical Manhood and Womanhood*, 263–79.

5. Margaret Fell, a leader among the early Quakers, published *Women's Speaking Justified, Proved and Allowed of by the Scriptures* in 1667 in London. She married George Fox, founder of the Quakers, in 1669. (See Ruth Tucker and Walter Liefeld, *Daughters of the Church*, 227–32.) The Quakers (Society of Friends) had no ordained clergy of either sex, but supported women speaking publicly under the inspiration of the Holy Spirit. Hassey writes, "In Colonial America virtually all women preachers belonged to the Society of Friends" (*No Time for Silence*, 74).

6. Tucker and Liefeld, *Daughters of the Church*, 14–15.

7. Ibid., 220–24, 225–27.

associated with sectarian movements and endure the scorn of respectable society.... But...there was no room for debate in theological circles. Women were admonished to keep silent in the churches, and the vast majority did.[8]

William Weinrich says that prior to the Reformation, "there never was recognized ordained female ministry in the west (or east) that involved teaching in the assembly and ministering at the altar."[9] After the Reformation, within Protestantism, Weinrich says, "The major Reformation and post-Reformation leaders assumed without question the practice of reserving the office of pastor and sacramental minister to men."[10]

Some understanding of the extent of approval of female clergy can be gained from census numbers. In 1880 there were 165 female ministers in the whole United States. These women ministers constituted 0.3 percent of all the clergy in the U.S. By 1920 there were 1,787 women clergy in the United States, or 1.4 percent of the clergy.[11] But the number of women pastors in the major evangelical groups was much smaller, since presumably these numbers include all the female clergy among liberal groups such as Unitarians, Universalists, and more liberal congregational churches, as well as women leaders in the Salvation Army and the Quakers. The 1920 number also includes any women clergy among early Pentecostal groups. But all of those combined made up only 1.4 percent of the total number of clergy in 1920. After we exclude a large proportion that were in liberal or sectarian groups, we find that the total number of women clergy in mainstream evangelical groups even in 1920 was exceptionally small.

— Answer #2: Our authority must be what the Bible teaches, not what some Christians have done at various times in the past.

This is the most important point about this study: The fundamental question is, What does the Bible teach about this? We may find it useful to read the arguments of evangelicals such as A. J. Gordon and Fredrik Franson to see if their interpretations of Scripture are persuasive (and Hassey helpfully summarizes their arguments

8.   Ibid., 243–44.
9.   Weinrich, "Women in the History of the Church," 277.
10.   Ibid.
11.   Hassey, *No Time for Silence*, 9.

on pp. 95–121). But Christians who take the Bible as their supreme authority are not free to adopt a position simply because some evangelical leader in the past has held that position. The question is, How did they understand the key passages on this topic? And do we think they were correct in their understanding? Are we willing to defend that understanding as the correct understanding of Scripture today?

Moreover, it is amazing that Hassey and others can find so few early evangelical leaders who advocate women's ordination or women as preachers and Bible teachers. The history of evangelicalism in the United States includes many millions of believers and hundreds of denominations and viewpoints, and it is surprising how few and how hesitant are the advocates among evangelicals for any public ministry for women until the mid-1970s.[12]

— Answer #3: Hassey's argument would have evangelicals today reject the godly wisdom of the majorities in these movements and adopt the rejected views of the minorities instead.

As Hassey herself points out, many of the denominations and institutions she examines later adopted policies that restricted the ordained pastoral ministry to men:

> Today, because of gender, female students at MBI and other Evangelical institutions are barred from pastoral training courses…. Why do many Evangelical groups who used women as pastors *then* now prohibit or discourage such ministry?[13]

Specifically, the Evangelical Free Church restricts ordination to men, in spite of the views of Franson and Princell. The Christian and Missionary Alliance restricts the eldership to men, in spite of the early views of A. B. Simpson. Many Bible colleges that formerly reported on women's pastoral ministries (apparently favorably, according to Hassey) now teach that only men should be pastors and elders in churches.

What happened? In various ways, the majority of wise, godly leaders in those

---

12. Modern evangelical advocacy of an egalitarian position probably began in 1974 with the book by Letha Scanzoni and Nancy Hardesty, *All We're Meant to Be*, which was followed quickly in 1975 by Paul Jewett's book, *Man as Male and Female*.

13. Hassey, *No Time for Silence*, xi.

movements, after careful study and reflection on Scripture, decided to adopt such policies. They rejected the egalitarian tendencies Hassey discovered here and there in the early days of those movements. In the decision-making process, the egalitarians lost.

But *Hassey would have us go back and say that the losers in the debate were right and the majority decision was wrong.* She would have us adopt the rejected views of the minority and reject the considered decision of the majority. But why? On what basis should the views of the minority be given privileged status and allowed to return now as established policy? Rather than respecting the wisdom and precedents of the vast majorities in earlier generations in these movements, Hassey's approach would have us reject that wisdom.

— Answer #4: Most early evangelical leaders who supported women's preaching were not egalitarians in the modern sense.

Modern egalitarians want evangelicals to go far beyond the views of the early leaders that Hassey quotes. Hassey points out that A. J. Gordon and Fredrik Franson were not egalitarian with respect to marriage, but supported "the husband's headship and wife's submission," as did Catherine Booth, who helped found the Salvation Army.[14] Though Franson encouraged women to preach, he did not write in support of women's ordination. Similarly, A. J. Gordon supported women's preaching but was unsure about women's ordination and women governing over congregations, thinking that 1 Timothy 2:12 might forbid such things.[15] And John Gustaf Princell also thought women could preach but was unwilling to advocate women in governing positions in churches.[16] Such positions are hardly the equivalent of modern egalitarian positions.

— Answer #5: There was great diversity and freedom in early American evangelicalism, along with a strong tradition of local church autonomy that allowed for the ordination of some women in specific local churches.

Freedom of religion has been a strong component of American history from its early days and found expression in the First Amendment to the Constitution in

---

14. Ibid., 109.
15. Ibid., 107, 109.
16. Ibid., 90.

1789. Evangelicalism has spawned hundreds of denominations and various splinter groups and sects. In addition to the denominations with highly developed governmental structures and strong authority over local congregations (such as the Episcopalians, Presbyterians, and Methodists), there were many denominations that gave autonomy to local congregations to decide their own affairs, and this included the freedom to ordain whomever they wished. Denominations with a strong emphasis on local church autonomy included many Baptist groups as well as many Free Churches. Hassey explains, "The Free Church congregational principle of the local autonomy of each church necessitated this openness to women."[17]

Where local church autonomy prevailed, it is not surprising that some small, rural churches would eventually have women pastors, especially if a church had a woman who had been trained at a Bible college and no men with similar training. But occasional cases like this, as Hassey reports, do not in themselves indicate denominational approval or majority assent, but rather an unwillingness to interfere with the strongly held principle of local church autonomy.

In such cases, a denomination's decision to forbid women's ordination would ordinarily come only after the national governing structure had become more developed, and only after the denomination reached a consensus that this was a matter of enough importance to justify overriding the strongly held principle of local church autonomy.

— Answer #6: The vast majority of evangelical churches and institutions did not approve of the ordination of women at any point in American history. The trend among several major denominations to approve the ordination of women only began in the 1950s, well after liberal theology had gained controlling influence in those denominations.

In the late nineteenth century, the vast majority of evangelical groups, including several large denominations that would become liberal in the twentieth century, rejected women's ordination to the pastorate. But the roots of a trend toward women's ordination among liberal denominations can already be seen in the late nineteenth century. In 1889, J. T. Sunderland published *The Liberal Christian*

---

17. Ibid., 91. Even today the "Statement of Faith" of the Evangelical Free Church of America says, "We believe that Jesus Christ is the Lord and Head of the Church, and that every local church has the right under Christ to decide and govern its own affairs" (Article 10).

Ministry, in which he said that one of the benefits of liberal Christianity, which rejected the view of the Bible as God's inspired Word, was that women had more freedom to minister in liberal churches. Hassey reports, "After praising Unitarian, Universalist, and Quaker female ministry, Sunderland wrote, 'no orthodox body has opened its regular ministry to women.'"[18]

A trend among liberal denominations to ordain women can also be seen in the extensive list compiled by Mark Chaves. Although there were a few exceptions prior to the 1950s, especially among some African-American, Baptistic, and Pentecostal groups,[19] the majority of large denominations in the United States did not approve women's ordination until 1956 or later, after most of them had come under the dominant influence of liberal theology (at least at their national leadership level). Here is the material from Mark Chaves's chart:[20]

Dates when major denominations began ordaining women in the United States:

Presbyterian Church in the USA (North)	1956
Methodist Church	1956
Church of the Brethren	1958
United Presbyterian Church, North America	1958
African Methodist Episcopal Church	1960
Presbyterian Church, US (South)	1964
Southern Baptist Convention	1964[21]
Evangelical United Brethren Church	1968
American Lutheran Church	1970
Lutheran Church in America	1970

---

18. J. T. Sunderland, *The Liberal Christian Ministry* (Boston: G. H. Ellis, 1889), as cited in Hassey, *No Time for Silence*, 2 and 222n6.

19. Among the larger denominations, the significant ones that ordained women prior to 1956 (according to Chaves's list) were Congregationalists (1853), Disciples of Christ (1888), the National Baptist Convention (1895), the Pentecostal Holiness Church (1895), the African Methodist Episcopal Zion Church (1898), the Northern Baptist Convention (1907), the Church of the Nazarene (1908), the Baptist General Conference (1918), the International Church of the Foursquare Gospel (1927), and the Assemblies of God (1935). See Mark Chaves, *Ordaining Women*, 16.

20. Mark Chaves, *Ordaining Women*, 16–17.

21. This Southern Baptist policy was revoked in 1984, after conservatives recaptured leadership of the denomination; see Chaves, *Ordaining Women*, 35, 89.

Mennonite Church	1973
Free Methodist Church, North America	1974
Evangelical Covenant Church	1976
Episcopal Church	1976
Reformed Church in America	1979

Even as of 2003, a number of large and influential denominations within the United States do not ordain women. These include the Southern Baptist Convention, the Presbyterian Church in America, the Lutheran Church—Missouri Synod, the Evangelical Free Church of America (in spite of the views of Free Church forefathers Fredrik Franson and John Gustaf Princell), and the Christian and Missionary Alliance (in spite of the views of the founder, A. B. Simpson). In addition, there are thousands of Bible churches and independent churches, many of them with several thousand members, that do not ordain women.

— Answer #7: Early Bible institutes were founded to train lay workers, not pastors, although some women students later became pastors.

Hassey points out at several places that the early Bible institutes (such as Moody and Northwestern and others) were not formed as seminaries to train pastors. They were schools for training lay workers in the churches, and they naturally admitted both men and women as students.[22] Hassey notes that prior to the founding of Moody Bible Institute, Dwight L. Moody said:

> I believe we need "gap men," men who are trained to fill the gap between the common people and the ministers. We are to raise up men and women who will be willing to lay down their lives alongside the laboring.[23]

Concerning the need for work among the urban poor, Moody said, "Give me women to work among this class of the population." Moody also wanted to solve the problem of "a chronic shortage of qualified Christian workers with a Bible education to assist in the inquiry room work connected with revivals."[24] With

22. Hassey, *No Time for Silence*, 14.
23. Ibid., 36.
24. Ibid.

this purpose, Moody founded The Bible Institute of the Chicago Evangelization Society in 1889 (which was renamed Moody Bible Institute in 1900).

And Hassey notes that some early Bible institutes explicitly distinguished the purposes for which they were training women from those for which they were training men, with an assumption that only men would be pastors.[25]

Some women graduates of these institutes spoke widely in public meetings in opposition to drunkenness and support of the temperance movement.[26] Others began to preach, and some became pastors of churches.[27]

Hassey makes much of the fact that alumni publications from schools such as Moody reported the ministries of these women, but it is not clear that those routine alumni reports indicated official endorsement of those ministries.[28]

In conclusion, given the incredible diversity of evangelicalism in America, and given the extensive religious freedom allowed in this country, it is not surprising that a few evangelicals supported women's preaching or women's ordination from time to time, or that there were some women preachers or even women pastors. But the overall picture that emerges is that these were the exceptions, and they constituted a tiny minority among all evangelicals in the United States, at least until the increasing influence of evangelical feminism in the 1980s. And even to this day, though it is difficult to ascertain exactly the number of ordained women in evangelical groups, it is certainly not very large.

— Answer #8: A broader perspective from the worldwide Christian church shows that egalitarianism is an unusual development primarily confined to European and American Protestantism in the last half of the twentieth century and is by no means representative of the church through history or around the world.

Roman Catholic author Richard John Neuhaus offered a broader perspective on this question in some comments in *First Things* in March of 1996:

---

25. Ibid. See 26 regarding Biola, and 27–29 regarding Philadelphia School of the Bible; she notes however that Moody, Northwestern, and other Bible institutes did not make such distinctions, at least not explicitly.

26. Ibid. See 13, 22, 33.

27. Hassey tells interesting stories about various women, such as the discussion of several Baptist and congregational women on 62–72.

28. See Grudem, EFBT, 466–68 for an analysis of what some of these reports actually signify.

Dr. Eugene Brand of the Lutheran World Federation (LWF)…addressing a recent consultation on women in Geneva…got carried away by the need to assure them that the LWF would "not sell out the ordination of women" to gain communion with the Roman Catholic or Orthodox churches. "We should not ask, 'Is it possible to ordain women?' We should ask, 'Is there any earthly reason why women should not be ordained?' The only answer to that question is no."

The only answer? In fidelity to a tradition of almost two thousand years, the three bodies that hold to a sacramental view of ministry in apostolic succession—Catholic, Orthodox, and Anglican—unanimously answered the question otherwise. In 1994 and 1995 the Catholic Church again—this time in a form that clearly makes the teaching unchangeable in the future—declared that the Church is not authorized to ordain women to the priesthood. As much as we can say "never" about anything in history, we can say that the Orthodox will never ordain women to the priesthood. The fact is that, among churches with a sacramental and apostolic view of ordination, the tradition was unbroken until 1974 when a few Episcopalian women were illegally ordained. The illegality was later regularized by the Episcopal Church in this country, and now the Church of England has followed suit. But the worldwide Anglican communion, counting fifty to sixty million members, is still divided on the question. The Catholic Church has more than a billion members, and the Orthodox approximately 200 million. It follows that, among the churches holding to a catholic view of ministry, those who have broken with the tradition—and that only within the last few years—claim about 3 percent of the membership. In addition, the great majority of Protestants who do not subscribe to a catholic view of priesthood (Baptist, Missouri Synod Lutherans, orthodox Calvinists, et al.) believe that ordaining women is precluded on biblical grounds. The inescapable conclusion is that ordaining women is a very recent North American–European innovation accepted by a very small part of world Christianity. Whether that very small part represents the wave of the future or a temporary aberration of our theologically confused times is a question about which people can disagree.

But to say that no is the "only answer" to the question of whether there is any reason why women should not be (or cannot be) ordained is to write off two millennia of tradition and the practice of the overwhelming majority of Christians in the world today....[29]

---

29. Richard John Neuhaus, "While We're At It," *First Things* 61 (March 1996): 69.

42

BLESSING ON MINISTRY

↶ EGALITARIAN CLAIM: God Has Evidently Blessed the Ministries of Many Women, Including Women Pastors. Who Are We to Oppose What God Has So Clearly Blessed?

Cindy Jacobs makes this argument:

> Women in numerous different ministries teach both men and women and are producing godly, lasting fruit for the Kingdom. Would that be happening if their work wasn't sanctioned by God? Wouldn't their ministries simply be dead and lifeless if God weren't anointing them?[1]

In personal conversation, people will sometimes say, "I heard Anne Graham Lotz preach, and it changed my mind about women preaching." Or they will hear Beth Moore preach at a conference and think, *This is such good Bible teaching. How can it be wrong?*

But is this reasoning true? Does the evident blessing of God on some women pastors prove that what they are doing is right?

---

1. Cindy Jacobs, *Women of Destiny*, 176. Sarah Sumner, *Men and Women in the Church*, argues that "Every generation produces gifted women who minister effectively to women and men" (49), women whose ministry God blesses (and she frequently uses herself as the leading example): See 15, 17–19, 20–21, 49, 51–53, 73–74, 95–96, 104, 187, 195–97, 226, 308–09, 315.

— Answer #1: Of course there will be some good results when a woman prays, trusts God, and teaches God's Word, because God's Word has power and because God in His grace often blesses us in spite of our mistakes. But that does not make the mistakes right, and God may withdraw His protection and blessing at any time.

It is not surprising to me that there is some measure of blessing when women act as pastors and teach the Word of God, whether in a local congregation, at a Bible conference, or before a television audience. This is because God's Word is powerful, and God brings blessing through His Word to those who hear it.

But the fact that God blesses the preaching of His Word does not make it right for a woman to be the preacher. God is a God of grace, and there are many times when He blesses His people even when they disobey Him.

One example where God brought blessing in spite of disobedience is the story of Samson in Judges 13–16. Even though Samson broke God's laws by taking a Philistine wife (Judges 14), sleeping with a prostitute at Gaza (Judges 16:1–3), and living with Delilah, a foreign woman he had not married (Judges 16:4–22), God still empowered him mightily to defeat the Philistines again and again. This does not mean that Samson's sin was right in God's sight, but only that God in His grace empowered Samson *in spite of his disobedience.* Eventually God's protection and power were withdrawn, "but he did not know that the LORD had left him" (Judges 16:20), and the Philistines captured and imprisoned him (v. 21).

If God waited until Christians were perfect before He brought blessing to their ministries, there would be no blessing on any ministry in this life! God's grace is given to us in spite of our failings. But that does not mean that it is right to disobey Scripture or that God will always give such blessing.

If a woman goes on serving as an elder or pastor, I believe she is doing so outside the will of God, and she has no guarantee of God's protection on her life. By continuing to act in ways contrary to Scripture, she puts herself spiritually in a dangerous position. I expect that eventually even the measure of blessing God has allowed on her ministry will be withdrawn (though I cannot presume that this will be true in every case).

— Answer #2: Arguments from the experience of blessing can go both ways: For two thousand years God has evidently blessed the ministries of millions of churches that have had only men as pastors and elders. Who are we to oppose what God has so clearly blessed?

Arguments based on experience are seldom conclusive. Even today, in the strongly egalitarian popular culture of the United States, by far the largest and most successful ministries (by any measure), the ministries that seem to have been most blessed by God, have men as senior pastors. Even those few large evangelical churches that have women as part of their pastoral team (such as Willow Creek Community Church) have a man (such as Bill Hybels) as the senior pastor, and men do most of the preaching. And evangelical churches with women pastors are few in comparison to the large number of churches that have only men as pastors and elders.

This fact should not be lightly dismissed. If it really were God's ideal for men and women to share equally in eldership and pastoral leadership roles, then at some point in the last two thousand years, and especially today, would we not expect to see a remarkable and unmistakable blessing of God on many churches that have an equal number of men and women as elders and that share the main Bible teaching responsibilities equally between men and women pastors?

And if the gender of pastors makes no difference to God, then why have we never seen God's evident blessing poured out abundantly on a church with *all women* pastors even once throughout the millions of churches that have existed in the last two thousand years?

— Answer #3: Liberal denominations that ordain women pastors have continually declined in membership and income.

Historian Ruth Tucker summarizes this trend:

> The role of women in the church in the twentieth century will perplex future historians.... Those historians who dig deeper will discover that the mainline churches that were offering women the greatest opportunities were simultaneously declining in membership and influence. Some of these churches, which once had stood firm on the historic orthodox faith,

were becoming too sophisticated to take the Bible at face value. The gains that have been made, then, are mixed at best.[2]

— Answer #4: Having women as pastors or elders erodes male leadership and brings increasing feminization of both the home and the church. It also erodes the authority of Scripture because people see it being disobeyed.

When people say there is "much blessing" from the ministries of women pastors, I do not think they are able to see all the consequences. Once a woman pastor and women elders are installed in a church, several other consequences will follow:

1. Many of the most conservative, faithful, Bible-believing members of the church will leave, convinced that the church is disobeying Scripture and that they cannot in good conscience support it any longer.[3]

2. Some of those who stay will still believe that the Bible teaches that women should not be elders, but they will support the leadership of the church. Many of them will think that the leaders they respect are encouraging a practice of disobedience to Scripture, and this will tend to erode people's confidence in Scripture in other areas as well.

3. Those who are persuaded that the Bible allows women as pastors will usually accept one or more of the methods of interpretation I discussed in previous chapters, methods that tend to erode and undermine the effective authority of Scripture in our lives. Therefore, they will be likely to adapt such methods in evading the force of other passages of Scripture in the future.

4. A church with female elders or pastors will tend to become more and more "feminized"[4] over time, with women holding most of the

---

2. Ruth Tucker, *Women in the Maze*, 184. See Grudem, EFBT, 477–78, for statistics on declining membership trends in several denominations that ordain women.

3. To take one example, I saw this happen at an influential evangelical church in Libertyville, Illinois, in 1996 and 1997. The pastor attempted over a period of months to add women to the governing board of the church, and as a result perhaps ten or more of the most conservative, most active families in the church left and joined the other main evangelical church in town, a Southern Baptist Church where I was an elder and where the pastor and church constitution clearly supported a complementarian position.

4. See Leon Podles, *The Church Impotent*, who notes that in 1952 the adult attenders on Sunday morning in typical Protestant churches were 53 percent female and 47 percent male, which was almost exactly the same proportion of women and men in the adult population in the U.S. But by 1986

major leadership positions and men constituting a smaller and smaller percentage of the congregation.

5. Male leadership in the home will also be eroded, for people will reason instinctively if not explicitly that if women can function as leaders in the family of God, the church, then why should women not be able to function as well as men in leadership roles in the home? This influence will not be sudden or immediate, but will increase over time.

All this is to say that the "evident blessing" God gives when women preach the Bible is not the only result of such preaching. There are significant negative consequences as well.

— Answer #5: What is right and wrong must be determined by the Bible, not by our experiences or our evaluation of the results of certain actions.

Determining right and wrong by means of results is often known as "the end justifies the means." It is a dangerous approach to take in ethical decisions because it so easily encourages disobedience to Scripture.

In 1966, Joseph Fletcher published *Situation Ethics: The New Morality.*[5] He argued that people at times needed to break God's moral laws in the Bible in order to do the greatest good for the greatest number of people. But as these ideas worked their way through American society, the "new morality" of Fletcher's situation ethics brought about a tremendous erosion of moral standards and widespread disobedience to all of God's moral laws.

If I say that women should be pastors because it brings good results, *even if the Bible says otherwise*, then I have simply capitulated to situation ethics. What is right and wrong must be determined by the teachings of Scripture, not by looking at the results of actions that violate Scripture and then saying those actions are right.

[4. *continued*] (after several decades of feminist influence in liberal denominations) the ratios were closer to 60 percent female and 40 percent male, with many congregations reporting a ratio of 65 percent to 35 percent (11–12). Podles focuses primarily on Roman Catholic and liberal Protestant churches in his study, and he concludes that, if present trends continue, the "Protestant clergy will be characteristically a female occupation, like nursing, within a generation" (xiii).

5. Joseph Fletcher, *Situation Ethics* (Philadelphia: Westminster Press, 1966).

━ Answer #6: Determining right and wrong on the basis of human experience alone is the foundation of liberalism in theology. Feminism takes us in that direction.

J. I. Packer explains that one of the characteristics of theological liberalism is "an optimistic view of cultured humanity's power to perceive God by reflecting on its experience."[6] Thus, *experience* rather than the Bible becomes the ultimate standard in theology. If we decide that women and men can have all the same roles in the church primarily because we have seen blessing on the work of women preachers and Bible teachers, such an egalitarian argument leads us toward theological liberalism.

6. J. I. Packer, "Liberalism and Conservatism in Theology" in Sinclair Ferguson and David Wright, *New Dictionary of Theology* (Leicester, UK: InterVarsity Press, 1988), 385.

43

CALLING

↶ EGALITARIAN CLAIM: If a Woman Has a Genuine Call from God for Pastoral Ministry, We Have No Right to Oppose That Call.

his argument is often made by women who believe that God has called them to become pastors. Millicent Hunter, whom *Charisma* magazine identifies as "pastor of 3,000-member Baptist Worship Center in Philadelphia," says that the current generation of women ministers is emerging with more boldness. "They are coming out of the woodwork with an 'I don't care what you think; this is what God called me to do' type of attitude."[1]

Sarah Sumner insists that God called her to be a theology professor:

> I didn't ask God to grant me the grace to enter seminary and complete my doctoral work. That was his idea. He designed the plan; he's the one who saw me through.[2]

She encourages other women to follow God's calling no matter what others may say:

> It is not Anne Graham Lotz's spiritual obligation to sit down with the leaders of the Southern Baptist Convention and convince them that God gave her as a preacher....

---

1. Millicent Hunter, as quoted in *Charisma* (May 2003), 40.
2. Sarah Sumner, *Men and Women in the Church*, 27.

If God gave her as a preacher, then she is a preacher, even if someone claims that that's impossible....You are who you are no matter what.... God decides your calling. God decides your spiritual giftedness.... If the Spirit of God has given you as a pastor, you are a pastor, even if you're not employed as one.[3]

Is this argument persuasive? Does God actually call some women to preach and teach His Word to men and women alike? Does He call some women to be pastors and elders?

— Answer #1: God never calls people to disobey His Word. Our decision on this matter must be based on the objective teaching of the Bible, not on some person's subjective experience, no matter how godly or sincere that person is.

This egalitarian claim is another form of the question, Will we take Scripture or experience as our ultimate guide?

I agree that people may have subjective experiences of God's presence and blessing that are genuine and real. But it is easy to make a mistake in understanding the meaning of those experiences. If a woman finds God's blessing and anointing when she preaches, then does that mean God is calling her to be a pastor, or does it mean that He is calling her to teach the Bible to women, in accordance with His Word, and that He will give much blessing in that task? If we had only the subjective experience alone to go on, it would be impossible to be certain that we had reached the right answer, because we would have only our own human interpretations of the event, not an interpretation given in God's own words. But in the Bible we have God's own words teaching us how to think about various ministries for women, and the Bible should be our guide in interpreting subjective experiences.

— Answer #2: What a woman perceives as a call from God to a pastoral ministry may be a genuine call to some other full-time ministry that is approved by Scripture.

Many ministries that include Bible teaching are open to women.[4] It may be that a strong sense of calling from God is in fact a calling from God to these kinds of ministries.

---

3. Ibid., 318.
4. See pp. 53–64, above, and Grudem, EFBT, 84–100.

PART ELEVEN

A BIBLICAL VISION OF MANHOOD AND WOMANHOOD FOR THE FUTURE

It is only in the last 150 years that we find some historical precedent for women pastors and Bible teachers, but it is not as strong as egalitarians would have us believe, and it is small compared with the entire history of the church. In any case, our final standard of what is right and wrong must be Scripture, not church history.

During the present controversy over women in leadership roles in the church, God has continued to allow a measure of blessing (for a time at least) on some churches that have women pastors and women elders, and on women who teach the Bible to congregations of men and women.

Looking forward to the future, we must decide whether we will follow His Word or allow ourselves to be led away from His Word by experiences that seem to bring blessing to people. Though not everyone will agree with me at this point, I believe this is a test of our faithfulness to God and to His Word in our generation. Eventually the consequences of each decision will become plain.

44

IS EVANGELICAL FEMINISM
A NEW PATH TO
LIBERALISM?

Some Disturbing Warning Signs

A s I have spent more and more time analyzing egalitarian arguments, I have concluded that evangelical feminism is becoming a new path to theological liberalism for evangelicals in our generation. When I use the phrase "theological liberalism," I mean a system of thinking that denies the complete truthfulness of the Bible as the Word of God and denies the unique and absolute authority of the Bible in our lives.

I have given extensive evidence for this trend in a recent book: *Evangelical Feminism: A New Path to Liberalism?*[1] I will not repeat the entire contents of that book here, but the overall argument is as follows:

1. Liberal Protestant denominations were the pioneers of evangelical feminism, and evangelical feminists today have adopted many of the arguments earlier used by theological liberals to advocate the ordination of women and to reject male headship in marriage. By contrast, the strongest opponents of women's ordination are found

---

1. Wayne Grudem, *Evangelical Feminism: A New Path to Liberalism?* (Wheaton: Crossway, 2006). I had summarized these same concerns in eighteen pages in Grudem, EFBT, 500–17, but now I have developed this argument much more extensively in 260 pages in *Evangelical Feminism: A New Path to Liberalism?*

among groups most firmly committed to the inerrancy of the Bible.

2. Many prominent evangelical feminist writers today advocate positions that deny or undermine the authority of Scripture, and many other egalitarian leaders endorse their books and take no public stance against those who deny the authority of Scripture. In twenty-five chapters in *Evangelical Feminism: A New Path to Liberalism?*, I document and explain twenty-five different ways in which the authority of Scripture is undermined or denied in current egalitarian writings.

3. Once the authority of Scripture is undermined or denied, certain consequences have predictably followed in denomination after denomination, and a number of these are already seen among evangelical feminists, as noted in the following points:

4. Recent trends now show that evangelical feminists are heading toward the denial of anything uniquely masculine, an androgynous Adam who is neither male nor female, and a Jesus whose manhood is not important. This step is already common in evangelical feminist writings.

5. The next step, also taken first by liberal Protestant denominations, is to advocate calling God "our Mother in heaven."[2] Leading evangelical feminist writers have now taken this step and some writings promoted by evangelical feminists even warn against the harm that comes from calling God "Father."

6. The next step that has happened in liberal denominations is incremental movement toward an endorsement of the moral legitimacy of homosexuality. Though only a small number of evangelical feminist writers have taken this step to this point, and though I am thankful that the egalitarian group Christians for Biblical Equality has remained clearly opposed to the moral legitimacy of homosexuality, this next step has been followed in liberal denominations as a predictable outworking of (a) the same methods used to undermine the authority of Scripture in order

---

2. I am grateful to see that the recent egalitarian book *Discovering Biblical Equality*, edited by Ronald W. Pierce and Rebecca Groothuis, contained (in its first printing) an essay by Judy Brown that warned against calling God our "Mother" (DBE, 293–94).

to deny any uniquely male leadership roles in the home or in the church, (b) the denial of differences between men's and women's roles in marriage and the church, and (c) the strong pressure for approval of homosexual conduct in the general culture.

7. The final step is the ordination of homosexuals and the promotion of homosexuals to high leadership positions in the church.

The common thread running through all of these trends is a rejection of the effective authority of Scripture in people's lives and that this is the bedrock principle of theological liberalism. That is why I believe the matters discussed in this book are so important for the future of the church.

45

THE CURRENT STATE
OF EVANGELICALISM
REGARDING BIBLICAL
MANHOOD AND
WOMANHOOD

A s I speak with people throughout much of the evangelical world, I find widespread awareness of an ongoing controversy over manhood and womanhood. In addition, there is much confusion both about what the Bible actually teaches and about how we should put these teachings into practice, whether in marriage or in the church. Yet I also sense a strong desire to know and to do God's will on these matters.

In this chapter I offer my assessment of the current state of evangelicalism on this question. For those who wish to see more detailed documentation for specific groups, I have included policy statements from various groups in an appendix to my book *Evangelical Feminism and Biblical Truth*.[1]

For the purposes of this chapter, the evangelical world can be divided into three groups: (1) complementarian, (2) egalitarian, and (3) undecided or uncommitted.

---

1. See Grudem, EFBT, Appendix 8, pp. 703–66.

AN OVERVIEW OF COMPLEMENTARIAN, EGALITARIAN, AND UNDECIDED GROUPS TODAY

COMPLEMENTARIAN GROUPS

1. Two-Point Complementarian

There are two different groups among those who hold that the Bible teaches different roles for men and women. The first group I call "Two-Point Complementarian" because they hold that men and women are equal in value but have different roles in (1) the home and (2) the church.

The other group, which I call "One-Point Complementarian," holds that men and women are equal in value but have different roles in (1) the home.

Three influential denominations are included among those that hold a Two-Point Complementarian position. The current leaders of these denominations have recently fought and won battles with liberalism, and they remember clearly that liberalism and women's ordination go hand in hand. These three denominations are the Southern Baptist Convention (at 16 million members, the largest Protestant denomination in the United States), the Lutheran Church—Missouri Synod (2.6 million members), and the smaller but very influential Presbyterian Church in America (316,000 members).[2]

Other Two-Point Complementarian groups include several denominations and organizations that historically have been strongly truth-based and doctrinally vigilant. Included in this group are the Evangelical Free Church of America, the Christian and Missionary Alliance, and the more recently formed Sovereign Grace Ministries (formerly PDI). Several seminaries also fall in this category, such as Westminster Seminary (Philadelphia and California), Reformed Seminary (Jackson, Orlando, and Charlotte), and Covenant Seminary in St. Louis, as well as Dallas Theological Seminary, The Master's Seminary, and now most or all of the Southern Baptist seminaries such as the Southern Baptist Theological Seminary in Louisville, Kentucky, and Southeastern Baptist Theological Seminary in Wake Forest, North Carolina.

Many Bible colleges also fall in this category, such as Moody Bible Institute

---

2. For more information on the recent history of these three denominations, see EFBT, 502–3.

in Chicago, and Northwestern College in St. Paul, Minnesota, as well as some Reformed colleges, such as Covenant College in Lookout Mountain, Tennessee.

Thousands of independent churches and Bible churches across the United States also fall into this category.

In the publishing world, book publishers such as Crossway, Multnomah, Moody, and Presbyterian and Reformed will publish only complementarian books. Among periodicals, *World* magazine's editorial policy supports a complementarian position.[3]

Finally, the Council on Biblical Manhood and Womanhood (CBMW) is a parachurch organization whose purpose is to define, defend, and promote a Two-Point Complementarian position, which it has done since 1988.[4]

2. One-Point Complementarian

An organization that holds a "One-Point Complementarian" position believes that men and women have equal value but they have different roles in (1) the home. In order to be in this category, an organization or group must be neutral regarding women as pastors or elders. (Those who advocate women's ordination I call egalitarian.) Many of these One-Point Complementarian groups may have leaders and members who are privately Two-Point Complementarians, but the official stance of the organization is only One-Point Complementarian.

Some parachurch organizations in this category are Focus on the Family and Promise Keepers. Both have decided not to take any official stand on the role of women in the church, but both uphold male headship in the home. In its official policies, Campus Crusade for Christ also falls in this category, since the organization has not taken any public stand on the role of women in ministry, while Family Life, a division of Campus Crusade under the direction of Dennis Rainey, clearly teaches male headship in the home at its "Weekend to Remember" marriage conferences.

Denominations do not usually fall in the One-Point Complementarian camp because in most cases they either approve or forbid the ordination of women. However, the Evangelical Presbyterian Church's official policy allows members and clergy to hold differing views on women's roles in the church.[5]

---

3. See the special issue of *World* on marriage and the family (May 20, 2000).

4. See www.cbmw.org.

5. The EPC statement is in Grudem EFBT, 751.

Egalitarian groups

Egalitarian groups hold that men and women are equal in value, but all roles in the home and the church are determined by gifts, abilities, and preferences, not by gender. I have put organizations in this category if the egalitarian viewpoint is the dominant emphasis in the group, though in some organizations, some people still hold to a complementarian position, while in other organizations an egalitarian position is the only one allowed.

1. Liberal denominations

When I call a denomination "liberal" here, I mean that liberalism is the dominant theological viewpoint, although in most or all of these groups there are more conservative believers who are saddened by the liberal direction of the denomination and stay to work for change. Egalitarianism is the dominant viewpoint in all theologically liberal denominations, and egalitarianism appears and gains strength as denominations move in a more liberal direction.[6]

By this I do not mean to say that all egalitarians are liberals. Some denominations have approved women's ordination for other reasons, which I will discuss in the following sections. But it is unquestionable that theological liberalism leads to the endorsement of women's ordination. While not all egalitarians are liberals, all liberals are egalitarians. There is no theologically liberal denomination or seminary in the United States today that opposes women's ordination.

2. Culturally sensitive egalitarians

Other egalitarian groups are not theologically liberal but are egalitarian for a variety of other reasons. One reason is that groups that emphasize *relating effectively to the culture* are attracted more strongly than other groups to the egalitarian trends in today's culture. Another characteristic of these groups is that, in their desire to have a positive influence on the culture, they place a higher value on effective results in ministry than they do on being sure they have correct doctrine or being sure they are faithful to the Bible in matters that seem to them to be second-order doctrines,

---

6. See Grudem, EFBT, 469–72, 500–05, as well as Wayne Grudem, *Evangelical Feminism: A New Path to Liberalism?*, for a discussion of the connection between liberalism and egalitarianism.

not doctrines of primary importance (and they put controversies over women's roles in this category).

Examples of culturally sensitive egalitarian groups are Willow Creek Community Church[7] in South Barrington, Illinois, and Fuller Seminary in Pasadena, California (Fuller has had an emphasis on gaining acceptance and influence in liberal denominations and in the liberal academic world ever since its founding in 1947). Another predominantly egalitarian institution is Regent College in Vancouver, British Columbia, and it too places a high value on understanding and relating effectively to the culture, especially at the academic and professional level.[8]

3. Experience-oriented egalitarians

Included in this category are groups where *effective ministry* or *a strong calling from God* take priority (in practice at least) over what seem to these groups to be controversial or confused doctrinal areas (and they often put controversies about men and women in that category).

The Assemblies of God fall in this category, as does the International Church of the Four Square Gospel.[9] The Toronto Airport Christian Fellowship (formerly a Vineyard church) also falls in this category, with its strong emphasis on a personal experience of the power of the Holy Spirit. I also put *Charisma* magazine here because since at least 1997 or 1998, women pastors and women in ministry have often received emphasis in *Charisma* and its sister publication, *Ministries Today*.[10]

---

7. See Grudem, EFBT, 759–60, for the policy statement of Willow Creek Community Church.

8. Two complementarian faculty members, J. I. Packer and Bruce Waltke, are still affiliated with Regent College, but they are of retirement age and both teach part-time. Several students have reported to me that the egalitarian position of Gordon Fee and others has been the dominant viewpoint they hear in class (though Fee has also now retired and teaches only part-time). Packer's successor as Sangwoo Youtong Chee Professor of Theology and Culture is John Stackhouse, who has recently published a new egalitarian book, *Finally Feminist* (Grand Rapids: Baker, 2005).

9. See the statement on women in ministry from the Assemblies of God in EFBT, Appendix 8, pp. 705–10, and notice how Scripture has effectively been neutralized for this question by the claim that there are differing views on these passages and it is not possible for the committee to decide between those different views. (See also EFBT, 371–76.)

10. See, for example, the article by Cindy Jacobs, "Women of God, Arise!" in *Charisma* (May 1998), 76–79, 110; Larry Keefauver, "Empower the Women," an editorial written by Keefauver as senior editor in *Ministries Today* (May/June 1998), 9; and the cover "Women of the Word" (March 1997). J. Lee Grady, the editor of *Charisma*, has published two books promoting an egalitarian position: *Ten Lies the Church Tells Women* and *Twenty-Five Tough Questions About Women and the Church*.

The Association of Vineyard Churches also falls in this category. When John Wimber was leading the Vineyard movement, he would not allow women to serve as elders in Vineyard churches.[11] However, after John Wimber's death in 1997, different churches and leaders had different views. On October 18, 2001, the national board published a statement saying that it had decided to allow each church to decide its own policy on this, effectively allowing women elders and pastors in the Vineyard movement.[12]

Other groups that place a high value on an experience of personal calling from God and experiences of fruitfulness in ministry are the Wesleyan Church, the Nazarene Church, and the Free Methodists.

4. Leader-influenced egalitarians

Other organizations within evangelicalism have adopted an egalitarian position primarily because of the influence of one or two strong leaders.

Included in this category is InterVarsity Christian Fellowship in the United States, which adopted a strong egalitarian position under the leadership of recent past president Steve Hayner. There are reports that InterVarsity staff members who held a complementarian position were not allowed to teach that position publicly under Hayner's leadership.[13] It appears from the books they publish that InterVarsity Press (USA) is also strongly egalitarian in its editorial policies. I do not

11. See "Vineyard Restricts Elders to Men," in *CBMW News* 1:1 (August 1995): 9 (at www.cbmw.org), with quotations from the March/April 1994 edition of *Vineyard Reflections*, a publication sent to Vineyard leaders. Wimber wrote, "I believe God has established a gender-based eldership of the church. I endorse the traditional [and what I consider the *scriptural*] view of a unique leadership role for men in marriage, family, and in the church.... Consequently I personally do not favor ordaining women as elders in the local church." (However, Wimber also explained that he did allow for women to preach to mixed congregations under the authority of the local church elders.)

12. See EFBT, Appendix 8, p. 711, for this statement of the Vineyard's current policy. Two egalitarian books in the bibliography are by Vineyard pastors: Rich Nathan, *Who Is My Enemy?* and Williams, *The Apostle Paul and Women in the Church*.

13. See "IVCF Affirms Egalitarianism," in CBMW *News* 1:1 (August 1995): 4, with reference to Steve Hayner's position paper, "Women in the Ministries of InterVarsity," October 1993 (see also EFBT 761–62.); Joe Maxwell, "Standing in the Gender Gap," *Christianity Today* (June 22, 1992), 69; and Jeff Robinson, "Louder than Words," www.Gender-News.com, May 10, 2004. http://www.gender-news.com/article.php?id=11 (accessed May 9, 2006).

think it has published a book from a complementarian position in the last twenty years, while it has published numerous egalitarian books.[14]

I also list Willow Creek Community Church in this category because of the strong influence of Dr. Gilbert Bilezikian, Wheaton College theology professor (now retired), who was an elder from the earliest beginnings of Willow Creek and whose book *Beyond Sex Roles* has been one of the most influential egalitarian books in the entire evangelical movement. (Willow Creek fits both this category and the earlier "culturally sensitive egalitarian" category.)

Finally, Christians for Biblical Equality (CBE) is a parachurch organization whose purpose is to define, defend, and promote an egalitarian position in the evangelical world, and it is thus a counterpart to the complementarian organization CBMW.

UNDECIDED OR UNCOMMITTED

Much of the rest of the evangelical world has not come to any clear conclusion on this issue, or has decided that it can allow both views to exist within the same organization. A number of evangelical seminaries are in this category, such as Trinity Evangelical Divinity School in Deerfield, Illinois, where I taught for twenty years. Though a majority of the faculty hold a Two-Point Complementarian position, a significant minority hold an egalitarian position on women in ministry. Gordon-Conwell Seminary similarly allows both viewpoints on its faculty, though the presence of Aida Spencer (full-time) and Catherine Kroeger (adjunct) as New Testament professors means that the egalitarian viewpoint has a much stronger presence at Gordon-Conwell than at most other evangelical seminaries (Spencer and Kroeger are both influential egalitarian writers and speakers). Wheaton College in Illinois and Bethel College and Seminary in St. Paul, Minnesota, similarly have both egalitarians and complementarians on the faculty.

Many other evangelical organizations would also fit in this category.

---

14. See the bibliography for a list of InterVarsity Press books advocating an egalitarian position. One chapter in Edmund Clowney's book *The Church*, 215–35, advocates a complementarian position, but this is only one chapter in one book, a book not primarily concerned with this question. I have been told that IVP is willing to publish a complementarian book on men and women, but I am not aware if any such book is scheduled. (In the United Kingdom, IVP-UK is a separate organization and it has not published several of the egalitarian titles published by IVP-US, and has published my book *Evangelical Feminism and Biblical Truth* (Leicester, UK: 2004.)

1. Male chauvinism has been the major problem through much of history.

For most cultures through most of history, the most serious deviation from biblical standards regarding men and women has not been feminism, but harsh and oppressive male chauvinism. It still exists today, not only in some families in the United States, but also in a number of cultures throughout the world. Many non-Christian religions, such as Islam, tragically oppress women and fail to treat them as equals in the image of God.[15]

The first page of the Bible corrects this, in Genesis 1:27, where we find that God created both man and woman in His image.[16] Much of the rest of the Bible goes on to affirm the equal dignity and value of women in the sight of God and that we must treat one another as equals in God's sight.

This truth has not always been fully recognized, even within the church. I believe that one of God's purposes in this present controversy is to correct some wrongful traditions and some wrongful assumptions of male superiority that have existed within churches and families in the evangelical world. In this and other issues, we should live with a constant expectation that over time the church will become more obedient to our Lord. I wrote in another context words that are also appropriate here:

> It has been about 1970 years since Pentecost, and during that time Jesus Christ has been gradually purifying and perfecting his church. In fact, Ephesians 5 tells us that "Christ loved the church and gave himself up for her, that he might sanctify her, having cleansed her by the washing of water with the word, that he might present the church to himself in splendor, without spot or wrinkle or any such thing, so that she might be holy and without blemish" (Ephesians 5:25–27). Throughout history, Jesus Christ has been purifying the church, working toward the goal of a beautiful, holy, mature, godly church.
>
> Sometimes that process of purification has been marked by specific historical events; for example, in 325 and 381, the Nicene Creed; in 451, the

---

15. See Grudem, EFBT, 26–28, 58–59.
16. See p. 20, above, and Grudem, EFBT, 25–28.

Chalcedonian Creed; in 1517, Martin Luther's 95 theses; even in 1978, the International Council on Biblical Inerrancy's Chicago Statement on Biblical Inerrancy. At other times, there has been no one defining moment, but a gradual rejection of misunderstanding and a growing consensus endorsing Biblical truth in some area. For example: the rejection of the militarism of the crusades and their attempt to use the sword to advance the church; or the realization that the Bible does not teach that the sun goes around the earth; or, in the 16th and 17th centuries, the marvelous advances in doctrinal synthesis that found expression in the great confessions of faith following the Reformation; or, in the 17th and 18th centuries, the realization that the civil government could and should allow religious freedom; or in the 19th century, the growing consensus that slavery was wrong and must be abolished; or in the 20th century, the growing consensus that abortion was contrary to Scripture. Other examples could be given, but the pattern should be clear: Jesus Christ has not given up his task of purifying his church. The long-term pattern has not been nineteen centuries of decline in the purity and doctrinal and ethical understanding of the church, but rather a pattern of gradual and sometimes explosive increase in understanding and purity.[17]

The church learns and grows and is purified through controversy. After a controversy has gone on for some time, the main body of recognized teachers and leaders among Bible-believing Christians will always make the right decision and will move forward with deeper understanding because Jesus Christ is Lord of His church, and He continues to protect and gradually to purify it. A minority will stick to wrong opinions and eventually become marginalized and then disappear, or they will have no significant, ongoing influence on the church. And so I think this controversy will progress until the church reaches a right decision and incorrect views are left behind, just as they have been in past controversies.

However, in speaking of errors of male superiority in the past, I do not mean

---

17. These two paragraphs are taken from Grudem, "Do We Act As If We Really Believe That 'The Bible Alone, and the Bible in Its Entirety, Is the Word of God Written'?" ETS presidential address, 1999, *Journal of the Evangelical Theological Society* 43/1 (March 2000): 13.

to imply that evangelical churches and families have been uniformly at fault. For example, one can read the Homilies of John Chrysostom (ca. 374–407) and find many beautiful admonitions about the love husbands should have for their wives and the dignity and respect with which they should treat them. Such emphases can be found in prominent writers throughout the history of the church. And many denominations and ministries today promote and encourage valid ministries for women as well as for men.[18]

Nevertheless, as we seek to resolve this current controversy, those of us who are complementarians must continually be asking: Can we do more to encourage and affirm the valuable ministries of women within scriptural guidelines? And in our hearts is there a genuine confidence in the equal value of men and women in the work of God's kingdom?

2. Egalitarianism is not advancing on the strength of exegetical arguments from Scripture.

As this controversy has progressed, more and more information has come to light. We have found more information about the meanings of words, about grammatical constructions, and about the larger biblical and historical backgrounds to the statements in Scripture.

These advances in scholarship have served to strengthen and confirm the complementarian position and to weaken the egalitarian position time and again. For example, the work of Andreas Köstenberger and H. Scott Baldwin was a significant advance in our understanding of the meaning of *authenteō* in 1 Timothy 2:12, showing that it means "have authority" or "exercise authority," rather than the negative meanings proposed by egalitarians.[19] The significant research of Richard Hove demonstrated that Galatians 3:28 ("There is neither male nor female, for you are all one in Christ Jesus") teaches the *unity* of *different persons with different*

---

18. I think of my local church, Scottsdale Bible Church, in Scottsdale, Arizona, which has a long history of promoting and encouraging valuable and visible ministries by women as well as men. Another example is Campus Crusade for Christ, which since its founding has had women as well as men in the front lines of campus ministry. And there are many other examples as well.

19. See EFBT 307–16 and pp. 185–191 above. The work of Köstenberger and Baldwin has now been supplemented by substantial new works by David Huttar and Albert Wolters (see above, pp. 187 and 192).

roles, not the *sameness* of men's and women's roles, as egalitarians have claimed.[20] Steven Baugh and others have shown that there were well-educated women at Ephesus, contrary to the claim of some egalitarians that Paul prohibited women from teaching because they did not have enough education.[21]

Yet another advance in our understanding has come through the research of M. H. Burer and Daniel B. Wallace showing that the word *episēmos* in Romans 16:7 means that Junia(s) is "well known *to the apostles*" rather than "well known *among the apostles*."[22] Another example would probably be my own work on the meaning of *kephalē* ("head"), which found over fifty examples where it means "person in authority." By contrast, no clear example has yet been produced of any text that says person A is the "head" of person B, and yet person A is not in a position of authority over person B (as the egalitarian position would require, in order to deny male leadership in those texts that say the husband is the head of the wife).[23]

The overall result of research like this is that the complementarian position is becoming more firmly established through detailed academic work, while egalitarian arguments are crumbling. Since this is the case, how does the egalitarian position advance?

3. How does the egalitarian position advance?

In spite of numerous setbacks in academic research on the meaning of Scripture, the egalitarian position continues to advance on a number of fronts in the evangelical world. Why is this? As I have participated in and observed this controversy for over twenty years, I have concluded that the egalitarian position advances through the following methods.

a. Incorrect interpretations of Scripture. A significant number of egalitarian claims that I have responded to in this book fall in this first category. Egalitarians have claimed things about the meaning of Scripture that do not hold up on close examination of the text itself. Others may differ with me when I say that these egalitarian claims are based on incorrect interpretations, and they are free to do so. In fact, I have written this book so that people will be able to consider the egalitarian posi-

---

20. See EFBT 184–85.
21. See EFBT 289–91.
22. See EFBT 224–25.
23. See EFBT 202–11.

tions and my responses and decide for themselves which viewpoint is persuasive.

Readers will have to examine the arguments and decide if they agree that these egalitarian claims are based on "incorrect interpretations of Scripture," as I have argued that they are.

b. Reading into Scripture things that aren't there. Several egalitarian claims are based on assertions that the Bible says something it actually does not say, such as the claim that Deborah led Israel into battle or that Paul tells women to "preach the Word."

c. Incorrect statements about the meanings of words in the Bible. Another category of egalitarian claims asserts that all of the English translations of the Bible are wrong, or that most or all of the standard Greek dictionaries are wrong, and that some new meaning should be accepted for key words that are in dispute in this controversy. One example is the claim that "head" means "source," in a sense that denies authority to the person who is called the "head" of someone else. Another example is the claim that Romans 16:2 says that Phoebe was a "leader" or "ruler" of many, and another is the claim that Ephesians 5:21 teaches that husbands and wives should "mutually submit" to one another, or the claim that "have authority" in 1 Timothy 2:12 means "misuse authority" or "murder" or "commit violence" or "proclaim oneself author of a man."

d. Incorrect statements about the history of the ancient or modern world. Over and over again, egalitarian writings claim things about the ancient world that are not true, such as that women were not well enough educated in the ancient world to serve as church leaders. In fact, the more information we gain from the ancient world, the less plausible this assumption becomes. Or egalitarian writings claim things that have not been proven by any verses of Scripture or any established facts, such as the claim that women were teaching false doctrine at Ephesus. These claims are repeated over and over again, and people begin to believe them, thinking that scholars must have some evidence for them, yet remaining unaware that no hard evidence supports these claims.

Related to this is the misleading claim that male headship in the home and the church leads to abuse and repression of women.

e. Methods of interpretation that reject the authority of Scripture and lead toward liberalism. Sometimes people say that this is "only a difference over Bible interpretation," and they conclude that both viewpoints should be allowed in the church.

(I agree that with some egalitarian claims it is only a difference of interpretation, and I have argued specific points about those interpretations in this book.)

However, another class of interpretations by egalitarians is different from this, and it is deeply troubling. That is a class of interpretations that do not proceed on the same assumptions about the authority of Scripture in our lives.

Egalitarian claims that implicitly or explicitly deny the authority of Scripture include claims that Genesis 1–2 is not historically accurate.

Another claim that fits this category is the idea that Paul and other New Testament authors were moving in a trajectory toward full inclusion of women in leadership, but they didn't reach that goal by the time the New Testament was completed; therefore, we should move beyond their teachings in the direction they were heading. Similar to the trajectory hermeneutic position is the view of Kevin Giles that we cannot decide doctrinal questions by citing Scripture passages, so we must decide them instead according to what the church has historically held. Still other claims that deny the authority of Scripture include the idea that a woman can teach and have authority over men if she does so under the authority of the pastor and elders, or that we do not have to obey certain New Testament commands even when we are engaged in the activities that they talk about simply because "we are not a church."

f. Rejecting Scripture as our authority and deciding this question on the basis of experience and personal inclination. Other egalitarian claims effectively place personal experience as a higher authority than Scripture. Included in this category are the arguments that we cannot oppose ministries that God has clearly blessed, so we should not waste time on obscure discussions about what the Bible might say about this, or that we cannot deny the validity of a woman's ministry if she has a genuine call from God to be a pastor.

g. Suppression of information. On a number of occasions I have observed a pattern of conduct by which a pastor will lead a church in an egalitarian direction through the suppression of relevant information and a refusal to allow a fair opportunity for any competent expressions of a complementarian position. Typically a pastor will read some egalitarian books and become convinced that they are right. He will then seek out allies or work to establish allies for his position as a dominant group on the board of elders or the church governing board. Then he will preach a series of sermons promoting the egalitarian viewpoint. He may also promote occasions in which women actually teach the Bible to mixed groups.

If anyone objects to what he is doing, he and his fellow leaders label that person as "divisive" and say that he or she is wrongly opposing the church's leadership. If any church members ask for an opportunity to express a complementarian position, they are told that "people already know that viewpoint, and they don't need to hear it again," even though many may have never heard a responsible defense of a complementarian view that included thoughtful interaction with egalitarian claims. Therefore all that these "instinctive complementarians" have to support their view is an instinctive or traditional preference, but they have no persuasive arguments or facts with which to answer the fruits of thirty years of academic research by egalitarian scholars.

When they try to cite Bible verses opposing the pastor's egalitarian agenda, he will answer with arguments from egalitarian scholars (such as those in this book). Often the pastor's arguments will not provide hard facts that people can inspect for themselves, but will take the form, "Scholar A and Scholar B say you are wrong, so you must be wrong." Such arguments seem hard to answer, because the instinctive complementarians lack technical training and lack the time and research facilities to find answers to the egalitarian scholars that the pastor quotes. In this way, the use of the Bible by the instinctive complementarians is effectively nullified.

It is thus a mismatch from the beginning. Even if opportunity is given for a forum to present a complementarian view, it may be at an inconvenient time or in a small room or will not be adequately publicized, and verbal commitments to allow such a meeting may be withdrawn or changed at the last minute. In every way possible, expression of a complementarian position will be minimized and marginalized and suppressed.[24]

4. Egalitarianism has two significant allies

As egalitarians attempt to gain influence in Christian organizations, they have two significant allies. The first is the secular culture, which in its more prominent expressions is strongly opposed to the authority of the Word of God, strongly opposed to the idea that any positions in society should be restricted to men,

---

24. For an example of suppressing the complementarian view by rude heckling from the audience, see Wallace Benn, "How Egalitarian Tactics Swayed Evangelicals in the Church of England," *CBMW News* 2:3 (June 1997): 14, reproduced in Grudem, EFBT, 541–43.

strongly opposed to the family as God created it to function, and (in many quarters) strongly opposed to authority in general. I recognize that not all people in our secular culture hold these positions, but a very influential part of our culture does, especially in the highly influential areas of the media, the entertainment industry, and secular universities.

The second ally of egalitarianism is a large group of Christian leaders who believe that the Bible teaches a complementarian position but who lack courage to teach about it or take a stand in favor of it. They are silent, "passive complementarians" who, in the face of relentless egalitarian pressure to change their organizations, simply give in more and more to appease a viewpoint that they privately believe the Bible does not teach.

This is similar to the situation conservatives in liberal denominations face regarding homosexuality where too many people who think it is wrong will not take a stand. As Robert Benne, member of the task force on homosexuality in the Evangelical Lutheran Church in America said, the presence of open homosexuals at every discussion makes it difficult for folks who are uncertain or just plain nice to voice objections or even reservations about the revisionist agenda. Most church people like to be polite and accepting, so they often accept that agenda out of the desire to "keep the peace in love."[25]

One of the leaders who helped conservatives retake control of the Southern Baptist Convention after a struggle of many years told me privately, "Our biggest problem in this struggle was not the moderates who opposed us. Our biggest problem was conservatives who agreed with us and refused to say anything or take a stand to support us."

How different was the ministry of the apostle Paul! He did not lack courage to stand up for unpopular teachings of God's Word. When he met with the elders of the church at Ephesus and recounted his three-year ministry among them, he was able to say with a clear conscience, "Therefore I testify to you this day that I am innocent of the blood of all of you, *for* I did not shrink from declaring to you the whole counsel of God" (Acts 20:26–27).

The word "for" indicates that Paul was giving the reason why he was "innocent of the blood of all of you." He said he would not be accountable before God for

25. *World*, Aug. 2, 2003, 21.

any failures in the church at Ephesus because he "did not shrink from declaring" to them "*the whole counsel of God.*" He did not hold back from teaching something just because it was unpopular. He did not hold back from teaching something because it would have created opposition and struggle and conflict. In good conscience he proclaimed everything that God's Word taught on every topic, whether popular or not. He proclaimed "the whole counsel of God." And he stood before God blameless for his stewardship of the ministry to the Ephesian church.

If the apostle Paul were alive today, planting churches and overseeing leaders in those churches, would he counsel them to shrink back from speaking and teaching clearly about biblical roles for men and women? Would he counsel them to shrink back from giving a clear testimony of God's will concerning one of the most disputed and yet most urgent topics in our entire society? Would he tell pastors simply to be silent about this topic so that there could be "peace in our time" in our churches and so that the resolution of the controversy would be left for others at another time and another place?

When Paul began to preach that people did not have to be circumcised in order to follow Christ, great persecution resulted, and his Jewish opponents pursued him from city to city, at one point even stoning him and leaving him for dead (Acts 14:19–23). But Paul did not compromise on the gospel of salvation *by faith alone in Christ alone*, not *by faith plus circumcision*. And when Paul later wrote to some of those very churches where he had been persecuted and even stoned and left for dead, he insisted on the purity of the gospel that he had proclaimed, and he said, "For am I now seeking the approval of man, or of God? Or am I trying to please man? If I were still trying to please man, I would not be a servant of Christ" (Galatians 1:10).

It is important for church leaders, in fact for all Christians, to ask themselves this same question.

EGALITARIANISM IS AN ENGINE THAT WILL PULL MANY DESTRUCTIVE CONSEQUENCES IN ITS TRAIN.

I have argued throughout this book that the complementarian position is confirmed in Scripture in many ways. And I have argued that this biblical position will lead Christian men and women to true joy and fulfillment as they live in accordance with the purposes God has given in His Word.

The other side of that teaching on the beauty and value of complementarianism is that the egalitarian position ultimately bears various kinds of destructive fruit in people's lives. I believe that an egalitarian position, with its constant blurring of the distinctions between men and women, will lead to a gender identity crisis in men and women, and especially in many of the children that they raise.[26] Men and women will be confused about what it means to be a man and what it means to be a woman, and how men and women should act in ways that are different from one another (topics that egalitarians will usually not teach on). Such a gender identity crisis will lead to increasing self-hatred in many people, to fear of marriage, to anger and violence that will stem from internal frustration (particularly in men), and to an increase in homosexual conduct.

As a result, I believe that the egalitarian position will lead to an increasing breakdown of families and a weakening and effeminization of the church.

In addition, egalitarianism will increasingly lead people to an acceptance of methods for interpreting Scripture that will then make it easy to relativize any of the unpopular moral commands of Scripture. If the many ways of denying the teaching of Scripture described in this book are applied to other unpopular teachings of Scripture, they can be readily dispensed with as well.

Therefore, I believe that ultimately the *effective* authority of Scripture to govern our lives is at stake in this controversy. The issue is not whether we *say* that we believe the Bible is the Word of God or that we believe it is without error, but the issue is whether we *actually obey it* when its teachings are unpopular and conflict with the dominant viewpoints in our culture. If we do not obey it, then the effective authority of God to govern His people and His church through His Word has been eroded.

EXPECTATIONS FOR THE FUTURE

I expect several different things will happen over the next ten years with this controversy.

1. The controversy will not go away until it has been resolved by the vast majority of evangelical groups and denominations. The pressures in the culture are so great

---

26. By contrast, for a positive perspective on raising boys to be boys, see James Dobson's recent book *Bringing Up Boys*. Dr. Dobson plans also to publish a book soon on bringing up girls. Many other excellent books on parenting are available from Focus on the Family (www.family.org) and from FamilyLife, a division of Campus Crusade for Christ (www.familylife.com).

that no church and no denomination and no parachurch organization can simply decide to avoid the controversy. Each group that has not done so will have to study this issue and reach a formal position on it. That position should then be spelled out in statements of faith (as with the Baptist Faith and Message statement of the Southern Baptist Convention) or in policy statements.[27] But until a group adopts a formal written policy on the roles of men and women in ministry and in marriage, the controversy will not go away; it will just be postponed.

2. *Once these written policies are established, change will be very difficult; the future direction of the group will be set.* Many people who differ with the policy (whatever it is) will leave and find another church or organization, and more people who agree with the policy will join. Therefore, establishing a written policy (one way or the other) will usually bring the controversy to an end within each group, at least for many years. As I explained earlier in this book at several points, I fear that many sincere Christians will make erroneous decisions on these questions because they were given only misleading or incorrect information on various aspects of the Bible's teachings about this issue.

3. *If a group endorses an egalitarian position, I believe that changes in traditionally held views in other areas of morality and doctrine will be rapid.* The controversy over men and women is not the only controversy in the church. Other beliefs being challenged today are the truthfulness of the Bible in all that it affirms, the existence of hell and the eternal punishment of those who do not believe in Christ, the necessity to hear about Jesus Christ and trust in Him personally for salvation, the idea that God knows all future human choices, the doctrine that Christ bore the wrath of God that was due us for our sins (the doctrine of penal substitutionary atonement), and the belief that homosexual conduct is contrary to the moral standards of Scripture.

Those are only a few of the teachings of Scripture being challenged in various quarters today. Not every group that endorses egalitarianism will also abandon these doctrines, but the pressures to abandon them will be strong. If an egalitarian church begins to abandon some of these other doctrines as well, it will be a strong indication that the church is moving rapidly toward a new kind of liberalism. As I explained in the previous chapter, I believe that egalitarianism will usher in a

---

27. Many sample policy statements are found in Grudem, EFBT, Appendix 8, pp. 703–66.

liberal view of Scripture, and it will eventually result in the loss of a number of other doctrines, such as those I have just named.

4. However, I do not think for a minute that the egalitarian position will win in this controversy. Jesus promised, "I will build my church" (Matthew 16:18), and I believe He will protect and preserve His church and bring it to greater and greater purity and strength. Therefore I believe that the vast majority of the church will endorse a Two-Point Complementarian view of manhood and womanhood, yet one that is somewhat revised from traditional views because it will bring a new delight in the beauty of our masculinity and femininity as something God created as "very good" in His sight (Genesis 1:31). We will increasingly recognize, as men and women, that our differences as well as our similarities are "very good" and a cause of joy and delight—for us as well as for God.

I believe the complementarian view that will ultimately triumph in the church will result in a new honoring of women as truly equal partners in the family and in the work of the kingdom. I believe it will bring in a new openness toward different ministries for women and a new appreciation for the valuable ministries of women in the home and in the church, yet with "some governing and teaching roles... restricted to men."[28] And I believe it will also bring a new depth of understanding of what God intended when He created marriage and the family and the church, and a new depth of understanding of God's wonderful purpose for us when we live according to His Word.

In this entire process, I believe that Jesus Christ will be purifying His church, according to His eternal and wise purpose,

> *That he might sanctify her*, having cleansed her by the washing of water with the word, *so that he might present the church to himself in splendor*, without spot or wrinkle or any such thing, that she might be holy and without blemish. (Ephesians 5:26–27)

He is the Lord of heaven and earth, and He will not fail.

---

28. Danvers Statement, Affirmation 6, p. 304–07 below.

THE DANVERS STATEMENT[1]

B *ackground:* The Danvers Statement was prepared by several evangelical leaders at an early Council on Biblical Manhood and Womanhood meeting in Danvers, Massachusetts, in December 1987. It was first published in final form by the CBMW in Wheaton, Illinois, in November 1988.

RATIONALE

We have been moved in our purpose by the following contemporary developments, which we observe with deep concern:

1. The widespread uncertainty and confusion in our culture regarding the complementary differences between masculinity and femininity;
2. the tragic effects of this confusion in unraveling the fabric of marriage woven by God out of the beautiful and diverse strands of manhood and womanhood;
3. the increasing promotion given to feminist egalitarianism with accompanying distortions or neglect of the glad harmony portrayed in Scripture between the loving, humble leadership of redeemed husbands and the intelligent, willing support of that leadership by redeemed wives;
4. the widespread ambivalence regarding the values of motherhood, vocational homemaking, and the many ministries historically performed by women;
5. the growing claims of legitimacy for sexual relationships which have biblically and historically been considered illicit or perverse, and the increase in pornographic portrayal of human sexuality;
6. the upsurge of physical and emotional abuse in the family;

---

1. The Danvers Statement can be obtained online at www.cbmw.org. More information about this and other issues related to biblical manhood and womanhood is available at that same website from the Council on Biblical Manhood and Womanhood.

7. the emergence of roles for men and women in church leadership that do not conform to biblical teaching but backfire in the crippling of biblically faithful witness;
8. the increasing prevalence and acceptance of hermeneutical oddities devised to reinterpret apparently plain meanings of biblical texts;
9. the consequent threat to biblical authority as the clarity of Scripture is jeopardized and the accessibility of its meaning to ordinary people is withdrawn into the restricted realm of technical ingenuity;
10. and behind all this, the apparent accommodation of some within the church to the spirit of the age at the expense of winsome, radical biblical authenticity, which in the power of the Holy Spirit may reform rather than reflect our ailing culture.

PURPOSES

Recognizing our own abiding sinfulness and fallibility, and acknowledging the genuine evangelical standing of many who do not agree with all of our convictions, nevertheless, moved by the preceding observations and by the hope that the noble biblical vision of sexual complementarity may yet win the mind and heart of Christ's church, we engage to pursue the following purposes:

1. To study and set forth the biblical view of the relationship between men and women, especially in the home and in the church.
2. To promote the publication of scholarly and popular materials representing this view.
3. To encourage the confidence of lay people to study and understand for themselves the teaching of Scripture, especially on the issue of relationships between men and women.
4. To encourage the considered and sensitive application of this biblical view in the appropriate spheres of life.
5. And thereby

   - to bring healing to persons and relationships injured by an inadequate grasp of God's will concerning manhood and womanhood,
   - to help both men and women realize their full ministry potential through a true understanding and practice of their God-given roles,

- and to promote the spread of the gospel among all peoples by fostering a biblical wholeness in relationships that will attract a fractured world.

AFFIRMATIONS

Based on our understanding of biblical teachings, we affirm the following:

1. Both Adam and Eve were created in God's image, equal before God as persons and distinct in their manhood and womanhood (Genesis 1:26–27; 2:18).
2. Distinctions in masculine and feminine roles are ordained by God as part of the created order, and should find an echo in every human heart (Genesis 2:18, 21–24; 1 Corinthians 11:7–9; 1 Timothy 2:12–14).
3. Adam's headship in marriage was established by God before the Fall, and was not a result of sin (Genesis 2:16–18, 21–24; 3:1–13; 1 Corinthians 11:7–9).
4. The Fall introduced distortions into the relationships between men and women (Genesis 3:1–7, 12, 16).

   - In the home, the husband's loving, humble headship tends to be replaced by domination or passivity; the wife's intelligent, willing submission tends to be replaced by usurpation or servility.
   - In the church, sin inclines men toward a worldly love of power or an abdication of spiritual responsibility, and inclines women to resist limitations on their roles or to neglect the use of their gifts in appropriate ministries.

5. The Old Testament, as well as the New Testament, manifests the equally high value and dignity which God attached to the roles of both men and women (Genesis 1:26–27; 2:18; Galatians 3:28). Both Old and New Testaments also affirm the principle of male headship in the family and in the covenant community (Genesis 2:18; Ephesian 5:21–33; Colossians 3:18–19; 1 Timothy 2:11–15).
6. Redemption in Christ aims at removing the distortions introduced by the curse.

- In the family, husbands should forsake harsh or selfish leadership and grow in love and care for their wives; wives should forsake resistance to their husbands' authority and grow in willing, joyful submission to their husbands' leadership (Ephesians 5:21–33; Colossians 3:18–19; Titus 2:3–5; 1 Peter 3:1–7).
- In the church, redemption in Christ gives men and women an equal share in the blessings of salvation; nevertheless, some governing and teaching roles within the church are restricted to men (Galatians 3:28; 1 Corinthians 11:2–16; 1 Timothy 2:11–15).

7. In all of life Christ is the supreme authority and guide for men and women, so that no earthly submission—domestic, religious, or civil—ever implies a mandate to follow a human authority into sin (Daniel 3:10–18; Acts 4:19–20; 5:27–29; 1 Peter 3:1–2).

8. In both men and women, a heartfelt sense of call to ministry should never be used to set aside biblical criteria for particular ministries (1 Timothy 2:11–15; 3:1–13; Titus 1:5–9). Rather, biblical teaching should remain the authority for testing our subjective discernment of God's will.

9. With half the world's population outside the reach of indigenous evangelism; with countless other lost people in those societies that have heard the gospel; with the stresses and miseries of sickness, malnutrition, homelessness, illiteracy, ignorance, aging, addiction, crime, incarceration, neuroses, and loneliness, no man or woman who feels a passion from God to make His grace known in word and deed need ever live without a fulfilling ministry for the glory of Christ and the good of this fallen world (1 Corinthians 12:7–21).

10. We are convinced that a denial or neglect of these principles will lead to increasingly destructive consequences in our families, our churches, and the culture at large.

We grant permission and encourage interested persons to use, reproduce, and distribute the Danvers Statement. Printed copies of the Danvers Statement in brochure form are available for a small fee from the Council on Biblical Manhood and Womanhood at www.cbmw.org or 2825 Lexington Road, Box 926, Louisville, KY 40280, or phone 502-897-4065 or 888-560-8210.

BIBLIOGRAPHY

The literature on this topic is immense, and I have not attempted to make this an exhaustive bibliography. I have included the books on this topic that are cited in this book, some other commonly used academic and popular books on the topic from both positions, and a few that focus on practical application for marriage. A longer bibliography, including journal articles on this topic, is found in Grudem, EFBT, 767-781.

One helpful source for further bibliographical information is the *Journal for Biblical Manhood and Womanhood (JBMW)* (2825 Lexington Road, Box 926, Louisville, KY 40280). Beginning with *JBMW* issue 6/1 (spring 2001), managing editor Rob Lister has published annually an extensive annotated bibliography for gender-related articles appearing in the previous year, using the categories "complementarian," "egalitarian," "non-evangelical," and "undeclared," and giving a one-paragraph summary of each article. *JBMW* is available online at www.cbmw.org.

In the list below, for books by evangelical authors that are clearly complementarian or egalitarian, I have designated them with a boldface [**comp.**] or [**egal.**] after each entry.

Akin, Daniel. *God on Sex*. Nashville, TN: Broadman and Holman Publishers, 2003. [**comp.**]

Aldredge-Clanton, Jann. *God, a Word for Girls and Boys*. Louisville, KY: Glad River Publications, 1993. [**egal.**]

Alsdurf, James and Phyllis. *Battered into Submission: The Tragedy of Wife Abuse in the Christian Home*. Downers Grove, IL: InterVarsity Press, 1989. [**egal.**]

Baldwin, Joyce. *Women Likewise*. London: Falcon Booklets, Church Pastoral Aid Society, 1973. [**egal.**]

Beck, James R. and Craig L. Blomberg, eds. *Two Views on Women in Ministry*. Grand Rapids, MI: Zondervan, 2001.

Belleville, Linda L. *Women Leaders and the Church: Three Crucial Questions*. Grand Rapids, MI: Baker Book House, 2000. [**egal.**]

Benton, John. *Gender Questions: Biblical Manhood and Womanhood in the Contemporary World*. Darlington, England: Evangelical Press, 2000. [**comp.**]

Bilezikian, Gilbert. *Beyond Sex Roles: What the Bible Says About a Woman's Place in Church and Family*, 2nd ed. Grand Rapids, MI: Baker Book House, 1985. [**egal.**]

———. *Community 101*. Grand Rapids, MI: Zondervan, 1997. [**egal.**]

Boldrey, Richard and Joyce Boldrey. *Chauvinist or Feminist? Paul's View of Women*. Grand Rapids, MI: Baker Book House, 1976. [**egal.**]

Boomsma, Clarence. *Male and Female, One in Christ: New Testament Teaching on Women in Office*. Grand Rapids, MI: Baker Book House, 1993. [**egal.**]

Bristow, John Temple. *What Paul Really Said About Women: An Apostle's Liberating Views on Equality in Marriage, Leadership, and Love*. San Francisco: HarperCollins, 1991. [**egal.**]

Brizendine, Louann. *The Female Brain*. New York: Morgan Road, 2006.

Brown, Ann. *Apology to Women: Christian Images of the Female Sex*. Downers Grove, IL: InterVarsity Press, 1991. [**egal.**]

Brown, Judy L. *Women Ministers According to Scripture*. Kearney, NE: Morris Publishing, 1996. [**egal.**]

Burke, H. Dale. *Different By Design*. Chicago: Moody Press, 2000. [**comp.**]

Bushnell, Katherine C. *God's Word to Women: One Hundred Bible Studies on Woman's Place in the Divine Economy*. North Collins, N.Y., n.d. (First published 1919, with no date indicated on the publication.) [**egal.**]

Calvin, John. *Institutes of the Christian Religion*, 2-vol. ed., trans. Ford Lewis Battles. Philadelphia: Westminster, 1960.

Campbell, Ken. *Marriage and Family in the Biblical World*. Downers Grove, IL: InterVarsity Press, 2003.

Chappell, Bryan. *Each for the Other*. Grand Rapids,

MI: Baker Book House, 1998. [comp.]

Chaves, Mark. *Ordaining Women: Culture and Conflict in Religious Organizations.* Cambridge, MA: Harvard University Press, 1997. [egal.]

Clark, Stephen B. *Man and Woman in Christ: An Examination of the Roles of Men and Women in Light of Scripture and the Social Sciences.* Ann Arbor, MI: Servant Books, 1980. [comp.]

Clouse, Bonnidell and Robert G. Clouse, eds. *Women in Ministry: Four Views.* Downers Grove, IL: InterVarsity Press, 1989.

Clowney, Edmund. *The Church.* Downers Grove, IL: InterVarsity Press, 1995. [comp.]

Cochrane, Pamela D. H. *Evangelical Feminism: A History.* New York: New York University Press, 2005.

Cook, Philip W. *Abused Men: The Hidden Side of Domestic Violence.* Westport, CT: Praeger, 1997.

Cooper, John. *A Cause for Division? Women in Office and the Unity of the Church.* Grand Rapids, MI: Calvin Theological Seminary, 1991. [egal.]

Cottrell, Jack. *Feminism and the Bible: An Introduction to Feminism for Christians.* Joplin, MO: College Press, 1992. [comp.]

Crabb, Larry. *Men and Women: Enjoying the Difference.* Grand Rapids, MI: Zondervan, 1991. [comp.]

Cunningham, Loren and David Joel Hamilton, with Janice Rogers. *Why Not Women? A Fresh Look at Scripture on Women in Missions, Ministry, and Leadership.* Seattle, Wash.: YWAM Publishing, 2000. [egal.]

Davis, Philip G. *Goddess Unmasked: The Rise of Neopagan Feminist Spirituality.* Dallas: Spence Publishing, 1998.

Dawes, Gregory W. *The Body in Question: Meaning and Metaphor in the Interpretation of Ephesians 5:21–33.* Leiden: Brill, 1998.

DeMoss, Nancy Leigh, ed. *Biblical Womanhood in the Home.* Wheaton, IL: Crossway Books, 2002. [comp.]

———. *Lies Women Believe and the Truth that Sets Them Free.* Chicago: Moody Press, 2001. [comp.]

———. *Walking in the Truth.* Chicago: Moody Press, 2002. [comp.]

Dobson, James. *Bringing Up Boys.* Wheaton, IL: Tyndale House Publishers, 2001. [comp.]

Doriani, Dan. *The Life of a God-Made Man.* Wheaton, IL: Crossway Books, 2001. [comp.]

———. *Women and Ministry: What the Bible Teaches.* Wheaton, IL: Crossway Books, 2003. [comp.]

Edwards, Brian, ed. *Men, Women and Authority: Serving Together in the Church.* Kent, England: Day One Publications, 1996. [comp.]

Epp, Eldon J. *Junia: The First Woman Apostle.* Minneapolis: Fortress, 2005.

Erickson, Millard. *God in Three Persons.* Grand Rapids, MI: Baker Book House, 1995.

Evans, Mary J. *Women in the Bible: An Overview of All the Crucial Passages on Women's Roles.* Downers Grove, IL: InterVarsity Press, 1983. [egal.]

Farrar, Steve. *Anchor Man.* Nashville: Thomas Nelson Publishers, 1998. [comp.]

———. *Point Man: How a Man Can Lead His Family.* rev. ed. Sisters, OR: Multnomah, 2003. [comp.]

Fee, Gordon D. *The First Epistle to the Corinthians.* New International Commentary on the New Testament. Grand Rapids, MI: Wm. B. Eerdmans Publishing Co., 1987. [egal.]

Finley, M. I. *Ancient Slavery and Modern Ideology.* New York: Viking Press, 1980.

Foh, Susan T. *Women and the Word of God: A Response to Biblical Feminism.* N.p.: Presbyterian and Reformed, 1980. [comp.]

France, R. T. *Women in the Church's Ministry: A Test Case for Biblical Interpretation.* Grand Rapids, MI: Wm. B. Eerdmans Publishing Co., 1995. [egal.]

Garland, Diana R. *Family Ministry: A Comprehensive Guide.* Downers Grove, IL: InterVarsity Press, 1999. [egal.]

George, Elizabeth. *A Woman's High Calling.* Eugene, OR: Harvest House Publishers, 2001. [comp.]

Gilder, George. *Men and Marriage.* Gretna, LA: Pelican Publishing, 1986.

Giles, Kevin. *The Trinity and Subordinationism: The Doctrine of God and the Contemporary Gender Debate.* Downers Grove, IL: InterVarsity Press, 2002. [egal.]

Goldberg, Steven. *The Inevitability of Patriarchy: Why Biological Differences Between Men and Women Always Produces Male Domination.* New York: William Morrow and Company, 1973.

Grady, J. Lee. *Ten Lies the Church Tells Women: How the Bible Has Been Misused to Keep Women in Spiritual Bondage.* Lake Mary, FL: Creation House, 2000. [**egal.**]

———. *Twenty-Five Tough Questions about Women and the Church: Answers from God's Word That Will Set Women Free.* Lake Mary, FL: Charisma House, 2003. [**egal.**]

Gray, John. *Men Are from Mars, Women Are from Venus.* New York: HarperCollins, 1992.

Grenz, Stanley, J. *Women in the Church: A Biblical Theology of Women in Ministry.* Downers Grove, IL: InterVarsity Press, 1995. [**egal.**]

Gritz, Sharon Hodgin. *Paul, Women Teachers, and the Mother Goddess at Ephesus: A Study of 1 Timothy 2:9–15 in Light of the Religious and Cultural Milieu of the First Century.* Lanham, MD: University Press of America, 1991.

Groothuis, Rebecca Merrill. *Women Caught in the Conflict: The Culture War Between Traditionalism and Feminism.* Grand Rapids, MI: Baker Book House, 1994. [**egal.**]

———. *The Feminist Bogeywoman: Questions and Answers About Evangelical Feminism.* Grand Rapids, MI: Baker Book House, 1995. [**egal.**]

———. *Good News for Women: A Biblical Picture of Gender Equality.* Grand Rapids, MI: Baker Book House, 1997. [**egal.**]

Grudem, Wayne, ed. *Biblical Foundations for Manhood and Womanhood.* Wheaton, IL: Crossway Books, 2002. [**comp.**]

———. *Evangelical Feminism: A New Path to Liberalism?* Wheaton, IL: Crossway Books, 2006. [**comp.**]

———. *Evangelical Feminism and Biblical Truth: An Analysis of More Than 100 Disputed Questions.* Sisters, OR: Multnomah, 2004. [**comp.**]

———. *Systematic Theology: An Introduction to Biblical Doctrine.* Leicester, England: InterVarsity Press, and Grand Rapids, MI: Zondervan, 1994.

Grudem, Wayne and Dennis Rainey, eds. *Pastoral Leadership for Manhood and Womanhood.* Wheaton, IL: Crossway Books, 2002. [**comp.**]

Gundry, Patricia. *Woman, Be Free!* Grand Rapids, MI: Zondervan, 1977. [**egal.**]

Hardenbrook, Weldon M. *Missing from Action: Vanishing Manhood in America.* Nashville: Thomas Nelson Publishers, 1987. [**comp.**]

Harper, Michael. *Equal and Different: Male and Female in Church and Family.* London: Hodder and Stoughton, 1994. [**comp.**]

Harris, Paul R. *Why Is Feminism So Hard to Resist?* Decatur, IL: Repristination Press, 1998. [**comp.**]

Hassey, Janette. *No Time for Silence: Evangelical Women in Public Ministry Around the Turn of the Century.* Grand Rapids, MI: Zondervan, 1986. [**egal.**]

Heimbach, Daniel R. *Pagan Sexuality: At the Center of the Contemporary Moral Crisis.* Southeastern Baptist Theological Seminary, 2001. [**comp.**]

———. *Counterfeit Sexuality: Defending Biblical Sexual Morality from Four Threats to God's Design for Biblical Sexual Behavior.* Colorado Springs: A Special Report from Focus on the Family, n.d. [**comp.**]

Hopko, Thomas, ed. *Women and the Priesthood.* Crestwood, NY: St. Vladimir's Seminary Press, 1983. [**comp.**]

House, H. Wayne. *The Role of Women in Ministry Today.* Grand Rapids, MI: Baker Book House, 1995. (Reprinted: Nashville: Thomas Nelson Publishers, 1990.) [**comp.**]

Hove, Richard. *Equality in Christ? Galatians 3:28 and the Gender Dispute.* Wheaton, IL: Crossway Books, 1999. [**comp.**]

Howe, Margaret E. *Women and Church Leadership.* Grand Rapids, MI: Zondervan, 1982. [**egal.**]

Hughes, Barbara. *Disciplines of a Godly Woman.* Wheaton, IL: Crossway Books, 2001. [**comp.**]

Hughes, R. Kent. *Disciplines of a Godly Man.* Wheaton, IL: Crossway Books, 1991. [**comp.**]

Hull, Gretchen Gaebelein. *Equal to Serve: Women and Men Working Together Revealing the Gospel.* Old Tappan, NJ: Revell, 1987, 1991. [**egal.**]

Hunt, Susan. *By Design.* Wheaton, IL: Crossway Books, 1994. [**comp.**]

———. *Spiritual Mothering.* Wheaton, IL: Crossway Books, 1992. [**comp.**]

Hunt, Susan and Peggy Hutcheson. *Leadership for Women in the Church.* Grand Rapids, MI: Zondervan, 1991. [**comp.**]

Hunt, Susan and Barbara Thompson. *The Legacy of*

Biblical Womanhood. Wheaton, IL: Crossway Books, 2003. [comp.]

Hurley, James B. *Man and Woman in Biblical Perspective.* Grand Rapids, MI: Zondervan, 1981. [comp.]

Inrig, Elizabeth. *Release Your Potential: Using Your Gifts in a Thriving Women's Ministry.* Chicago: Moody Press, 2001. [comp.]

Jacobs, Cindy. *Women of Destiny: Releasing You to Fulfill God's Call in Your Life and in the Church.* Ventura, CA: Regal Books, 1998. [egal.]

James, Carolyn Custis. *When Life and Beliefs Collide: How Knowing God Makes a Difference.* Grand Rapids, MI: Zondervan, 2001.

James, Sharon. *God's Design for Women: Biblical Womanhood for Today.* Darlington, England: Evangelical Press, 2002. [comp.]

Jepsen, Dee. *Women: Beyond Equal Rights.* Waco, TX: Word Books, 1984. [comp.]

Jewett, Paul K. *Man As Male and Female: A Study in Sexual Relationships from a Theological Point of View.* Grand Rapids, MI: Wm. B. Eerdmans Publishing Co., 1975. [egal.]

Kassian, Mary A. *Women, Creation and the Fall.* Wheaton, IL: Crossway Books, 1990. [comp.]

———. *The Feminist Gospel: The Movement to Unite Feminism with the Church.* Wheaton, IL: Crossway Books, 1992. [comp.]

Keener, Craig S. *Paul, Women and Wives: Marriage and Women's Ministry in the Letters of Paul.* Peabody, MA: Hendrickson, 1992. [egal.]

Kimmel, Tim. *Basic Training for a Few Good Men.* Nashville: Thomas Nelson Publishers, 1997. [comp.]

Knight, George W. III. *The Role Relationship of Men and Women: New Testament Teaching.* Chicago: Moody Press, 1985. [comp.]

———. *The Pastoral Epistles.* New International Greek Testament Commentary. Grand Rapids, MI: Wm. B. Eerdmans Publishing Co., 1992. [comp.]

Köstenberger, Andreas J., Thomas R. Schreiner, and H. Scott Baldwin, eds. *Women in the Church: A Fresh Analysis of 1 Timothy 2:9–15.* Grand Rapids, MI: Baker Book House, 1995. [comp.]

Köstenberger, Andreas J., and Thomas R. Schreiner, eds. *Women in the Church: An Analysis and Application of 1 Timothy 2:9-15.* Second edition. Grand Rapids:

Baker, 2005. [a revised edition of the 1995 volume, *Women in the Church*] [comp.]

Kroeger, Catherine Clark and James R. Beck, eds. *Women, Abuse, and the Bible: How Scripture Can Be Used to Hurt or Heal.* Grand Rapids, MI: Baker Book House, 1996. [egal.]

Kroeger, Catherine Clark and Mary J. Evans, eds. *The IVP Women's Bible Commentary.* Downers Grove, IL: InterVarsity Press, 2002. [egal.]

Kroeger, Richard Clark and Catherine Clark Kroeger. *I Suffer Not a Woman: Rethinking 1 Timothy 2:11–15 in Light of Ancient Evidence.* Grand Rapids, MI: Baker Book House, 1992. [egal.]

Lepine, Bob. *The Christian Husband.* Ann Arbor, MI.: Servant Publications, 1999. [comp.]

Lewis, Robert. *Real Family Values: Leading Your Family into the 21st Century with Clarity and Conviction.* Sisters, OR: Multnomah Publishers, 2000. [comp.]

———. *Raising a Modern-Day Knight.* Colorado Springs: Focus on the Family, 1997. [comp.]

Lewis, Robert and William Hendricks. *Rocking the Roles: Building a Win-Win Marriage.* Colorado Springs: NavPress, 1991. [comp.]

Lundy, Daniel G. *Women, the Bible and the Church: Currents of Change in the Evangelical World.* Richmond Hill, Ontario: Canadian Christian Publications, 1993. [comp.]

Lutz, Lorry. *Women as Risk-Takers for God: Finding Your Role in the Neighborhood, Church, and World.* Grand Rapids, MI: Baker Book House, 1997. [egal.]

Mahaney, Carolyn. *Feminine Appeal: Seven Virtues of a Godly Wife and Mother.* Wheaton, IL: Crossway Books, 2003. [comp.]

Malcolm, Kari Torjesen. *Women at the Crossroads: A Path Beyond Feminism and Traditionalism.* Downers Grove, IL: InterVarsity Press, 1982. [egal.]

Marshall, I. Howard. *A Critical and Exegetical Commentary on the Pastoral Epistles, ICC.* Edinburgh: T&T Clark, 1999. [egal.]

Martin, Faith. *Call Me Blessed: The Emerging Christian Woman.* Grand Rapids, MI: Wm. B. Eerdmans Publishing Co., 1988. [egal.]

Martin, Francis. *The Feminist Question: Feminist Theology in the Light of Christian Tradition.* Grand Rapids, MI: Wm. B. Eerdmans Publishing Co., 1994.

Mickelsen, Alvera, ed. *Women, Authority and the Bible: Some of Today's Leading Evangelicals Seek to Break Through a Critical Impasse.* Downers Grove, IL: InterVarsity Press, 1986. [egal.]

Mitchell, Patrick. *The Scandal of Gender: Early Christian Teaching on the Man and the Woman.* Salisbury, MA: Regina Orthodox Press, 1998. [comp.]

Molenkott, Virginia. *Women, Men, and the Bible.* Nashville: Abingdon Press, 1977. [egal.]

Mounce, William D. *Pastoral Epistles.* Word Biblical Commentary, vol. 46. Nashville: Thomas Nelson, 2000. [comp.]

Nathan, Rich. "Is the Feminist My Enemy?" in *Who Is My Enemy?* Grand Rapids, MI: Zondervan, 2002. [egal.]

Neuer, Werner. *Man and Woman in Christian Perspective.* Trans. Gordon Wenham. London: Hodder and Stoughton, 1990. [comp.]

Nicole, Roger. "A Tale of Two Marriages," in *Standing Forth: Collected Writings of Roger Nicole.* Rosshire, Great Britain: Christian Focus, 2002. [egal.]

O'Brien, Peter T. *The Letter to the Ephesians.* Pillar New Testament Commentary. Cambridge: Apollos, and Grand Rapids, MI: Wm. B. Eerdmans Publishing Co., 1999. [comp.]

O'Leary, Dale. *The Gender Agenda: Redefining Equality.* Lafayette, LA: Vital Issues Press, 1997. [comp.]

Orthodox Church in America. *Women and Men in the Church: A Study of the Community of Women and Men in the Church.* Syosset, New York: Department of Religious Education, 1980.

Osburn, Carroll D., ed. *Essays on Women in Earliest Christianity.* Volumes 1 and 2. Joplin, MO: College Press Publishing Company, 1995. [egal.]

———. *Women in the Church: Refocusing the Discussion.* Abilene, TX: Restoration Perspectives, 1994. [egal.]

Otto, Donna. *The Stay-at-Home Mom.* Eugene, OR: Harvest House Publishers, 1991. [comp.]

Passno, Diane. *Feminism: Mystique or Mistake? Rediscovering God's Liberating Plan for Women.* Wheaton, IL: Tyndale House Publishers, 2000. [comp.]

Patterson, Dorothy. *A Woman Seeking God.* Nashville: Broadman and Holman Publishers, 1992. [comp.]

Patterson, Dorothy and Rhonda Kelley, eds. *The Woman's Study Bible.* Nashville: Thomas Nelson Publishers, 1995. [comp.]

Paul, John II. *On the Dignity and Vocation of Women.* Boston: St. Paul Books and Media, 1988.

Peace, Martha. *The Excellent Wife.* Bemidji, MN: Focus, 1999. [comp.]

Perriman, Andrew. *Speaking of Women: Interpreting Paul.* Leicester, England: InterVarsity Press, 1998. [egal.]

Pierce, Ronald W., and Rebecca Merrill Groothuis. *Discovering Biblical Equality: Complementarity without Hierarchy.* Downers Grove, Ill.: InterVarsity, 2004. [egal.]

Piper, John and Wayne Grudem, eds. *Recovering Biblical Manhood and Womanhood: A Response to Evangelical Feminism.* Wheaton, IL: Crossway Books, 1991. [comp.]

Podles, Leon J. *The Church Impotent: The Feminization of Christianity.* Dallas: Spence Publishing, 1999.

Rainey, Dennis. *A Call to Family Reformation.* Little Rock, AR: Family Life, 1996. [comp.]

———. *Ministering to Twenty-First Century Families.* Nashville: Word, 2001. [comp.]

———. *One Home at a Time.* Colorado Springs: Focus on the Family Publishing, 1997. [comp.]

Rainey, Dennis and Barbara. *The New Building Your Mate's Self-Esteem.* Nashville: Thomas Nelson Publishers, 1995. [comp.]

Rosberg, Gary and Barbara. *Divorce-Proof Your Marriage.* Wheaton, IL: Tyndale House Publishers, 2002. [comp.]

Saucy, Robert L. and Judith K. TenElshof, eds. *Women and Men in Ministry: A Complementary Perspective.* Chicago: Moody Press, 2001. [comp.]

Scanzoni, Letha and Nancy Hardesty. *All We're Meant to Be.* Waco, TX: Word Books, 1974. [egal.]

Smith, F. LaGard. *Men of Strength for Women of God.* Eugene, OR: Harvest House Publishers, 1989. [comp.]

Smith, Paul R. *Is It Okay to Call God "Mother"? Considering the Feminine Face of God.* Peabody, MA: Hendrickson Publishers, 1993. [egal.]

Spencer, Aída Besançon. *Beyond the Curse: Women Called to Ministry.* Nashville: Thomas Nelson Publishers, 1985. [egal.]

Stendahl, Krister. *The Bible and the Role of Women: A Case Study in Hermeneutics.* Trans. Emilie T. Sanders. Philadelphia: Fortress Press, 1966, 1st Swedish ed. 1958. [egal.]

Stackhouse, John G. *Finally Feminist: A Pragmatic Christian Understanding of Gender.* Grand Rapids: Baker, 2005. [**egal.**]

Storkey, Elaine. *Origins of Difference: The Gender Debate Revisited.* Grand Rapids, MI: Baker Book House, 2001. [**egal.**]

Strauch, Alexander. *Biblical Eldership.* Littleton, CO: Lewis and Roth Publishers, 1995. [**comp.**]

———. *The New Testament Deacon: Minister of Mercy.* Littleton, CO: Lewis and Roth Publishers, 1992. [**comp.**]

Sumner, Sarah. *Men and Women in the Church: Building Consensus on Christian Leadership.* Downers Grove, IL: InterVarsity Press, 2003. [**egal.**]

Tannen, Debra. *You Just Don't Understand: Women and Men in Conversation.* New York: Ballantine Books, 1990.

Thiselton, Anthony. *First Epistle to the Corinthians, NIGTC.* Grand Rapids, MI: Wm. B. Eerdmans Publishing Co., 2000. [**egal.**]

Trombley, Charles. *Who Said Women Can't Teach?* South Plainfield, NJ: Bridge Publishing, 1985. [**egal.**]

Tucker, Ruth A. *Women in the Maze: Questions and Answers on Biblical Equality.* Downers Grove, IL: InterVarsity Press, 1992. [**egal.**]

Tucker, Ruth A. and Walter Liefeld. *Daughters of the Church: Women and Ministry from New Testament Times to the Present.* Grand Rapids, MI: Zondervan, 1987. [**egal.**]

Van Leeuwen, Mary Stewart. *Gender and Grace: Love, Work and Parenting in a Changing World.* Downers Grove, IL: InterVarsity Press, 1990. [**egal.**]

Webb, William J. *Slaves, Women and Homosexuals: Exploring the Hermeneutics of Cultural Analysis.* Downers Grove, IL: InterVarsity Press, 2001. [**egal.**]

Weber, Linda. *Mom, You're Incredible.* Colorado Springs: Focus on the Family Publishing, 1994. [**comp.**]

———. *Woman of Splendor.* Nashville: Broadman and Holman Publishers, 1999. [**comp.**]

Weber, Stu. *Four Pillars of a Man's Heart.* Sisters, OR: Multnomah Publishers, 1997. [**comp.**]

———. *Tender Warrior.* Sisters, OR: Multnomah Publishers, 1993. [**comp.**]

Weld, Theodore. *The Bible Against Slavery,* 4th ed. New York: American Anti-Slavery Society, 1838.

Williams, Don. *The Apostle Paul and Women in the Church.* Ventura, CA: Regal Books, 1979. [**egal.**]

Winter, Bruce W. *After Paul Left Corinth.* Grand Rapids, MI: Wm. B. Eerdmans Publishing Co., 2001.

Witherington, Ben III. *Women and the Genesis of Christianity.* Cambridge: Cambridge University Press, 1990.

Witherington, Ben III. *Women in the Earliest Churches.* Society for New Testament Studies Monograph Series.

INDEXES

Name Index

Note: Biblical names, ancient names, and modern names are combined in this single index.

Are men's and women's roles interchangeable?

Egalitarians, or evangelical feminists, consider men's and women's roles in the home and church to be interchangeable. In this most exhaustive analysis ever published on this topic, Bible scholar Wayne Grudem considers over a hundred egalitarian arguments and finds them contrary to the Bible. According to Grudem, the Bible teaches that God values men and women equally. However, their roles in home and church are complementary to each other, not interchangeable. Arguing against both feminism on the left and male chauvinism on the right, his carefully researched handbook is a valuable resource defending the complementarian viewpoint.